HISTORY OF THE CHURCH
AND STATE IN NORWAY.

From a Photograph by]

[K. Knudsen, Bergen.

TRONDHJEM CATHEDRAL

(partly restored).

HISTORY OF THE CHURCH AND STATE IN NORWAY

FROM THE TENTH TO THE SIXTEENTH CENTURY

BY THOMAS B. WILLSON, M.A.

WESTMINSTER
ARCHIBALD CONSTABLE & CO LTD
2 WHITEHALL GARDENS
1903

BRADBURY, AGNEW, & CO. LD., PRINTERS,
LONDON AND TONBRIDGE.

PREFACE.

ENGLISH readers are more or less familiar with the most striking events in the history of Norway in the heroic days, but so far as I have been able to discover, no English writer has endeavoured to trace the history of the Church in Norway, from its foundation in the time of Olaf Tryg-vessøn, down to the period of the Reformation. If I am correct in this, the omission seems a strange one, as the Church in Norway was the only daughter of that of England to be found in Europe. Her missionaries, it is true, laboured in many parts of the Continent, but I think that in no country, except Norway, could it be said, that they helped to found and nurture a national Church, where none before existed.

Under these circumstances, I have for a long time wished to supply English readers with a history of this Church; and a close acquaintance with Norway, extending over thirty years, makes it, I hope, not altogether presumptuous to attempt the task. With this object in view, I obtained, some ten years ago (through my friend, the late Pastor Andreas Hansen), the kind permission of Dr. A. Chr. Bang, now Bishop of Christiania, to translate his valuable *Udsigt over den Norske Kirkes Historie under Katholicismen.* Further consideration, however, showed me that this work presupposed an acquaintance with the history of the Norwegian Church, such as few English readers possessed, and which was necessary in order fully to appreciate this valuable survey. I felt, therefore, that a history of the Church on broad lines, and avoiding mere technical details,

*

might prove of interest, and so the present work was
undertaken.

Further study of the subject led me to call this book a
"History of the Church and State in Norway," as I think it
will be found that in Norway, Church and State were more
closely connected than in any other country in Europe.
As the work is indeed primarily a history of Norway from
its ecclesiastical side, I have therefore not followed more
closely than it seemed necessary, the various purely civil
events and the warlike expeditions to other lands in the
early days.

The main object I have had in view was to trace the
history of the growth, development, vigorous life, and
subsequent decline and fall of that Church, of which the
foundations were mainly laid by the English fellow-helpers
of Olaf Trygvessøn and Olaf the Saint, at the end of the
tenth and beginning of the eleventh centuries. I have
further wished to show the way in which that Church was
related to the State, and the struggle which it had for
supremacy, closely akin to that carried on about the same
time in other countries of Europe.

The story is a deeply interesting one, and in this I
hope the reader will agree with me. If not, then
the fault is that of the narrator, and not of the events
narrated.

Elsewhere will be found a fairly comprehensive list of
authorities employed; but I wish to acknowledge fully
my obligations to my predecessors who have written on
this subject in modern times, especially to the writings of
such wonderful learning and research as those of the late
Professor Rudolf Keyser in *Den Norske Kirkes Historie
under Katholicismen*, Dr. Konrad Maurer in *Die Bekehrung
des Norwegischen Stammes zum Christenthume*, and to
the more recent works of Bishop Bang, Absalon Taranger,
A. D. Jørgensen, and the late Professor Dr. R. T. Nissen.

Lastly, I must express my gratitude to those who have assisted me in the preparation of this work, especially to Professor Dr. Yngvar Nielsen, Rector of the University of Christiania, for advice respecting original authorities and also for much useful information ; to Pastor S. Holst Jensen, for reading the proofs of the entire work, and for many valuable suggestions and corrections ; to the Very Rev. G. W. Kitchen, D.D., Dean of Durham, for advice on many points ; to Mr. Clement O. Skilbeck, for his admirable picture for the title page, of St. Olaf and his design for the cover ; to Herr Konservator H. Schetelig and the authorities of the Bergen Museum, for permission to photograph some of their antiquarian treasures ; to my son, Mr. Olaf Willson, B.A., for many references in English and foreign authorities, for his appendix on the Norwegian *stavkirker*, and for the index ; and above all, to my wife, without whose unfailing aid and encouragement this work would probably never have been completed.

T. B. WILLSON.

Shooter's Hill, Kent,
March, 1903.

TABLE OF CONTENTS.

CONTENTS.

LIST OF ILLUSTRATIONS.

MAP OF THE THREE SCANDINAVIAN KINGDOMS.

LIST OF THE PRINCIPAL AUTHORITIES.

In the following list will be found the principal authorities, both mediæval and modern, used in this history. The list is not, however, by any means an exhaustive one.

The *Heimskringla* of Snorre Sturlassøn (b. 1178, d. 1241). From the earliest times down to the battle of Re, 1177.

The *Sverre's Saga, Haakon's, Guthorm's and Inge's Saga, Haakon Haakonssøn's Saga*, by Karl Jonssøn, Sturla Thordssøn and others. From 1177 to 1263.

Fagrskinna. A history from Halfdan the Black to Sverre.

Agrip. A fragment of great value, probably from 1190. From Halfdan to Sigurd Jorsalfarer.

Flateyarbok. A MS. from the island of Flatey (Iceland) : a collection of various Sagas to 1395.

Saga of Olaf Trygvessøn, by Odd, a monk of Thingøre, in Iceland.

Olaf den helliges Saga, edited by Munch and Unger (Christiania), 1853.

Bishop Arne's Saga, and *Bishop Laurentius's Saga*. 13th century.

Danorum Historiæ, by Saxo-Grammaticus.

Historia de Antiquitate regum Norwegiensium, by Theodoricus Monachus : in Langebek's *Scriptores rerum Danicarum*, Vol. V.

Gesta Hammaburgensis Ecclesiæ Pontificum, by Adam of Bremen.

The following Chronicles in places referring to Norway :—

Anglo-Saxon Chronicle : Florence of Worcester, William of Malmesbury, Simeon of Durham, Roger de Hoveden, Matthew Paris, William of Jumièges.

Norges Gamle Love (The Old Laws of Norway), Vols. I.—V. (Christiania), 1846—95. A collection of the ancient ecclesiastical and civil legislation, and other documents, from the earliest times to 1387.

Diplomatarium Norvegicum. A collection of documents relating to Norway ; first volume issued in 1849, and the remainder at intervals since that date.

Det Norske Folks Historie, by P. A. Munch, in eight vols. (Christiania), the two last relating to the union period.

Norges Historie to 1387, by Rudolf Keyser, two vols. (Christiania).

Udsigt over det Norske Folks Historie, four vols. } By J. E. Sars (Christiania).

Illustreret Norges Historie, by O. A. Øverland (Christiania).

De første Konger af den Oldenborgske Slægt
Grevens Feide } By C. Paludan-Müller (Copenhagen).

Det Norske Kirkes Historie under Katholicismen, two vols. } By Rudolf Keyser (Christiania).

Die Bekehrung des Norwegischen Stammes zum Christenthume, two vols. } By Dr. Konrad Maurer (München).

Udsigt over den Norske Kirkes Historie under Katholicismen } By Bishop Dr. A. Chr. Bang (Christiania).

De Nordiske Kirkers Historie, by R. T. Nissen (Christiania).

Den Nordiske Kirkes Grundlæggelse og første Udvikling } By A. D. Jørgensen (Copenhagen).

Den Angelsaksiske Kirkes Inflydelse paa den Norske. } By Absalon Taranger (Christiania).

De Norske Klostres Historie, by C. C. A. Lange (Christiania).

Den Danske Kirkes Historie før Reformationen } By L. Helveg (Copenhagen).

Norges Helgener, by Prof. Ludvig Daae (Christiania).

Passio et miracula beati Olaui, edited by F. Metcalfe, M.A. (Oxford, Clarendon Press).

Throndhjem i Fortid og Nutid (997—1897). Various authors.

Bergen fra de Ældste Tider indtil Nutiden. } By Professor Dr. Yngvar Nielsen.

Den Sorte Død i det 14de Aarhundrede, by Dr. A. L. Faye (Christiania).

The introduction to Laing's translation of the " Heimskringla," by Rasmus B. Anderson, in four vols. (London), 1889.

CHAPTER I.

HEATHEN NORWAY IN THE EARLIEST TIMES.

The Coming of the Northmen—Their Religion—Temples—Festivals
—Geographical Divisions—Local Government.

THE Norwegians are a branch of the great stream of
Teutonic migration, which flowed from its original home in
Asia over the northern part of Europe. At what time
these invaders displaced the aboriginal inhabitants of the
Scandinavian peninsula, we have no certain means of
ascertaining, though some have affirmed that Odin was an
historical personage who, some three centuries before the
Christian era, led his victorious hosts across Europe. We
may take it, however, that about that time these Teutonic
tribes crossed the narrow seas between the Scandinavian
and North German lands, and established themselves on the
great peninsula. Gradually they drove back the primitive
peoples they found thinly scattered over the country, men
most probably of Mongolian origin, and whose descendants
still survive in the wandering Finns and Lapps of the far
north of Norway and Sweden.

The entire Scandinavian peninsula was at that time
largely covered with dense forests, and in these the invaders
established themselves, and gradually clearing open spaces,
in time proceeded to cultivate the land. Eventually they
worked their way down to the western and north-western
coasts, and quickly became expert in seamanship, and in
reaping the rich harvest which the well-stocked waters
of the North Sea afforded them. The acquaintance thus
gained with the ocean, and especially the tempestuous

B

North Sea, soon made them the most skilled sailors in Europe, and the way in which this sea power was in later centuries developed, can easily be traced in European history.

Like the other Teutonic nations of whom Tacitus tells us, they were all free men, and had with them slaves or thralls, who were generally captives taken in war. These were mere chattels, and their lives were at their masters' disposal, but they might, and sometimes did, obtain their freedom.

The settlers did not live in towns or villages, but each man had his own farm or *gaard*, though, for protection's sake in earlier times, they were usually not very far off from one another. This absence of towns, and division of the land into freeholds, was a characteristic of the Norwegians, and exercised a very remarkable influence over their subsequent history; for it was always the country parts, and not the towns, where the preponderating political power lay, and the free landowners, unfettered by feudalism, and practically without an aristocracy (the chiefs were only the larger landowners), controlled and directed the policy of the nation, meeting in the assemblies, or *Things*, where all free men had an equal voice.

In religion they were practically the same as many of the other Germanic tribes, but we have the advantage of possessing a full account of their theories of the Universe and the gods, in the very remarkable early literature of Iceland which has been preserved for us. In the older Edda, which is chiefly concerned with the mythology of the North, we have the Vøluspaa poem, one of the earliest and most picturesque accounts of the faith of the Northmen.

As the heathen beliefs and practices must naturally have much to do with the beginnings of Christianity in Norway, it is necessary we should have some knowledge of them.

The universe, in the old Norse mythology, was divided into Muspelheim and Niffelheim, the former the abode of light and fire, and the latter a dark and gloomy land of ice and snow. Between these lay Ginnungagap, a swelling deep "without form and void," and in which there was no life. Deep down in Niffelheim there was a well from which an ice-cold stream sprang, and flowed into Ginnungagap, and the spray from this, meeting the warmth and fire of Muspelheim, produced the Giant or Jotun, Ymer and his cow Audhumbla. On the milk of this cow the Jotun lived, and the evil race of the Jotuns sprang from him. The cow licked the salt from the rocks, whence sprang Bure, whose grandson was Odin. The Giant Ymer was killed by Odin and his brothers, and from his dead body, which was cast into Ginnungagap, the world was formed. His flesh was the earth, his blood the sea, his hair the trees, his bones the mountains, etc. All of the race of Jotuns were drowned in Ymer's blood, except one who with his wife escaped in a boat; their descendants were allowed to live beyond the utmost bounds of the sea in Jotunheim. The interior of the earth was peopled by dwarfs or Trolds, usually malign spirits.

The earth having been created there were yet no men upon it, so Odin and his two companions, Høner and Løder, went down to it, and finding two trees, formed from them the first man and woman, Ask and Embla.

The home of the Gods was Asgaard, with its beautiful hall Valhalla, where they feasted and where the Valkyries attended on them, and did their bidding. The gods were known as the *Æser*, or Aser, a name said to be derived from a word signifying a spiritual being, and the belief in the gods was called the *Asatro*.

At the head of the gods was Odin, the all-father, whose wife was Frigg, the all-nourishing. Their son was Thor, the Thunderer, the benefactor of the world, and the friend of mankind, to whom the Norwegians seem to have assigned a higher rank than Odin, to whom the other Teutonic tribes gave the highest place. Thor was the relentless foe of the Trolds and Jotuns, against whom he waged war with his far-famed hammer Mjølnir.

The other chief Æser were Niørd, the giver of riches and the ruler of the winds and protector of sailors. His daughter was Freya, the Venus of the North. Then there was Baldur the Beautiful, the Sun God, who was killed by the evil Loki, one of the race of the Jotuns, whom the gods had taken as one of themselves. Braga, the son of Odin, was the god of the spirits of the dead.

In addition to these and many others, there were local gods and household gods, held in veneration in certain places, and not universally reckoned amongst the inhabitants of Asgaard, and only worshipped by certain families. These survived in Norway for centuries after the introduction of Christianity, though of course only worshipped in secret, and the household divinities actually survived down to our own day, and may possibly still exist.

We must not lose sight of the Trolds, the spirits of the mountains and the forests, whose power was always dreaded, and whom the people were always ready to propitiate with offerings. Against them, as we have seen, Thor waged war, and when the faith of the "white Christ" vanquished the Asatro, we find St. Olaf takes the place of the Thunderer as their opponent and conqueror. Troldom was always in Christian times an offence of the greatest magnitude, and we find constant ecclesiastical legislation on the subject.

The worship of the gods was probably in the earliest days conducted in the open air, and in a grove of trees, but later we know temples or *Hovs* were built, and these we frequently meet with in the first days of Christianity in Norway.

The temples were in shape very much the same as the

earlier Christian churches, and there seems little doubt that some of them were adapted to Christian worship on the overthrow of the heathen gods. The sites of the temples, at any rate, were utilized for building churches which survive down to our own day.

The *Hov* usually consisted of what we might call a nave and chancel or apse. In the nave there was one, or sometimes two doors which were placed in the long side of the building, and not in what we would call the west wall. In the centre of this nave there was a large flat fireplace, where the flesh of the sacrifice was cooked and eaten, the smoke of the fire escaping through holes in the roof. Along the side of the walls ran benches, and in the middle of these, or sometimes near the door, were what were called the *høisæde* (high seats) with their *stolper* or pillars, where the chief sat who officiated at the sacrificial rites. In the partially enclosed apse or chancel, stood the altar of sacrifice which was placed on a slight elevation above the floor of the building. On this altar the victim, usually an animal, sometimes a human being, was slain and the blood caught in copper bowls kept for the purpose. This blood was then sprinkled on the altar, the walls, the images, and the worshippers.

On the altar was a golden ring which the officiant carried during the ceremonies, and on it all oaths were sworn at the *Thing*. Behind the altar was the image of the principal god, usually Thor, and ranged in a semi-circle were other images.

When the sacrifice was over, the flesh of the victim was cooked in great pots which hung over the fire, and the feast began. The people brought their own supplies of beer as well as the animals used in sacrifice. There were no priests as a separate caste (a fact which had a very important influence afterwards in the spread of Christianity), but the chief man of the district acted in that capacity.* When the feasting began the horns were filled with beer, and were blessed in honour of the gods. Then the *skaals* were drunk, to Odin or Thor for victory; to Niørd and Freya for good crops and peace; and to Braga for the souls of the dead.

There were three great festival *blots*, or sacrifices, held every year: the winter *blot*, on October 14th, the midwinter, or Jul, at first on January 12th, afterwards transferred to Christmas;† and lastly, the summer *blot*, on April 14th.

In addition to the regular temples built of wood, there were also altars which were erected in the open air; these were called *Hørg*, and the word still survives in the names of several places in Norway.‡

The temples were of two classes, the public and the private ones. The former were the *Hovs*, belonging to each *fylke* or division of the country, and these were again divided into *herreds*, where there were also temples.

The other class consisted of what might be called private chapels, where some wealthy chief kept one up at his own expense. The public ones were supported by landed property assigned to them, and partly by taxation.

The temples were sacred, and any one desecrating them or breaking the peace in them was liable to outlawry. This was not uncommon, as the feasting and frequent *skaals* drunk, often led to very deadly quarrels in the course of the celebration of the *blots*.

Pilgrimages were made to the more famous temples, and were undertaken in later days even from so great a distance as Iceland.

Such was the religion of the Norwegians in the ancient times, and we have given these particulars with regard to it, as it is necessary we should bear them in mind when

---

* These offerings might also be made by women.
† See p. 26.
‡ In Voss and Hordaland, also in names of mountains.

we come to deal with the struggle between the forces of heathenism and Christianity. We shall see that the early Christian missionaries were fully conscious of the advisability of adapting as far as they could the heathen customs to Christian usages, and making the transition as easy as possible for their rude converts.

In order to follow the course of events in the history of Norway, we should understand something of the geographical divisions of the country in mediæval times, and carefully study the map.

In the early days the whole country was divided into what were called *fylker*, literally " folk land," the districts inhabited by certain folk. These districts were mostly greater than the largest of the English shires in modern times, but they varied considerably in area. They corresponded somewhat to the *amts* into which Norway is now divided. These *fylker* had mostly a petty king or chief over them, usually the largest and most powerful landowner, but to him the people paid no taxes—he was only their chief and leader in time of war. The *fylker* were again subdivided into *herreds* or hundreds, and the chief man there was the *Herse*.

The population consisted of the Bønder and their thralls. It is difficult to find an English word which will accurately render the meaning of the word *Bonde*, the singular of Bønder. To translate it as some have done, by the word peasant, conveys an entirely incorrect meaning. The Norwegian *Bonde* was a free man dwelling on his own land, having no lord over him to whom he was under any of the obligations of feudalism. His obligations were to defend the country when attacked, and to contribute to the support of the *Hov*. This tenure of the land was called Odel, and any attempts to interfere with it met with the strongest opposition. The Bønder, however, sometimes let out a portion of their land which they might not require, to others, but these *Leilændinger,* as they were called, were also free men.

In all the subsequent history, it is important to bear in mind that Bønder were really the depositaries of all political power, and that they formed a class which was in many respects unique in Europe. In later days their power was curtailed and reduced, but the absence in Norway of the feudalism which prevailed over the most of Europe gave them an influence in the history of their land which was very remarkable.

Local self-government prevailed in Norway from the earliest times. The Bønder met in councils called *Things,* where the affairs of the district were settled. There were *Things* for each *fylke* and *herred,* to decide the more local questions, and there were also the greater assemblies of the people, in centres where many of the *fylker* were grouped together, and where the laws were made. Thus we find for the northern *fylker* there was the great Frosta *Thing,* which met at Frosta on the Trondhjem Fjord, and which legislated for Trøndelagen and Haalogaland; the Gula Thing for the western and southern *fylker;* and the Eidsiva *Thing* for the more central parts. These gatherings were the parliaments of Norway; at them the kings were chosen, and we find that, in order to secure uniformity in the laws proposed by the early Christian kings, they were obliged to have the consent of each of these assemblies of the free men of Norway.

In the early days the northern *fylker,* and especially the fertile district of Trøndelagen, enjoyed the greatest political power, and the candidate for the crown who secured the adherence of the Frosta *Thing* was almost certain to be successful with the other assemblies. Trøndelagen was also the stronghold of heathenism, and the two Olafs met there with more opposition in their efforts on behalf of Christianity than in any other part of the land.

The far north of Norway, with its sparse population of Lapps and Finns, had practically no part in the history of the country; it remained heathen for centuries after the rest of the land had been converted, and afforded an outlet for the crusading zeal of the kings, in the days when the Saracens were left in undisturbed possession of the Holy Land, and the fierce enthusiasm of the eleventh and twelfth centuries had passed away.

CHAPTER II.

THE FOUNDING OF THE KINGDOM.

Halfdan the Black—Harald Haarfagre—The Consolidation of the Kingdom—Internal Government—Repressive Measures and their Results—Harald's Sons—Erik Bloodaxe—Haakon—Harald's Death and Creed.

IT is not until the middle of the ninth century that we begin to emerge from the mythical period of Norwegian history, and come to the reign of Halfdan Svarte, or Halfdan the Black, who was a petty king over the region lying to the west and north of what is now the Christiania Fjord, but at that time known as Vestfold.

His father was Halfdan Hvitbein (the white leg), who came of the mythical race of the Ynglinger, said to have been descended from the goddess Freya. This race came from Sweden and settled in that part of Norway before mentioned. Halfdan Hvitbein was a prudent chief, and encouraged commerce and agriculture in his dominions. Halfdan the Black increased his father's possessions to a considerable extent in a northern direction, and was the originator of the famous Eidsiva law, which was, for many generations, the law for that part of Norway, as the Frosta law was for Trøndelagen. This collection of laws derived its name from having been promulgated at the Thing held at Eidsvold, a spot close to the southern end of the great Miøsen lake, and where the present constitution of Norway was drawn up in 1814.

In 860, Halfdan was returning from a feast at Hadeland in the spring of the year, and when crossing the Rands Fjord at Røkenvik, the ice, which was then beginning to thaw, gave way under the royal sledge. His retainers, rushing to his rescue, only made matters worse, and the king and his immediate followers were drowned. His death was the cause of much grief to his people, who had enjoyed under his rule a time of great prosperity, and a succession of good harvests, a manifest proof of the favour of the gods. In order to secure a continuance of these benefits, they decided to divide his body into four portions, and to bury them in different parts of his dominions.

Halfdan left behind him an only son, named Harald, then a child of only ten years of age. His mother was Ragnhild, a wise and prudent woman, and granddaughter of Harald Klak, King of Jutland. Before her son's birth she dreamt that she was holding a thorn in her hand, which grew to be a great tree which struck its roots deep down into the earth, and the top of which reached to heaven. It had wide-spreading branches, which covered the whole of Norway and the countries around it. The lower part of the tree was red as blood, and the branches above were white as snow.

The child whose future greatness was thus foreshadowed by the dream was the far-famed Harald Haarfagre, the founder of the kingdom of Norway, and progenitor of a race of kings which, with a few brief interruptions, ruled over Norway for close upon four hundred years.

The early days of Harald were passed under the wise guidance and direction of his uncle Guthorm, who skilfully piloted the youthful monarch through the various dangers to which he was exposed, and reduced to submission many of the neighbouring petty kings.

When Harald grew to manhood he sought as his wife the beautiful Gyda, daughter of King Erik of Hordaland. She declined his advances, and declared she would marry none of these petty kings. She told the king's messengers to carry back to him her final decision : " I will not be his wife until, for my sake, he has conquered the whole of Norway." When Harald received this message he declared that Gyda had spoken well. "I call God, who made me, to witness," he said, "that never will I have my hair cut or combed until I have conquered the whole of Norway, with *skat*, duties, and lordships, or die in the attempt."

Harald kept his word. Aided by his uncle and the famous Jarl, Ragnvald of Møre (the district now known as Nordmøre, Romsdal, and Søndmøre), and his own great courage and strength, he rapidly conquered one petty kingdom after another, and defeating the jarls or kings who ruled over them, soon consolidated his kingdom. It was not, however, until after the great naval battle of Hafrsfjord, near Stavanger (872), that the opposition of the local rulers was crushed and Harald everywhere acknowledged as overlord of Norway. Immediately after the battle his long and matted hair was cut by Ragnvald Jarl, and his bright golden locks gained him the name of the Fair-haired, or Haarfagre. Soon after this he claimed the hand of the scornful beauty who had declined his suit in his earlier days.

When he had established his kingdom he quickly made his power everywhere felt; lawlessness of all kinds was repressed with a stern hand, and the poor and the oppressed looked up to the king with gratitude, and were ready to defend him against all comers.

Harald, however, decided to introduce changes which were distasteful to both the Bønder and the Jarls, and the enforcement of which led to very important results for other nations besides his own. The land of Norway, as we have seen, was held by what was called Odel tenure; in other words, the owners were free from payment of *skat*, and were only obliged, when called upon, to follow their leaders in the defence of the land from the attacks of enemies.

The king wished them to hold their land as fiefs from

the crown, and this naturally provoked much hostility. Over each *fylke*, or group of *fylker*, the king appointed a jarl, and extorted from the unwilling people the payment of *skat*, or tribute. He also further compelled the chief men in the districts to take service under him, and become a part of his immediate following.

Changes of this nature were not likely to be quietly acquiesced in by a people so independent as the hardy Norwegian Bønder, but the power of the king was too great to admit of successful resistance, and the alternative lay between submission to the royal authority or migration. Many of the chiefs and principal men chose the latter. They took ship and left their native land, and established themselves in the Shetlands, Orkneys, and Hebrides. Others went further and, after various raids, founded a kingdom in Dublin, and settlements in various places on the Irish coast as well as the Isle of Man. They also established themselves on the Færoe Islands, where previously Irish monks had made a home for themselves. The most important settlement, however, was made in Iceland, where an independent state was founded, which in later years became famous for its learning and literature, and from whence the colonization of Greenland and part of the coast of North America was carried out.

Another of Harald Haarfagre's reforms led to results which may be said to have permanently affected the history of Europe. It was customary for those who fitted out Viking expeditions to levy enforced contributions in money and kind from the people along the coast; these extortions were known as *strandhug*. Harald, with the intention of protecting his people, sternly forbade the practice, and decreed outlawry as the punishment for a breach of his law. A notable offender was soon forthcoming. Ragnvald Jarl, the king's greatest supporter, and the champion of his early days, had a son named Rolf, who,

from his great size and weight, and because none of the
small Norwegian horses or ponies could carry him, received
the surname of the Ganger, or walker. This man was
one of the boldest spirits in the Viking days, and on one
occasion, when coming home from an expedition, he allowed
his followers to make a raid on the cattle and goods of
the farmers in Viken. A weaker king might have hesitated to enforce the law against the son of his old friend.
But Harald did not hesitate. The law must be obeyed;
and Rolf the Ganger was banished from Norway. He went
to what was then known as Neustria, and extorted the
concession of a "Danelag" from Charles III. A century
and a half later his descendant, William Duke of Normandy,
sat on the throne of England. Had *strandhug* not been
illegal, or had a weaker monarch than Harald Haarfagre
ruled over Norway, how different might have been the
history and destiny of England !

Harald had a numerous family by his different wives,
and towards the end of his long reign he adopted the very
unwise expedient of dividing his kingdom among them,
but leaving his eldest and favourite son Erik, who was surnamed *Blodøkse* (Bloodaxe), from his prowess in war, as overlord of the various smaller kingdoms. Such an arrangement
led to its natural results. Erik determined to overthrow
the power of his brothers, and caused Bjørn *Farmand*
(the Merchant), who ruled over the district about Tønsberg,
to be treacherously murdered. He proceeded to attack
Halfdan, who was king in Trøndelagen, but the latter was
warned in time, and collecting men and ships, made so good
a defence that Erik was forced to go to his father for protection. After this a truce was arranged by friends on
both sides, and thus for a time things resumed a more
peaceful condition.

In 921, Harald in his old age, had a son by a mistress
named Thora of Moster, who, from her great height, was

known as Moster *stang*, or pole. This son was named Haakon, and his appearance on the scene was naturally displeasing to the other sons of the king, who had grown to man's estate, and were to divide the kingdom between them. Harald saw the danger to which the boy's life would be exposed if he allowed him to remain in Norway, so he sent him to England, while still a very little child, to the court of Athelstan, where he remained until his father's death. In England the child was baptized and brought up as a Christian, and afterwards was the means of first bringing Christianity into Norway.

In 930, at the age of eighty, the old King decided to surrender all his authority into the hands of Erik, and to carry into force the arrangement which he had made before. Three years afterwards he died at his residence at Hauge, close to the present town of Haugesund, a little to the north of Stavanger. Where he died, there he was buried. On a mound overlooking the sea, and swept by the winds of the Northern Ocean, the greatest man that Norway had yet seen was laid to rest. On the top of the mound which was heaped over the body of the great warrior and ruler, the usual *bautasten*, or memorial stone, was erected ; and in after days, when his descendants sailed along the coast in their war ships to battle against foreign enemies or rebellious subjects, they saw it from afar, and remembered the man who had welded into one the divided kingdoms of Norway, and made it for the first time one of the nations of Europe. In days of anarchy and oppression, when Danish or other races sought for supremacy over Norway, men turned to the descendants of Harald the Fair-haired, thinking that of his line there must ever be a ruler and a chief, who would bring back to them again, the days when justice to all would be neither " sold, delayed, or denied," and when Norway would be united under its own king.

During the long reign of Harald, Norway remained

altogether pagan.   The king himself seems to have had but little faith in the old gods, though he conformed to all the usages connected with the heathen sacrifices at the three great feasts of the year—in January, April, and October.   He had doubtless heard and known of the Christian faith from his intercourse with England and Denmark; but he seems, if the Sagas are to be trusted, to have had a comparatively simple and characteristic creed: " He believed in the God who was the strongest and had created all things and ruled all things."

CHAPTER III.

THE FIRST CONTACT WITH CHRISTIANITY.

The Religious Results of Viking Cruises—Northmen in the British Isles—Enforced Baptism—Half Christianity—The Missions from Hamburg and Bremen—Ansgar's Life and Work.

In order to understand the way in which the heathen Norwegians first learned of the Christian faith, it is necessary to retrace our steps. It was in the last quarter of the eighth century, or about eighty or ninety years before the accession of Harald Haarfagre, that the Viking expeditions began, which, for nearly three hundred years, made the Northmen the terror of North-Western Europe, and of certain districts in the Mediterranean as well. The adventurous chiefs from Norway, Sweden, and Denmark set forth in their long ships, each rowed by from twenty to forty men, and passing quickly over the waters of the North Sea, began to harry the coasts of England, Scotland, Ireland, and Northern France.

Readers of English history are familiar with the entry in the Anglo-Saxon Chronicle under the year 787, which tells of the first appearance of these dreaded foes ; and we know the way in which, from being at first mere marauding expeditions, they were continued until settlements and kingdoms were established in the north-east of England, the Orkneys and Shetlands, Dublin, and the Isle of Man. We are, however, not concerned so much with the political as the religious results of these expeditions, for they were the means by which, as far as we can learn, the heathen Norwegians were first brought in contact with Christianity.

In England and Ireland they came to countries where,

especially in the latter, the Christian faith had for some centuries entirely possessed the land, and had to a considerable extent tamed the wilder passions of the Saxon and Keltic races.   When the warriors came ashore from their ships the churches and monasteries naturally offered a tempting prey on account of their unprotected state, and the Northmen quickly availed themselves of the treasure which they found there.   They also undoubtedly learned of the Christian faith from the captives they had taken, and from seeing something, as they often did, during more peaceful visits, of the stately worship and ritual of the Church, which was not without its influence on the fierce Northmen.

The tenets of Christianity, however, did not naturally commend themselves to those who placed fighting in the very forefront of the duty of man, and to whom the clash of arms and the carnage of the battle would appeal more forcibly than the most stately service of the Church, with all the accessories of music and banners.

In places where the invaders settled for the winter, instead of returning back, or where, for one or another cause, they were detained, there were not wanting faithful priests, who, taking their lives in their hands, tried to win the fierce Vikings to the faith of Christ, at least, so far as to consent to be baptized, or if they would not do that, to allow themselves to be what was called *primsigne* (*prima signatio*), signed with the cross, a sort of half-way house to Christianity.

In these efforts they were not infrequently successful, but it must be borne in mind that compliance with the entreaties of the priests and others, did not at all necessarily imply the acceptance of a real faith in Christianity.   On the contrary, we know that when the Viking marauders found themselves in a position from which they could not well extricate themselves, and were surrounded by their enemies, it was not at all uncommon for the chief and his followers to allow themselves to be baptized *en masse*, as it usually offered a way of escape, and further enriched them with presents of handsome baptismal robes. Indeed, it appears an undoubted fact that it was not an unknown thing for Viking chiefs and their followers to be baptized several times over in different countries or places.

It is, of course, true that there were genuine conversions to Christianity among the Norwegians, but many of the earliest baptisms were of the nature described.

When, however, after some years the Norwegians and Northmen settled themselves in districts they had conquered, then real progress was made in the propagation of the faith, and they became, as in Dublin, in Cumbria, and the Danelag, as faithful and earnest Christians as those who had taught them the faith.

This, however, was outside the Norwegian kingdom. In Norway it only helped to break down the ancient faith in the gods. Many of the great men, like King Harald Haarfagre, were indifferent to the old religion, and only believed in the God who was the strongest and ruled all.

Some of the Vikings followed a middle course, like that adopted by the colonists whom the kings of Assyria placed in the cities of Samaria. They were baptized and they took Christ into their worship. The Sagas tell us of one of these, Helge the Thin, of Iceland, who had thus been converted. When he was ashore on his farm he worshipped Christ, but when he was at sea, or in any position of danger, he offered his prayers and sacrifices to Thor.

It may be wondered why it was that Christianity did not first come to Norway from the South, instead of from the British Isles ; but the explanation is not a difficult one. The latter countries had already been christianized, while between Norway and the Christianity of the revived Western

Empire there was still a solid mass of heathenism. The Kaiser, Karl the Great, after reducing the Saxons to submission, was anxious to bring the Northern nations to Christianity, partly from religious and partly from political motives, so that he might be made more secure from attack. Nothing, however, seems to have been done in his day, but under Ludvig the Pious an attempt was made to evangelize the Danes, and he appealed to Ebbo, the Archbishop of Rheims, to send a missionary to them. The Pope (Paschal I.) also wrote a letter commending the work. Such, however, was the terror which spread over the north-west of Europe at the ravages of the Vikings, that at first no one was found to volunteer, until at last the famous Ansgar, "the Apostle of the North," a monk of Corvei, near Amiens, undertook the task.

He began his work in Holstein, accompanied by his faithful friend Autbert. After two years' labours he was obliged to flee to the court of the Emperor, and the work appeared to have failed. Just at that time, however, Bjørn, the King of Sweden, sent a messenger to the Kaiser asking for a Christian teacher, and Ansgar was sent in 830. After various adventures and dangers, Ansgar reached Birk (Sigtuna), and laboured with much success for a year and a half, when he returned with a letter to the Kaiser. Ludvig saw the importance of establishing an episcopal see near to the mission field, and selected Hamburg as the spot, and in 834 Ansgar was consecrated as Archbishop by the Archbishop of Metz and several other prelates. Shortly afterwards Gautbert was consecrated Bishop of Sweden.

Thus the work progressed, but troubles were yet to come. In 845 the heathen King Erik, of Jylland, in Denmark, attacked Hamburg and burned the cathedral, library, and monastery to the ground, and Ansgar escaped only with his life. The Swedes at the same time attacked Gautbert and destroyed his mission. Ludvig the Pious was now dead, and his sons divided the Empire, Ludvig the German having the portion which most concerned Ansgar.

At this time the bishopric of Bremen was vacant, and Ludvig decided to transfer the archiepiscopal see to that town in 849, and it was made the metropolitan see for the Northern nations, and independent of Köln, in which it was formerly situated.

The work again prospered. King Erik, the destroyer of Hamburg, became favourable to Christianity, and granted a place for a church in Slesvig, where, in 850, the first church in Denmark was erected, and dedicated to the Blessed Virgin. In 856 Ansgar's active life ended at the comparatively early age of sixty-four.

Thus it happened that Christianity had gained a hold in Sweden and Denmark a considerable time before it first appeared in Norway; but it is strange that there was practically no attempt made to christianize Norway from either Denmark or Sweden. To the British Isles, to England especially, the honour of having brought the faith of Christ to Norway is almost entirely due, and the Church in Norway was a daughter of the Anglo-Saxon Church.

A notice of the foundation of the metropolitan see of Bremen is necessary here, as it was for a considerable period the province in which the Norwegian Church was situated; and to the famous Chronicle of Adam of Bremen we are indebted for many interesting references to early Christianity in Norway.

CHAPTER IV.

HAAKON THE GOOD AND THE FIRST ATTEMPT TO INTRODUCE CHRISTIANITY.

Erik and Gunhild's unpopularity—Coming of Haakon—Erik driven out—Haakon a Christian—His tentative Efforts on behalf of the Faith—Formal Attempt at the Frosta *Thing*—Its Failure—Haakon's Lapse, his Death, and Burial.

On the death of Harald Haarfagre, in 933, his eldest son, Erik Blodøkse, became overlord of Norway, in accordance with the arrangement made by his father. He was a cruel and overbearing man, but of undoubted courage in battle, as his surname implies. He was never popular with the people, and the murder of his brother Bjørn made it plain that he intended, when he had the opportunity, to murder or drive away his other brothers from the small kingdoms their father had allotted to them, and to become, as his father had been before him, the sole king in the land.

The unpopularity of Erik was increased tenfold by reason of his queen Gunhild, whom he had married several years before. She was a native of Haalogaland and renowned for her beauty, and Erik had met her in one of his northern journeys. In addition to her beauty, she is said to have possessed the very doubtful recommendation of a knowledge of sorcery, which she had learned from the Finns of the North, and this did not tend to increase her popularity. There can be no doubt whatever, that she was a wicked and ambitious woman, who, playing the part of a Northern Jezebel in the royal court, proved the king's evil genius.

The tyrannical rule of Erik, and the universal hatred with which his wife was regarded, provoked discontent on

all sides, and in little more than a year he was driven
from the land.

When King Harald Haarfagre died, there was living at
the court of Athelstan his youngest son Haakon, who, as
we have seen, had been dispatched thither for safety by
the old king. During his residence in England he had
been baptized and brought up in the Christian faith.
When his father died, in 933, he was a lad of about
fourteen, but tall and handsome, and bearing a very striking
resemblance to his fair-haired father. When tidings of
Harald's death reached England, Athelstan at once determined to supply his foster-son with the equipment necessary
to enable him to proceed to Norway and claim his share
in his father's kingdom. Among the many gifts bestowed
by the king upon the young prince, we read of a magnificent sword, with a hilt of gold and a blade of such
strength and temper, that it would cleave a millstone ;
from this fact it was given the name of *Kvernbit* (the
quern cutter), and it never failed Haakon in any battle
during the whole of his long and adventurous career.
With ships and men supplied by the English king, the
young chief set sail for his native land and proceeded at
once to Trøndelagen, to the great chief Sigurd Jarl of
Hlade, a spot close to the present city of Trondhjem,
which at that time was not yet in existence.

The powerful jarl at once espoused the cause of Haakon,
from whom he received the promise of greatly extended
power, when he obtained the kingdom. The first step to
be taken was to summon the *Thing* to meet, which Sigurd
lost no time in doing. When the bønder were assembled,
Sigurd addressed them on Haakon's behalf, and presented
the young prince to them. When he began to speak the
older men at once recognized him as a true son of Haarfagre, and cried out with joy that it was the old monarch
who had become young once more.

Haakon, doubtless under the wise guidance of Sigurd, promised the people that if they helped him to gain the kingdom, he would restore the much-prized Odel rights, of which they had been deprived by his father, whose action in this respect had been most unpopular among the bønder, and which only the strong hand of Harald had been able to enforce.

The promise of this great concession settled the matter, with one accord the people at the *Thing* took him as king. With the help of Sigurd Jarl the conflict did not last long; the hatred of King Erik, and especially of Queen Gunhild, was so intense that few were found to defend his cause, and in little more than a year, in 935, Erik and Gunhild were driven from Norway, and took refuge at first in Denmark. From thence Erik passed into England, and received the kingdom of Northumbria from Athelstan, and afterwards (in the reign of Edmund) fell in the battle of Stainmoor, the exact date of which is uncertain, but it was probably fought between 950 and 954.*

When Haakon's authority as overlord of Norway was everywhere accepted, and he had made the people happy and contented by the removal of their grievances, he felt the time had come to attempt the formal introduction of Christianity into Norway, by securing its recognition at the *Things*.

In many ways it was a favourable moment. The Viking expeditions had made Christianity known to many, and if they were not prepared to accept the new faith, at any rate their belief in the old gods of their forefathers was shaken, and the great personal popularity of the king was much in his favour. It is true that his chief supporter, the great Jarl of Hlade, was still a zealous heathen, but his loyalty to his young monarch was undoubted, and in the subsequent

* "The Battle of Stainmoor," by W. G. Collingwood, in the Cumberland and Westmoreland Antiquarian Society's "Transactions," Vol. II.

struggles he saved him in many moments of great personal danger.

It seems most reasonable to believe that amongst the retinue with which his English foster-father had supplied him, there would probably have been found at least one priest, who would carry on the religious instruction of the young prince, and also that a considerable number, if not all, of his English supporters were Christians. When Haakon's power was established, very likely many of these returned to England, and the king was left with but a few Christians in his immediate following. The personal influence of Haakon seems to have induced a few of his heathen subjects to be baptized, and to abandon the old sacrifices.

When this was done Haakon took a more decisive step. He sent a message to England to ask that a bishop and priests should be sent out to Norway to aid him in his work.

We have no certain means of knowing whether a bishop responded to this invitation, but there is a list given by William of Malmesbury in "De Antiquitate Glastoniensis Ecclesiæ," of bishops who had been monks of that famous foundation; amongst them we find the name of "Sigefridus Norwegensis Episcopus." There are many conflicting opinions as to the identity of this man with Haakon's helper. Three other bishops have been claimed as William's "Norwegensis Episcopus." *

It is plainly stated by Snorre that Haakon had churches built, and placed priests to minister in them, and these churches were erected in the Møre and Romsdal districts where Haakon chiefly resided. They were probably only wooden churches, and they quickly perished after the failure of Haakon to procure the recognition of Christianity. The bishop and priests were either murdered or fled back again to England.

At the commencement of his reign Haakon had not taken

* See Appendix I.

any official part in the usual sacrifices to the gods, but this did not excite suspicion because it was understood that being only a lad he wished those duties to be performed by deputy, which was accordingly done. Haakon, however, did nothing rashly, and wisely decided not to force Christianity on his people all at once. Among various tentative measures he secured (apparently without opposition) the transference of the great *Julefest*, held early in January, to the time of the Christian festival of Christmas, and made its duration the same.

Thus the years passed by, and Haakon waited for his opportunity. In or about the year 950, after having reigned for sixteen years, and having had for some time the government in his own hands, he felt he was strong enough to make the attempt. His first step was to bring the question before the local *Things* in Møre and Romsdal districts, in which he frequently resided, and where he felt his personal influence would be considerable. These assemblies, however, seeing the importance of the question, excused themselves on the ground that it lay beyond their powers, and should be considered by the great Frosta *Thing* to whose laws they were subject. To this Haakon agreed, and prepared to bring the matter before the great assembly of the North. The Frosta *Thing* was usually held at midsummer, when the days were longest, and night in those regions practically unknown. From all the eight *fylker* of Trøndelagen the people flocked to the yearly meeting, and the gathering on this occasion was unusually large. The *Thing* having been opened with the usual formalities, King Haakon rose and addressed the people. The critical moment so long looked forward to by the king, had now come, and the first formal attempt to procure the recognition of Christianity in Norway was now to be made.

Haakon began with an earnest appeal to the people to embrace the faith in which he had been brought up, to permit themselves to be baptized, to believe in the one God and His Son Jesus Christ. The people listened in silence. Had the king stopped there, it is possible he might have met with, at any rate, a partial success; but when he proceeded to tell them they must not work on Sundays, and that, further, they must be prepared to follow the Christian usage and fast on Fridays, then the cries of dissent broke out. The idea of abstinence from food was not at all an acceptable one to the Northmen, and to abstain from work on Sundays might often mean the partial loss of the hay harvest, or failure in securing a good haul of fish. Haakon, however, was very plain in setting before them all that the acceptance of Christianity would entail.

When the king had ended, there stood up in the council one Asbjørn of Medalhus, a wealthy bonde from a place now called Melhus in Guldal, near Trondhjem. He told the king that the people willingly acknowledged the benefits which had come to them from his wise and kindly rule, especially in the restoration to them of their Odel rights and privileges. But he declared in no uncertain tones that they would not give up the faith of their fathers, and accept the thraldom which it seemed the king wished to force upon them. If he insisted on this, then they would choose another king, but they had no desire to quarrel with him so long as they were left to worship the gods of their forefathers. This speech was received with shouts of applause by the people, and it was at once apparent that the assembly was entirely hostile to Haakon's proposed innovations.

Then Sigurd Jarl stood up in defence of the young monarch. He hastened to explain to the people that they were under a mistake in supposing that Haakon wished to force his views on them, or to cause any break in the friendship which existed between them. With this he quieted the people, and the proceedings terminated, the victory remaining with the heathen party.

Having thus thwarted the king, the believers in the old gods were determined to press home their advantage, and an opportunity for this soon presented itself.   At the usual festival held in October, when the winter sacrifices were offered, the Odin's *mindebæger* (the horn of beer to be drunk to Odin) was handed to the king.   Before drinking it he made the sign of the cross over it.   At this the watchful heathen protested, but the wily Jarl Sigurd explained that the king, believing in his own strength, dedicated the horn to Thor instead of Odin, by making over it the sign of *Mjølnir* (Thor's hammer), and so the incident passed.

The crisis, however, soon came.   At the *Julefest* the heathen party resolved there should be no more tem- porizing.   They made it clear to the king that either he must join in the heathen ceremonies or forfeit his crown. Sigurd Jarl saw the danger, and with difficulty persuaded Haakon to give way.   The feast was held, and the king ate some of the horse-flesh and drank of all the necessary horns of beer to the gods, this time without making the sign of the cross, and thus openly sealed his adherence to the Asa faith.   But he left the feast heavy and displeased, and intending to come back with a powerful force and revenge himself on the bønder, but for the time the triumph of Odin and Thor over "the White Christ" was complete.

It is easy for us to condemn Haakon for his apostacy, but we must remember the position in which he was placed.   Cut off from the support of those in England among whom he had been brought up, surrounded by heathen, many of whom he had good cause to love, and with the certainty of losing his kingdom, if not his life, if he refused to join in the idol feasts, his kind-heartedness and good-nature, as well as the pressure of circumstances, all combined to make him yield an outward compliance with the demands of the heathen party. All through the rest of his life he seems to have felt deeply his abandonment of the faith, and his failure to spread it in his kingdom. He was doubtless sincere in his intention to make another effort on behalf of Christianity when a convenient opportunity presented itself, but the " convenient season" never came.

After these events, fresh trouble was in store for Haakon and his kingdom. His brother, Erik Bloodaxe of Northumberland, was slain in battle, and his sons determined to attempt to regain the kingdom from which their father had been driven by Haakon. Queen Gunhild went with them to Denmark, where the king, Harald Gormssøn, was ready to give them assistance. They made several descents upon Norway, and Haakon was obliged to summon to his aid all his available forces, and he dared not weaken his strength by any question of religion.

The attacks of Gunhild's sons were repulsed with great loss to them, but they only retired to Denmark for fresh help, and appeared again and again on the coast. This state of things lasted till the close of Haakon's life.

In 960 the king was paying a visit at Fitjar, on the large island of Stord, in Søndhordland, off the entrance to the great Hardanger Fjord. While there, with but a small force, he was surprised by the fleet of Harald Graafell, the eldest of Erik's sons. The enemy were in overwhelming force, but Haakon and his men disdained to seek safety in flight. A fierce battle ensued, in which, after a desperate struggle, Harald Graafell's forces were defeated and forced to fly. Just at the very end of the battle Haakon was mortally wounded by an arrow. Before his death, having no son, he named his nephew Harald as his successor. Then, we are told, the sorrow for his abandonment of the faith filled the king's mind. "If life is granted to me,"

he said to his followers, "I will betake myself to a land of
Christian men, and do penance and atone for my sin
against God, but if I die here in heathenism, then bury me
as you wish yourselves."

His men, with tears, told him they would carry his body
over to England, and give it Christian burial.   But the
dying king shook his head.   " I am not worthy of it," he
said.   " I have lived as a heathen, and, therefore, as a
heathen should I be buried."

As a heathen he was laid to rest.   He was buried on his
estate at Sæheim, in Nordhordland.   All men mourned for
him, friends and foes alike, and "men said such a good
king would never come to Norway again."   The love and
veneration of his people marked him out among the kings
as Haakon the Good.

CHAPTER V.

HARALD GRAAFELL; AND THE HEATHEN REACTION UNDER HAAKON JARL.

Norway under Gunhild's Sons—Graafell murdered in Denmark—
Haakon Jarl rules Norway under Harald Blaatand of Denmark
—Haakon Jarl's enforced Baptism—Danish Missionaries in Viken
—Adam of Bremen's Testimony—The Results of this Work—
Norwegian Church a Daughter of the English Church—Haakon
Jarl and the Jomsvikings—The Battle at Livaag—Haakon's Evil
Deeds and the Coming Deliverer.

The death of Haakon the Good was followed by a period
of anarchy and struggles with foreign foes, which lasted
for some thirty-five years, and caused much suffering and
want in the land.

Haakon, on his deathbed, had expressed the wish that
his nephew Harald, surnamed Graafell, should succeed
him. He was the eldest of the five sons of Erik Blodøkse,
and with them he shared the portions of Norway ruled
over by Haakon, namely, the northern and north-western
divisions, for it must be remembered that the grandsons
of Harald Haarfagre held the petty kingdoms in Viken
(the country around the Christiania Fjord), which he had
bestowed on their fathers.

Harald Graafell, however, was the overlord of the
portions where his brothers ruled. As they were mainly
guided by the universally detested Gunhild, they soon
became very unpopular. Following the example of their
father, they endeavoured to extend their authority by the
treacherous murder of King Trygve,* the son of Olaf, and

---

* The father of the great Olaf Trygvessøn, who at the time of this
murder was not yet born, see p. 40.

Gudrød, the son of their father's victim, Bjørn, both kings in Viken. Sigurd Jarl was another obstacle in their way, and he, too, was slain. The people of Trøndelagen immediately supported his son, Haakon Jarl, and Gunhild's sons soon found to their cost what a mistake they had made in killing his father. At first, however, they were partially successful, and Haakon Jarl was obliged to take refuge with Harald *Blaatand* (blue tooth), king of Denmark.

Harald Graafell and his brothers were nominal Christians, as they had been baptized when in England, and in Norway during their time the ancient heathen system was still further weakened. The brothers do not seem to have attempted to obtain any official recognition of Christianity from the *Things*, as Haakon did—indeed, their zeal for the propagation of the faith was of a very negative character, and manifested itself chiefly in the destruction and plunder of the heathen temples wherever they went, and enriching themselves and their followers with the spoils. No attempt was made to force Christianity on the people, nor were, as far as we can see, any churches erected or rebuilt in any part of Norway. Men were free to worship as they thought fit, and the example of the sons of Gunhild was not likely to prepossess the heathen in favour of the faith which they nominally professed. These were years of bad harvests, and distress was everywhere prevalent; the fish forsook the shores, and famine and sickness stalked through the land. In these calamities the people saw the wrath of the gods whose temples had been destroyed, and who were not propitiated with sacrifices. Universal discontent prevailed.

About the year 970 (the exact date is doubtful) Harald Graafell was treacherously induced to visit Denmark, and when there was attacked and slain. This was the opportunity which Harald Blaatand was looking for to assert his supremacy over Norway. He at once set sail with a powerful fleet to Trøndelagen; and, as there was no one to oppose him (two of Harald Graafell's brothers were already dead, and Gunhild and the others fled to the Orkneys), he had no difficulty in having himself acknowledged as king. Haakon Jarl was left as governor over the north and western *fylker*, and the district of Viken was under Harald's immediate care. Haakon was, as a vassal, bound to assist his overlord Harald whenever called upon.

Now came, in the region ruled over by Haakon, a veritable heathen reaction. The jarl was a devout adherent of the ancient faith, and set to work immediately to rebuild the temples and to celebrate once more the heathen festivals at the appointed seasons. The first year of Haakon's rule was signalized by the return of the herrings to the coast, which they had forsaken, and a prosperous harvest ; so the people recognized in this that the anger of the gods was appeased and the evil averted from the land.

It was not long before Harald Blaatand had to summon his vassal Haakon to his aid. The young Kaiser Otto II., who had succeeded his father in 973, invaded Denmark in 975, in order to bring that kingdom more completely into subjection (as Harald had designs of rejecting the suzerainty which Otto I. had imposed on him), and also for the purpose of forcibly advancing Christianity in Denmark. Considerable progress had been made, as we have seen, under Ansgar, the Archbishop of Bremen, and a church had been erected at Slesvig ; but the king still remained a heathen.

In obedience to Harald's call, Haakon Jarl raised an army and fleet, and came to the aid of his overlord. After a short resistance, however, Harald was defeated, and the Kaiser offered him terms of peace on condition that he should be baptized. We are told that the holy Bishop Poppo preached to the king and his army, and the result was that both Harald and all his forces were baptized.

The Danish king, having thus accepted Christianity, decided that his vassal must do the same, and sent for

Haakon, who had taken refuge in his ships, and obliged him also to be baptized. Then, having supplied him "with priests and other learned men," he dispatched him to Norway.

Whatever may have been the sincerity of Harald in embracing Christianity, Haakon soon made it clear that he still remained a heathen. He set sail, and at the first possible opportunity put his ecclesiastics ashore and harried the coast of Sweden until he came to Norway, and, setting Harald at defiance, went overland to Trøndelagen. In revenge for this, the Danish king invaded the west coast of Norway and ravaged the country with fire and sword; but when Haakon had collected his fleet and came to resist the attack, Harald sailed back again into Denmark.

It is necessary at this point to advert to the missionary efforts which were made in the district of Viken, at this time directly subject to the Danish Crown. Harald, after his conversion to the faith under the persuasive eloquence and miracles of Bishop Poppo, did all in his power to promote the christianizing of his heathen subjects both in Denmark and Norway. For some details of this we are indebted to the "Gesta Hammaburgensis Ecclesiæ Pontificum" of Adam of Bremen, a chronicle of great value in connection with the early history of Christianity in the North; but, being naturally a very zealous supporter of the see of Bremen, it is probable that he may have been inclined to estimate more highly than it deserved, the work of the missionaries sent from Bremen to Norway; and possibly, also, to look with a not altogether impartial eye on the English Church's missionaries, to whose efforts mainly, as we shall see, the spread of the faith in Norway is due.

Adam mentions that Liafdag, who in 948 was consecrated to the see of Ribe, in Denmark, was the most famous among the early bishops and renowned for his miracles, and that he had preached "beyond the sea, that is in Sweden and Norway."

Snorre mentions that Harald, after his conversion, sent, amongst other men, "two jarls to Norway, who were to preach Christianity; which was also done in Viken, where King Harald's power prevailed." There they baptized many men, but after Harald's death they relapsed. Snorre does not give us the names of these "jarls," but in the Saga of the Jomsvikings they are mentioned under the very uncouth names of Urguthrjøtr and Brimiskjarr. Who these "jarls" were we have no means of knowing. It seems doubtful if they were jarls at all. Some suppose that if jarls were sent, they had priests with them, who were subsequently credited with having been jarls.

There seems no doubt whatever that there was, before Olaf Trygvessøn's day a certain amount of missionary work in Viken which was not altogether destitute of results, but that this was not a little magnified by the Bremen authorities later on, when the great work of the English bishops and priests, under the two Olafs, was made manifest.

The scholiast of Adam says, speaking of the labours of Olaf Trygvessøn's bishop : "Though before him our missionaries, Liafdag, Poppo, and Odinkar, had preached to that nation. This can we say : our missionaries laboured, and the English entered into their labours."* It is only fair to add that Adam himself takes a more liberal view when he says, with reference to the work of the two Churches : "The mother-Church of Hamburg bears no grudge if even foreigners have done good to her children, saying with the apostle :† *Quidam prædicant per invidiam et contentionem, quidam autem propter bonam voluntatem et caritatem. Quid enim? Dum omni modo sive per occasionem sive per veritatem Christus annuncietur, et in hoc gaudeo et gaudebo*'" (Phil. I., 16–18).

* Adam, Scholiast, 142.
† Adam II., c. 35.

It would be altogether unfair to fail to recognize the work of the missionaries sent forth by the see of Bremen to evangelize the North. But it seems pretty clear that the result of their efforts in Viken (the only part of Norway where they claim to have laboured) were not of a very lasting character, and that no attempt was made to organize the Church there, on any stable foundation, as St. Olaf did in his work throughout Norway. The claim of Bremen to have founded what might be called a rival Church to that established by the English missionaries cannot, indeed, be seriously considered. The Christianity of Viken seems, openly at least, to have disappeared under the heathen rule of Haakon Jarl; and, later on, the severing of the connection with the Danish Crown, when the district was incorporated in Olaf Trygvessøn's kingdom, brought Viken, like the rest of Norway, into the organization founded by the English missionaries; and the efforts of those sent forth from the see of Bremen were confined, for a considerable time at least, to the two other Scandinavian kingdoms.

The question seems to be fairly summed up by Keyser in the following words: "The direct and indirect results of the efforts of the German-Bremen Church in Norway were confined to individual conversions, or attempts at conversion, in Viken, whilst they never succeeded in forming any special Church community. On the other hand, Christianity over the whole of Norway, both with respect to the permanent conversion of the people and ecclesiastical organization, proceeded exclusively from England; in other words, *the Norwegian Church was wholly and completely a daughter of the English Church.*" *

Harald Blaatand did not long survive his failure to coerce his rebellious vassal Haakon Jarl. His death was the result of a wound, received in a battle fought against

* Keyser, *Den Norske Kirkes Historie,* Vol. I., p. 32.

his son Svein Tjugeskjæg (the forked beard), who had raised
an insurrection against him. On his father's death, Svein
was accepted as king of Denmark. The new king did not
forget the fact that his father had been the overlord of
Norway, and at once decided to take steps to bring
Haakon to submission to his authority. For this purpose
he called to his assistance the famous Jomsvikings.

This very remarkable guild of fighting men lived, when
ashore, in their stronghold at Jom, or Jumne, in Pomerania.
They were the heathen prototypes of the military orders
of later days, and lived under very strict rules and discipline. No one over fifty years, or under eighteen, was
admitted into their company, and women were strictly
excluded from their fortress. Around it there grew up a
town, with some considerable trade. The Jomsvikings
were very zealous heathen, and made it a distinct condition that none should come to the town who intended
to preach Christianity. Adam of Bremen, however, bears
witness to the fact that with this exception "no more
honest or kindly race could be found." The fierce courage
and endurance of these Vikings made their assistance much
sought for in local warfare.

The chief of the Jomsvikings at this time was Sigvald
Jarl, and to him Svein addressed himself. After the
usual negotiations Sigvald undertook within three years
to kill or to drive away from Norway, the rebellious
Haakon Jarl.

At the close of 978 the Jomsvikings set sail with a
powerful fleet, and reached the neighbourhood of Rogaland
at the time of the *Julefest*. Meanwhile Haakon had
received tidings of the approach of these formidable foes,
but nothing daunted he assembled a powerful fleet and
determined to defend his land. The Jomsviking force
sailed north, and, doubling the peninsula of Stadt, finally
came to battle with Haakon in the bay of Livaag, on the

island of Hareidland, which lies a little to the south of the
present town of Aalesund. There ensued one of the most
sanguinary battles ever fought in Norway. Haakon Jarl
and his son Erik fought with dauntless courage, but were
able to make little impression on the fierce Jomsvikings.
As the fight went on it seemed as if victory must rest
with the invaders. Then Haakon, in his extremity,
adopted a desperate and horrible expedient, the truth of
which there seems no reason to doubt, as we know such
practices were found among the heathen Norsemen.
Following the example of the king of Moab, he sought
to propitiate the gods with a human sacrifice. Leaving
his men to fight, he went hurriedly ashore, and there
offered up his little seven-year-old son Erling as a sacrifice
to the gods. Then followed a terrible storm, and the hail
beat with violence in the faces of the Vikings, and at last
they began to give way. Finally fortune declared itself
for Haakon, and the redoubtable Sigvald Jarl was forced
to fly with only twenty-five ships.

Haakon was now free from attack from Denmark, and
his authority was supreme over the north and west, and
it seemed as if he would be able to establish his family as
overlords of Norway as Harald Haarfagre had done.
But after the great victory at Livaag, when his power was
at its height, he became careless and secure, and soon his
cruelties and lust displeased even his heathen subjects, and
the land was filled with discontent. The forcible seizure
of the beautiful wife of Orm Lyrgia, one of the most
powerful of the bønder in Trøndelagen, brought matters to
a crisis. A deliverer of the race of the fair-haired Harald
was found in Olaf Trygvessøn, the most striking and
heroic character presented to us in the history of the
introduction of Christianity into Norway.

CHAPTER VI.

OLAF TRYGVESSØN, AND THE TRIUMPH OF THE WHITE CHRIST.

OLAF TRYGVESSØN may well be called the founder of the Norwegian Church, though the work of organization was carried out by the more widely-known Olaf the Saint. He was not, it is true, the first Christian king in the land, for Haakon the Good, and Harald Graafell, were both nominal Christians, and the former, before his lapse, had made a very sincere effort to induce his people to receive the faith. But he lacked what Olaf possessed, the burning zeal of a great missionary, albeit this zeal was at times evinced in a manner more suggestive of the followers of Mahomet than of Christ—and also (what was of no small importance) the strong argument of fighting men and ships, without which, it must be confessed, Olaf's conversions to Christianity would but seldom have taken place.

The early life of Olaf Trygvessøn, as recorded in the Sagas, is full of the strangest adventures, and it is difficult to determine how much of it is legendary. It is unnecessary for our purpose to follow all the incidents of his early days as set forth there; it is enough to confine ourselves to the principal events about which there is not much doubt.

Olaf Trygvessøn was, as his name indicates, the son of Trygve (the grandson of Harald Haarfagre), and one of the smaller kings who ruled in Viken. Trygve was, as we know, murdered by Gunhild's sons about the year 963. On her husband's death his wife, Astrid, fled for her life and took refuge on an island in the Randsfjord, a large lake in Hadeland, accompanied by her faithful foster-father, Torolv Luseskjæg. Soon after she gave birth to a son, who was named Olaf after his grandfather.* For some years Astrid and her child were pursued from place to place by the remorseless malignity of Queen Gunhild, and were often in extreme peril of their lives. Finding it unsafe to remain any longer in Norway, she eventually took refuge with her brother Sigurd, who had been for some time one of the principal men at the court of King Valdemar of Gardarike, a large district of Western Russia, at that time in Scandinavian hands.

Here Olaf remained until about his eighteenth year, when, in accordance with the practice of those times, he started on a Viking cruise with other adventurous spirits. He went to Vendland and Denmark, and soon collected a body of followers who acknowledged him as their chief. England, at this time under the feeble rule of Ethelred II., the Redeless, offered a very tempting field for Viking raids, and to that country and to the coasts of Scotland and Ireland Olaf and his followers accordingly went. He, in common with others, received from Ethelred considerable sums of money to abstain from plundering. After several years spent around the coasts of the British Isles, he came

---

* The heathen Norsemen had a ceremony resembling baptism, in which water was poured upon the child when he was named.

to the Scilly Isles, where, we are told, he was baptized by a holy man, probably a hermit, who foretold his future greatness, and instructed him in the Christian faith. He then went back to England, having made peace with Ethelred. This was in 994. Florence of Worcester tells us that this agreement was after some severe fighting, and adds a notice of another important event in Olaf's life. "Ælfheah (St. Alphege), Bishop of Winchester, and the noble ealdorman Ethelward, went to King Olaf by order of King Ethelred, and having given hostages, conducted him with honour to the royal vill of Andover, where the king was residing. The king treated him with great distinction, and, causing him to be confirmed by the bishop, adopted him as his son and made him a royal present. He on his part promised King Ethelred he would never again invade England, and afterwards returning to his fleet, sailed for his own kingdom at the beginning of summer and faithfully kept his promise." He did not, however, return immediately to Norway, for early the next year we find him in Dublin with his brother-in-law, Olaf Kvaran, who ruled over the kingdom the Northmen had founded there.

It was not likely that tidings of such a mighty warrior as Olaf had proved himself to be, would fail to come to the ears of Haakon Jarl, now in the height of his power, and remembering that he was the great-grandson of Harald Haarfagre, and therefore heir to the crown of Norway, the crafty jarl determined, if possible, to decoy him to his native land, and make away with him. For this purpose he accordingly dispatched an emissary, Thore Klakka, to Dublin in order to see if he could induce him to go to Norway. Thore was a very plausible man, and answered all Olaf's questions in a manner which gained him his confidence. He insinuated that as Haakon was disliked, the people would willingly welcome a descendant of Haarfagre as a deliverer. After a good many interviews he induced Olaf to make the attempt, which the young chief was nothing loth to do, and with five ships he set sail from Dublin accompanied by the traitorous Thore Klakka.

Sailing north, Olaf paid a passing visit to the Orkneys, where he had the good fortune to surprise the jarl, Sigurd Lodvessøn, who, not expecting such a visitor, had only one ship with him.

What followed was a typical example of the method which Olaf adopted in spreading the faith. He sent a courteous message to the jarl inviting him to come on board his ship. After conversing for some time on various topics and hospitably entertaining the jarl, Olaf explained to his guest that the time had now come for him to be baptized. It was only natural that the jarl should demur at first to this unusual proposal, but Olaf explained with equal clearness that the only alternative was his immediate execution. Under such circumstances Sigurd did not hesitate any longer, and was then and there baptized with all his followers, and swearing allegiance to Olaf, gave his son over as a hostage for his good faith.

After this promising beginning, Olaf continued his voyage to Norway. Instead of sailing direct to Trøndelagen he made for the west coast, and landed on the eastern side of the small island of Moster, which lies south of the great island of Stord, and inside the marvellous *skjærgaard*, or island belt, which almost everywhere protects the coast of Norway from the North Sea. There, close to the place where the present village of Mosterhavn and the ancient stone church stand, Olaf Trygvessøn again set foot upon his native land. We are told that his first act upon landing was to have mass sung in a tent which he erected on the shore, on the spot where the church now stands, thus emphasizing by this ceremony the missionary side of his expedition. He had with him his friend and counsellor Bishop Sigurd, a man of English race, and several priests who were selected for their acquaintance with the language of the Northmen, but all trained up in the ways of Anglo-Saxon Christianity.

From Moster they sailed north to Trøndelagen, where, instead of the power of the jarl Haakon being at its height, as the traitor Klakka had imagined, they found that his violations of the homes of the bønder, had raised the whole district in rebellion against him.

The great-grandson of Harald Haarfagre was welcomed as a deliverer, and accepted as a leader of the insurrection. The end of the jarl was not long in coming. He took refuge with a single thrall in the house of his mistress Thora, in Guldalen. When Olaf and his men arrived there in search of the jarl, she concealed him under the pigsty, where he was murdered by his servant, who brought the jarl's head to Olaf, and was rewarded by having his own head immediately cut off.

Thus perished miserably the last great heathen ruler of Norway. We cannot fail to recognize the courage and ability which Haakon manifested, especially in the earlier part of his rule. Nor can we deny to him the credit of a sincere attachment to the faith of the old gods of his fore-fathers. His enforced baptism in Denmark, he at once showed, had been merely a compliance with *force majeure*, and in no way binding on him. Had he restrained his evil passions in his later days and not excited against himself the hostility of his fellow heathen, it is quite possible that the attack of Olaf might not have been successful, and that for a much longer period heathenism might have retained its hold in the North. But his crimes and outrages everywhere raised opposition, and at a great *Thing* for all the *fylker* of Trøndelagen, held immediately after Haakon's death, Olaf was unanimously chosen as king, and began in 995 the short but remarkable reign which had so much to do with the future history of his native land.

Almost immediately after his being chosen king in

Trøndelagen, Olaf's authority was accepted throughout the land. One *Thing* after another welcomed him, and even those provinces in the south-east, which had been subject to the Danish Crown, renounced their allegiance to it, and all the petty kings of Norway accepted Olaf as their over-lord. Thus in one short year the extraordinary "magnetic attractiveness" of Olaf Trygvessøn once more welded Norway into a single nation. Olaf was indeed a born leader of men, and a typical representative of a Norseman in the heroic days. Tall and unmatched in all athletic exercises, his skill in arms was also unequalled, and his dauntless courage won everywhere for him, the devotion of his followers and the respect and fear of his foes. His failings were those of the times in which he lived. There can be no denying that on many occasions he was guilty of permitting very horrible cruelty to be practised on those who had fallen into his hands, and this, when done in the propagation of the faith, showed that, in common with most of the Christian kings of Europe in his day, his missionary spirit was more in consonance with the Old than the New Testament. His dealings with the opposite sex were not always free from blame—indeed, there seems no reason to doubt that he had more than one wife living at the same time—but in this also he only reflected the life of the age in which he lived. He is to be judged by the standard of the tenth century, and not of the twentieth, and, bearing that in mind, we cannot fail to recognize him as a great and noble man, and a most sincere and devoted believer in the faith of Christ. In many ways he was superior to his more famous namesake Olaf the Saint, but he lacked the great gifts of organization which Olaf Haraldssøn possessed, and which left its impress on all the subsequent history of the Church in Norway.

When Olaf had established his authority, he was ready to begin his work of spreading Christianity over the country.

He had very wisely kept that in the background at first, and indeed we may wonder that the people of Trøndelagen, who had been always the chief supporters of the old gods, had not extracted conditions from Olaf before electing him as king, for they must have known that he was a Christian, and had Bishop Sigurd and his priests along with him.

Such, however, was the hatred which the crimes of Haakon Jarl had aroused, that they were only too glad to take Olaf as their king, especially when his great popularity and immediate descent from Harald Haarfagre, had in it so much to commend him to them.

Olaf further showed his wisdom in commencing his work of christianizing the people in Viken instead of Trøndelagen. This he did for two reasons. First, because Viken was the district where the missionaries sent out from Bremen had worked ; and although the results of their labours were not very great, and what they had accomplished was mostly swept away in the heathen reaction under Haakon Jarl, still there was a certain amount of familiarity with the facts of Christianity still surviving among the people. Secondly, however, there was a stronger reason. In Viken the king was among his own people, and in the district where his father and grandfather had ruled. Olaf rightly estimated that the ties of relationship and family connection, when supported by the glamour of his name and his might in battle, would help him most materially.

In this he was not disappointed. His kinsmen to whom he explained his intention of christianizing Norway were ready to fall in with his plans and were at once baptized.* This example on the part of the chiefs was quickly

* Amongst these, according to one account, was Sigurd Syr, the chief or king of Ringerike and stepfather of St. Olaf ; and on a subsequent visit in 998 it is said that the future king and saint, then two years old, was baptized, Olaf Trygvessøn standing as his godfather. On this point, however, see p. 61.

followed by the general body of their adherents, and in a short time all had been baptized, and nominally accepted Christianity.

After this good beginning, Olaf decided to work northwards along the coast. The people of Agder and Hordaland agreed after some persuasion. At Rogaland the people came to the *Thing* fully armed, and intending to resist the king; but the Saga records with great joy, that one after another, the three principal men who were chosen as spokesmen for the heathen party, and deputed to reply to the king, all broke down the moment they attempted to speak, and, there being no one to defend heathenism, the result was that all were baptized.

Then Olaf proceeded to meet the Gula *Thing*, the great assembly of the West of Norway, as the Frosta *Thing* was for Trøndelagen, and the Eidsiva for the central parts. This was usually held at Evenvik, in a fertile valley on the rocky coast, just south of the entrance of the great Sogne Fjord. At that time the valleys and mountain sides were clothed with great forests, where all is now bare and devoid of trees, and only the roots of great pines which are from time to time dug up, attest the different character which the face of the country at that time presented.

When the *Thing* was "set," as the expression was, the king was listened to, while he made his customary appeal to the people on behalf of the faith. Ølmod the Old was the spokesman of the chiefs, and declared that if the king intended to use force they would resist to the uttermost, but if he wished to be friendly they would on their part keep on good terms with him, and he concluded by suggesting that the king should give his sister Astrid in marriage to Erling Skjalgssøn. To this Olaf agreed, and after some difficulty persuaded Astrid to consent, and the result was finally that the chiefs and people were all baptized.

The next *Thing* was that held at Dragseid, a spot situated

From a Photograph by]   *[T Olaf Willson.*

**PART OF AN ALTAR PIECE FROM AUSTEVOLD
CHURCH, NORDHORDLAND.**

(15th Century.)

St. Sunniva in the centre, with St. Peter and St. Mary Magdalene.
Now in Bergen Museum

[To face p. 46.

on the neck of the great peninsula of Stadt, a little north of the Nordfjord. This *Thing* was attended by the people of Søndmøre and the Romsdal, as well as by those from the Firda *fylker*, the country between Nordfjord and Sogne Fjord. Here Olaf was apparently more peremptory. He gave them the simple alternative of baptism or fighting, and as he was the strongest the bønder agreed to be baptized.

Close to Dragseid is the small island of Selje. According to some accounts, it was at this time that the king discovered, or was informed of, the existence of the body of St. Sunniva, who had met her death on this island. As the saint was subsequently recognized as one of the three patrons of Norway, it is well to relate her story here.

According to the "Acta Sanctorum in Selio," it was in the time of the Kaiser Otto I. (936—973) that "Sweet Sunniva the blessed" lived. She was the daughter of an Irish king, and to escape marriage with a heathen prince, she fled from her home and embarked in three ships with a number of men, women, and children, who along with her desired to escape " from the raging storms of an evil world." Without oars or ship-gear they committed themselves to the sea, and the storm and tempest carried them across the North Sea* and finally landed them on the little island of Selje. The people on the mainland saw the strangers, and proceeded to attack them. Sunniva and her companions fled for refuge to a cave on the island, and prayed that death might come to deliver them from their heathen foes. The prayer was heard, and a *stenskred* (stone avalanche) fell and closed the entrance to the cave and all perished. Later on some merchants sailing past the island, saw a light, and going ashore found a human head, which emitted a

* It is not a little remarkable that an exactly similar instance to this, occurred in our own day, in the case of Elizabeth Mouath, who was blown across the North Sea in a fishing-smack from the Shetlands to the island of Lepsø, a little north of Selje.

fragrant odour. They went to Olaf Trygvessøn and told the tale. The king then with Bishop Sigurd went to the island, and after searching they discovered the body of St. Sunniva perfectly preserved. A church was erected on the island and a cloister established, and from Selje later on, many teachers went out to spread the faith. It seems most probable, on the whole, that the visit of Olaf and Bishop Sigurd to Selje, took place after he had gone to Nidaros, and when his work of christianizing the north was further advanced. Selje was subsequently the seat of a bishopric, which was transferred to Bergen at the end of the eleventh century; but it remained an important monastic centre down to the sixteenth century, and may well be called the "holy isle" of Norway.

Olaf was now rapidly approaching Trøndelagen, where the first real opposition to his efforts to spread the faith was to be encountered. Sailing with his fleet into the Trondhjem Fjord, the king made at once for Hlade, where the famous heathen temple stood, on the estate of his predecessor Haakon Jarl.

His movements seem to have taken the people by surprise; the district was the stronghold of heathenism, and the inhabitants, though the most powerful in Norway, were unprepared to defend their gods. Olaf acted with his usual promptitude; landing his men, they plundered and destroyed the temple, and the king carried off in triumph a gold ring which Haakon Jarl had placed on the temple door. This open attack on the religion of the people immediately roused the district. The bønder at once sent round the *hærpil*, or war arrow, and the people flocked to defend their gods. Not finding himself strong enough, Olaf decided to move north to Haalogaland (the district along the coast, north of Namsos) and see what he could do with the inhabitants there; but they had been warned, and their three chiefs, Haarek of Thjotta, Hjort of Vaage, and Eivind

Kinnriva, collected their forces to withstand the king, and finding himself thus foiled Olaf sailed southwards. When he reached the Trondhjem Fjord the bønder had gone back again to their farms.

Olaf at this time (996—7) founded the town of Nidaros, the present city of Trondhjem. He selected as the site, the spot where the Nid flows into the fjord. At this place the river takes a great bend before entering the sea, and the king with much wisdom placed the buildings in such a position, that the river formed on almost two sides a natural moat which would protect them from attack by a land force. Here he built a rough kind of palace, and here also he erected a church, most likely of timber, and dedicated it to St. Clement, bishop of Rome. The king by his founding of the town shewed that he felt the importance of attracting traders to the country, and raising up a force which might be useful against the power of the bønder.

Olaf now considered he was strong enough to summon a meeting of the *Thing* at Frosta in the autumn of 996. The bønder, however, were not to be caught napping. They came to the gathering fully armed, and having as their leader and speaker, the powerful chief who was known as Jernskjægge (the iron beard) of Upphaug. The *Thing* being set, Olaf rose and addressed them, and urged the acceptance of Christianity. At once cries of dissent were heard, and they tried to stop the king, reminding him of the way in which Haakon the Good's similar proposal was met at the same place.

Olaf quickly saw that he was not strong enough to resist the power of the bønder on this occasion, and so he began to speak kindly to them, and skilfully averted an outbreak, promising that he would meet them at Mæren later on, and join in the great *blot*, or sacrificial feast, held there in the January following. After this the *Thing* broke up, and Olaf and his men went back to Hlade, on the outskirts of his newly-founded town of Nidaros, and the bønder returned to their farms.

The king, however, had no idea of abandoning his crusade against heathenism, but he went to work craftily. When the time approached for the *blot* at Mæren, he invited to a feast all the principal men of the districts close to Nidaros, and they responded to the invitation, apparently without suspicion. Olaf had taken the precaution of having a number of ships and picked men ready close at hand. The chiefs were received with great cordiality by the king, and, as was customary, all drank heavily at the feast. Next morning the king was up early and had Mass said, and then brought his men ashore. When the chiefs had awakened after their night's carouse, Olaf called them to a meeting. Then the humour of the king was seen. With a delightful appearance of sincerity he gravely explained to them that at the Frosta *Thing* they had insisted he should follow the example of Haakon and sacrifice to the gods; he was therefore resolved that the forthcoming festival should be one of no ordinary grandeur and solemnity. Hitherto they had been accustomed to offer a miserable thrall as a sacrifice to the gods, but he intended to do better than that. Then to the horror of his guests he mentioned the names of six of the principal men before him, and announced his intention to offer *them* up as a sacrifice. We can well imagine the terror of the chiefs when they found themselves in the king's power. They at once begged for mercy, and Olaf readily promised it on condition, that they were all then and there baptized, and further that they would give hostages for their future good behaviour. These terms they willingly accepted, and they were sent away. The opposition of the inner Trondhjem district was thus practically broken.

In January, 997, came the great gathering at Mæren, where Olaf had promised to take part in the sacrifices. Both sides came fully armed. The *Thing* assembled, and the people demanded that the king should keep his promise. Olaf then proceeded with Jernskjægge and others to the *hov* or temple ; all who entered were unarmed, but the king placed outside a body of men fully armed to be ready for emergencies. In his hand Olaf bore a golden staff ; when they came to the image of Thor, the king with this staff struck down the idol. At once his men, taking this as a signal, overturned the other idols. In the confusion which arose, Jernskjægge sought to escape, but when he came out of the temple he was killed by the king's men. Then Olaf came out and addressed the excited multitude, giving them the usual alternative baptism or immediate battle. The heathen, seeing their leader slain and having no hope of success, chose baptism, and they were, as usual, at once baptized and sent to their homes. After this there seems to have been no open resistance in Trøndelagen to Olaf's efforts on behalf of Christianity.

In order to conciliate the bønder it was arranged that the king should marry Jernskjægge's daughter Gudrun, but as she attempted to assassinate him on the evening of the marriage, she was put away. Then, it seems, Olaf sought the hand of the proud and ambitious Sigrid, the widow of Erik of Sweden. He did his wooing by deputy, and sent her as a gift the gold ring he had taken from Haakon Jarl's *hov* at Hlade. The queen accepted the offering ; but on discovering that the ring was not pure gold, but only copper gilt, she was very angry. A meeting with Olaf was, however, arranged to be held at Konghelle. The queen found that the Norwegian monarch expected that she would, as a preliminary step, be baptized, but to this she indignantly declined to submit. Olaf was very angry, and exclaimed, "Why should I marry a heathen hound like you ? " and so far forgot himself as to strike her on the face with his glove. "This will be your bane," said the furious queen as they parted. Her words came true, as we shall see. Soon after she married Svein Tjugeskjæg, the king of Denmark, who was quite ready to dispute Olaf's possession of Norway, from whence his jarl had been driven by the coming of Olaf in 995.

Having upturned heathenism in Trøndelagen, Olaf in 998 and 999 turned his attention again to Haalogaland, where the chiefs had resisted his first attempt. By a stratagem he got Haarek of Thjotta into his power and had him baptized, and on his promising to be faithful to him sent him back to the north. Haarek repaid the king by capturing Eivind Kinnriva and sending him to Nidaros. The king's threats were of no avail against this brave heathen, and the consequence was he was put to death with horrible cruelty. Now there were but two heathen chiefs left, Raud of Godø, and Hjort, and the king went north against them; they were soon defeated. Hjort was, after an exciting chase, shot by the king himself when he had been brought to bay by Olaf's famous dog Vige, and Raud, who was taken prisoner, and followed the example of Eivind, was barbarously put to death. So ended the open heathen resistance in the north. Before this expedition Olaf had spent the winter in Viken, and seems to have attempted to christianize the Oplands, the country around and north of the Miøsen lake, but did not do much there, and the final uprooting of heathenism in that part was the work of St. Olaf.

In the space of about four years Norway, through the vigorous measures of King Olaf, had thus practically become Christian. The methods adopted were not such as would commend themselves to us at the present day, and there can be no doubt that as the work went on, and the power of the king increased, he became much more cruel towards those who resisted him. One could wish that for the sake of Olaf's name the accounts of the cruelties which were perpetrated in Haalogaland were not true; but there seems

no reason to doubt them for a moment, and the writers of
the Sagas gloried in them as marks of the king's power
and, from their point of view, as acceptable to God.

The short and brilliant reign of Olaf Trygvessøn was now
drawing to a close. We have seen how the rejected Queen
Sigrid had vowed vengeance on the king, and almost immediately after the incident narrated above, had married
King Svein of Denmark. Just at that time Olaf had
married Thyra, the sister of King Svein, who had been
wife of King Burislaf of Vendland, but had separated from
him and taken refuge in Norway. This marriage much
incensed Svein, and his union with Sigrid made another
enemy for Olaf in the Danish court.

Queen Thyra's insistance on her husband making an expedition to Vendland to recover some of her estates, was
for a long time disregarded by the king ; but at last he gave
way, and in the summer of the year 1000 he set out with
a powerful fleet, and, without encountering opposition,
secured his wife's property.

This was the chance for which Svein and Sigrid were
watching, and which Erik Jarl (son of Haakon) and his
brother Svein hailed as an opportunity for avenging their
father's death. When Olaf was returning home—by the
treacherous advice of Sigvald the Jomsviking, who was
bribed by King Svein—he was induced to allow his fleet
to scatter, and was attacked, when he had only eleven ships,
by the fleet of the Danish king and Erik Jarl.

The ships of the enemy were lying in wait beside the
little island of Svolder, near Rügen, and when the advance
part of Olaf's fleet had passed out of sight, emerged from
their shelter and attacked the king and the ten ships which
were with him. A fierce fight ensued. Olaf fought with
that dauntless courage which had ever sustained him, but
the odds were overwhelming. Nearly all his men were
slain, the king himself was wounded, and, seeing that all

was lost and he was in danger of being taken prisoner, he with his devoted friend Kolbjørn Stallare, sprang overboard, one from each side of the ship. Kolbjørn held his shield under him and was picked up at once by Erik's men, who mistook him for the king, but Olaf, who held his shield over his head, disappeared and was seen no more. There can be no manner of doubt that the king was drowned ; but his body was never recovered, and tradition had it that he escaped and went on a pilgrimage to the Holy Land, and died in extreme old age in a Syrian monastery.

Thus ended the life of this remarkable man, who in such a short space had effected so great a change in the history of his native land. Of his character and methods we have already spoken, and of the results which followed from his missionary efforts we shall speak further on, when we come to the reign of his famous namesake. His death was a fitting close to his strange and eventful life. He passed away as the Norsemen of old thought it noblest to do, in the midst of the fight. Like Frederick Barbarossa, like other great warriors and kings, famous in history or legend, the mystery of his ending threw a glamour of romance about his name ; and often in after days it may have been that many a Norseman looked for an hour when the hero of the race of the fair-haired Harald would come back again, and lead them to victory against the enemies of the " White Christ" and of the land which they loved so well.

Before closing this chapter it is necessary to allude to the work of spreading Christianity in Iceland, which was mostly accomplished under the king's direction ; for though Iceland was then an independent State, it was in closest connection with Norway, from whence its earliest Norse inhabitants had come in the reign of Harald Haarfagre.

The first Christians in Iceland were the Irish monks who had sought refuge there about the eighth century, at

a time when Ireland was the great missionary church of
the West, and had sent its missionaries to spread the faith
all over the Continent, as well as in Scotland and the
north of England.   St. Gall, labouring in Switzerland, and
St. Columbanus at Bobbio, in the north of Italy, had carried
the light of the Gospel among the barbarian races who had
established themselves in the land of the fallen Western
Empire.

The Irish hermits found in Iceland a quiet resting-place
in dark and troublous times, and when the freedom-loving
Northmen, who declined to submit to the rule of Harald
Haarfagre, came to Iceland they found before them some of
these pious men, who had braved the perils of the unknown
seas and settled there.

These Northmen were of course heathen, and carried with
them the worship of their forefathers, and soon erected
their temples to Odin and Thor, and drove the hermits to
seek some other retreat.

The first efforts to evangelize the new settlers were made,
some fifteen years before the accession of Olaf Trygvessøn,
by an Icelander named Thorvald Kodranssøn, who had been
a Viking, but who had come under the influence of Bishop
Frederick of Saxony, who baptized him. This man induced
the bishop to accompany him to Iceland in 981, and
together they did a good deal of work in the part of the
country lying in the east and north. At first there does
not seem to have been much opposition, but when they
tried to induce the *Althing* to accept the faith, the heathen
chiefs, as in the *Things* of Norway, were at once violent in
their opposition. The controversy at one gathering became
so acute that Thorvald in rage slew two of his opponents,
and was then driven from the country.

No further attempt seems to have been made until after
Olaf had been accepted as king in Norway, when he sent
one of his men, an Icelander, named Stefner Thorgilssøn,

to resume the work. He commenced his labours in the south and west; but his zeal aroused the heathen, and he was banished from the land, and returned to Norway to King Olaf. Meanwhile the king had, in the usual way, baptized any Icelanders whom he met with in Norway, and sent them back pledged to advance Christianity in their own country.

Olaf now sent a missionary of another kind. When he first came to Norway he had with him, among the priests with Bishop Sigurd, a man named Teodbrand, who was a Saxon priest, said to be the son of a nobleman. This man was first acquainted with Olaf in his early Viking days, and followed his adventurous life before 994. He was a clever man and a very eloquent speaker, but of a most violent temper, and acted in many ways in a manner very contrary to his calling. After 995 he was placed in charge of the church which had been erected on the island of Moster, in Hordaland, and there enforced his doctrines with many " apostolic blows and knocks," and seems to have lived more as a Viking than a Christian priest.

Tidings of his misconduct came to Olaf, and he sent for him to Nidaros and lectured him with great severity. Teodbrand was much alarmed, and asked the king to allow him to atone for his evil deeds by undertaking some difficult and dangerous work. Thereupon Olaf ordered him at once to Iceland. When he got there his eloquence and zeal had considerable effect; but Teodbrand, or Thangbrand, as he was also called, soon broke out again and killed two of his antagonists, and in 998—9 returned to Norway to the king. In spite of this unworthy missionary, Christianity continued to make progress in Iceland, and the influence of two of the chiefs, Gissur the White and Hjalte Skjæggessøn, who had become Christians, was so great that in the year 1000 the *Althing* accepted Christianity as the religion of the island.

The inhabitants of the Færoe Islands,* under their chief
Sigmund Bretessøn, also embraced Christianity.

It was about the year 1000 that the Northmen from Iceland and Greenland, attempted to colonize the part of North
America known to them as Vinland, so called because the
vine grew wild there. This region, which is generally
thought to have been one of the New England States, was
first discovered by Leif Erikssøn, son of Erik the Red (the
first explorer of Greenland), who, returning from Norway
to Greenland, was driven out of his course by a gale of
wind. After a precarious existence as a Norse colony, it
was finally abandoned, but the knowledge of the continent
of North America always survived in Iceland, and Leif
Erikssøn, not Christopher Columbus, has the right to be
regarded as the undoubted *Discoverer* of America.

In this connection, it is most interesting to note that
Adam of Bremen, in the second half of the eleventh
century, mentions Vinland. He speaks of it as " an island
(or region) . . . which is called Vinland because vines
grow there wild, producing excellent wine, and fruit
abounds there which has not been planted "; then he adds,
" non fabulosa opinione sed certa comperimus ratione
Danorum" (*Gesta Hamm. Eccles. Pont.*, Bk. IV., c. 38).

* The name here given is the conventional English one, and
undoubtedly incorrect. It should be *Færøerne* Færø = island of sheep
or cattle. Øerne = the islands. " Færoe Islands " is a pleonasm.

CHAPTER VII.

ST. OLAF, KING AND MARTYR.

THE events of the fifteen years which elapsed between
the battle of Svolder and the coming of Olaf Haraldssøn to
claim the inheritance of the race of Harald Haarfagre,
need not, from a purely ecclesiastical point of view, detain
us long.

After the death of Olaf Trygvessøn, Norway reverted to
a position similar to that of the days of Haakon Jarl. It
ceased to be a kingdom, and became a vassal State of
Denmark. The allies who compassed the death of Olaf
divided the spoil. Erik Jarl got the lion's share, and
practically held all the west of Norway from Haalogaland
to Lindesnæs. Olaf of Sweden (the son of Queen Sigrid),
who had helped at Svolder, received the country east and
south of the present city of Christiania, called Ranrike,

and also four *fylker* in the north. Svein of Denmark obtained Viken and Agder. Svein, Erik Jarl's brother, held the parts of the country allotted to the kings of Sweden and Denmark, and so the two brothers between them ruled the whole of Norway.

The two jarls were (unlike their father) Christians, and they seemed to have ruled well in their several districts; but they made no efforts to spread Christianity, and in their time every man did that which was right in his own eyes in all matters of religion. They had only one rival in the land, and that was Erling Skjalgssøn, who had married Astrid, sister of King Olaf, and resided at Sole, in Jæderen, a few miles from the present city of Stavanger. His authority extended over a large part of the surrounding country, and the brothers did not deem it prudent to attack him.

Erik Jarl had as his great supporter in the north, Einar Thamberskjelver, a noted archer, who had fought alongside King Olaf at Svolder, but had accepted the alliance offered him by Erik, and the compact was cemented by his marriage with Bergliot, the sister of the jarl.

After the death of Svein in 1013 Knut the Great called on his vassal Erik for aid in his invasion of England, and to this call he responded, leaving his son Haakon in his place, with his uncle Einar as his guardian.

Such was briefly the state of affairs when Olaf Haraldssøn made his appearance to claim his kingdom. We must now, however, retrace our steps and consider the early life of the future saint of Norway.

Harald Grenske, the father of Olaf, was one of the petty kings who ruled in Vestfold, the country to the west of the Christiania Fjord. He was grandson of Bjørn Farmand, and therefore great-grandson of the mighty Haarfagre. He received the name of Grenske from having been brought up in the district called Grønland (now part of the

Telemark), where, in his early days, he had as his foster-sister the future far-famed Queen Sigrid.   Harald married Aasta Gudbrandsdatter, a wise and prudent woman; but she does not seem to have had much influence over her rather worthless husband.   When Queen Sigrid was first left a widow, Harald Grenske, although his wife was living, at once became a suitor for her hand.   After first receiving his advances favourably, the haughty queen had the house in which Harald was staying burned down one night, and he perished in the flames, Sigrid remarking that she did not want any of these small kings!

Very soon after her faithless husband's death, Aasta gave birth to Olaf, who thus, like his namesake, the son of Trygve, was born after his father's violent death.   Some little time after this Aasta married Sigurd Syr, petty king of Ringerike, and another great-grandson of Harald Haarfagre.

In his stepfather's home Olaf grew up a strong and active lad.   At the early age of twelve years he, as was then customary, started on a Viking cruise (1007).   In this, his first voyage, which was to the Baltic, he had as his instructor in the art of war his foster-father Rane.   After a time the scene of their exploits was changed to England, then a promising field for the Northmen, who were eager for plunder.   In 1009 Olaf seems to have been in England with Thorkel the Tall, and to have joined in the various attacks which were made on that unfortunate country during the reign of Ethelred II.

In 1012, however, we find him and his friend fighting on the side of Ethelred in the defence of London against the attack of Svein, and it was on that occasion that "London bridge was broken down," in accordance with the stratagem of Olaf, who, protecting his ships from the Danes who manned the bridge, destroyed the piles which supported it and finally broke it in two.   Notwithstanding this, the cause of Svein at last triumphed; Ethelred was obliged to fly to Normandy, and Olaf, faithful to his ally, followed him to that country, and was soon at home among the Norwegian settlers there.   Svein died in 1014, and Ethelred was recalled to England.

It would seem most probable that it was during his stay in Normandy that Olaf was baptized.   It is true that Snorre states that the future saint had received that sacrament when a child of "three winters old," during the visit paid by Olaf Trygvessøn to Ringerike about the year 997, when a number of people in that part of the country were baptized.   Snorre's account seems reasonable enough at first sight, but we have, however, evidence to the contrary, which renders it more probable that his baptism was deferred until his visit to Normandy.   That he was a believer in the Christian faith when he came to England is most probable, but that he had not yet been baptized seems equally clear.

William of Jumièges, in his Chronicle, says : "The Duke [Richard] . . . called to his aid two kings, with an army of Pagans—Olaf, King of the Norwegians, and Lacman, King of the Swedes."   Then he mentions their going to Rouen, "where the Duke Richard welcomed them royally. . . . Then King Olaf, being attracted by the Christian religion, as were also some of his followers ; and on the exhortation of Robert Archbishop [of Rouen], was converted to the faith of Christ, was washed in baptism and anointed with holy oil by the archbishop, and, full of joy at the grace he had received, returned straightway to his own kingdom."

In the "Passio et Miracula Beati Olaui," * the work of the great Archbishop Eystein, the same statement meets us : "He, when he had learned the truth of the Gospel in England, confessed the faith with all his heart, and with

* Cap. I.

zealous devotion of mind hastened to seek the grace of
baptism in the city of Rouen. Then, being purified by
the font of Salvation, he was immediately changed to
another man ; and, as the apostle says, he was buried with
Christ by baptism into Death. . . . He despised every
sort of vain pleasure, and the glory of an earthly kingdom
became as dross in comparison with the sweetness of the
heavenly one. Although he held a kingly position, he was
poor in spirit."

In "Breviarium Nidrosiense," these words just quoted
formed the first lection which was used in the service
appointed for July 28th, the vigil of St. Olaf. It seems
clear, therefore, that the Norwegian Church believed that
Olaf was baptized during this visit to Normandy.

His baptism, and confirmation which must have immediately followed it, undoubtedly served to deepen the religious
feelings of Olaf, and filled him with the desire to carry on
and complete the work which his great kinsman and namesake had begun in his native land ; but just at the moment
there seemed no immediate prospect of a successful
attempt to claim the throne of Norway, and so he waited.

According to one account, he meditated passing some
time on a pilgrimage to the Holy Land, but was warned in
a dream that he should desist and, instead of this, assert
his claim to the inheritance of his fathers.

Olaf was a man of very great discretion, and was not
ready to endanger his chances of success by any premature
move. He felt sure, from what he knew of the position of
affairs both in Denmark and England, that the time would
not be long before he would have a chance of asserting his
claims. And in this he was not wrong.

The opportunity for which Olaf was waiting soon came.
Knut the Great, who had succeeded his father Svein,
summoned Erik Jarl to aid him in his invasion of England,
and Olaf felt that this was the time to attempt to take

possession of the kingdom of his great ancestor Harald
Haarfagre. He returned to England, and sailed along the
coast to Northumbria, plundering as he went. Finally he
set sail with two large ships and two hundred and sixty
picked men. After a stormy passage they came safely to
the island of Selje without meeting any opposition. On
landing, Olaf stumbled and fell on one knee. " I have
fallen," he cried to his followers. " You have not fallen,
O King," said his foster-father Rane; "you have only
taken a firm hold of the land." " So be it if God wills,"
said Olaf.

As a Heaven-sent leader, Olaf proved to be singularly
fortunate at the outset. He was proceeding south from
Selje, and when a little north of the Sogne Fjord he had
the good luck to capture the young jarl Haakon Erikssøn,
who was not expecting the invader in that part of the
country. Instead of putting the young man to death, as
some advised, Olaf set him free, having first obliged him
to swear that he would never oppose his claims on Norway.
This generous treatment was, for the time at least, rewarded,
and the young jarl went at once to his uncle, King Knut.
How far he kept the promise we shall see later on.

After this encouraging beginning, Olaf continued his
journey round the coast until he came to Viken, where he
was received with open arms by his amiable stepfather,
Sigurd Syr. This petty king at once called a *Thing*, and
at it Olaf was chosen as king without any opposition. He
was still, however, very far from the overlordship of
Norway.

Leaving Viken with a small but resolute body of men, he
went north in the winter, and crossing over the Dovre
Fjeld, appeared suddenly at Nidaros, to the astonishment of
the Jarl Svein, who, after a narrow escape of being taken
prisoner, fled to the south. The people of Trøndelagen,
however, were deeply attached to the family of the jarl of

Hlade, and, recovering from their first surprise, attacked Olaf at Nidaros and forced him to return again to Viken. He then saw that if he was to be ultimately successful, he must set to work in a more systematic manner.

Seeing how essential it was to have the supremacy at sea, he spent the winter of 1015—16 in getting together a fleet and equipping it with a body of trained men. His opponent Jarl Svein did the same thing in the north, and, when the spring was come, sailed south to attack his daring invader.

The two fleets encountered each other at Nesjar, or Nesje, at the entrance of the Langesund, near the present town of Frederiksværn. There, on Palm Sunday, April 3rd, 1016, a decisive battle was fought and the jarl, being signally defeated, fled to Sweden, intending to fit out a fresh fleet, but died soon after his arrival in that country.

The victory at Nesje secured Norway to Olaf. Knut was then too busy with the conquest of England to be able to send men to support his vassal's cause in Norway, and in a very short time *Thing* after *Thing* acknowledged Olaf's authority, and he became undisputed monarch of the whole land ; and once more, as in the days of Olaf Trygvessøn, Norway was ruled by the firm hand of one man.

It was not to be expected that Olaf, king of Sweden, would at once acquiesce in this new state of affairs. He sent his men to collect taxes in those provinces which Jarl Svein had held under him. This Olaf Haraldssøn promptly resented, and the unfortunate officials were either killed or driven away. Matters appeared for a time to be in a very critical state ; but the people of neither nation wished for war, and at a great *Thing* held at Upsala matters were for a time peaceably arranged.

To strengthen the defences of Norway on the side of Sweden, Olaf founded the town of Borg (or Sarpsborg, as it is now called), at the mouth of the Glommen, near the Swedish frontier, and there he built a church. Thus, political difficulties being for the time settled, Olaf was able to devote himself to the internal affairs of his country, and to the completion of the work which Olaf Trygvessøn had begun, in the establishment, on a firm basis, of Christianity in Norway.

Olaf Haraldssøn was now in his twenty-second year—a very youthful monarch, it is true, but one of very varied experience. He had begun his active life and shared in war at the very early age of twelve years, so that when he became king he had a wider knowledge of the world and its ways, than that which fell to the lot of most of his contemporaries in the North.

In person, King Olaf was not of the commanding stature of most of the Norsemen. He was of middle height, but very strongly built, and inclined to stoutness, which led his enemies to bestow on him the nickname of Olaf Digre. Like most of the chiefs of his time, he was very skilful in the use of weapons. His hair was auburn in colour, inclining to red, and indeed the description of David answers very much to that of Olaf—"he was ruddy and withal of a beautiful countenance, and goodly to look upon." His eyes (all the writers of the Sagas remark) were very piercing, and when he was angry his men dared not look him in the face.* In his inflexible will and determination to carry out whatever he had undertaken he resembled his

---

* Sigvat the Skald thus describes the effect of Olaf's glance on his rebellious subjects, in his last fight at Stiklestad :—

> " I think I saw them shrink with fear :
> Who would not shrink from foeman's spear,
> When Olaf's lion-eye was cast
> On them, and called up all the past ?

> " Clear as the serpent's eye his look,
> No Trondhjem man could stand but shook
> Beneath its glance, and skulked away
> Knowing his king, and cursed the day."
>
> (Laing's Translation of the Heimskringla.)

C.S.N.   F

great ancestor Haarfagre. Very generous to his friends, and often to his enemies when they fell into his power, he was nevertheless sometimes very cruel to those who resisted his will, especially where Christianity was concerned. Of the depth and sincerity of his belief in the Christian faith, his life and death gave proof, and although a vast amount of legend has gathered round the "Royal Saint" of Norway, we can, notwithstanding, very easily form an accurate estimate of the character of the man.

It is well here to consider what was the state of the country with respect to Christianity when Olaf was ready to commence his work.

We have seen the way in which Olaf Trygvessøn went through the length and breadth of the land, giving the people the alternative of baptism or the sword, and that after a very few years the great majority of his subjects had been baptized. It is perfectly clear that in cases of enforced baptism, it would have exercised no influence whatever on the lives of those who had received it, except in the comparatively few districts where the king had had churches built and priests (more spiritually-minded, let us hope, than Thangbrand) placed to teach the people the faith.

At first sight, it seems to us almost incredible that in such a short space of time a large body of heathen should have submitted, even nominally, to receive Christianity, although backed up by force of arms. There is, however, one important consideration which must not be overlooked, and to which we have before alluded.* There was no regular heathen priesthood to organize the opposition to the efforts of the king. The priestly offices at the *blots* were performed by the head of the family, or the chief of the district. This absence of a priestly caste was an immense help in the rapid spread of Christianity. When, therefore, the chief, or some of the principal bønder of the

* Chap. i., p. 6.

fylke had been baptized, most of their people followed like a flock of sheep. If the chief allowed the *hov* to be demolished there was no other place in which the worship of the gods could take place.

We may wonder why it was that Olaf Trygvessøn and Olaf the Saint, who had at any rate some fair instruction in the Christian faith, and were accompanied in their journeys and work by such good men as Bishops Sigurd and Grimkell, should have acted in a way which might naturally seem to us now, to actually profane the sacrament of holy baptism. We must, however, remember that in acting in this way they were only following exactly, the precedent set before them by the restorer of the Western Empire, Karl the Great, in his dealings with the Saxons and other heathen nations of northern Europe.

In those days, and in the minds of the two Olafs and their teachers, holy baptism, even when thus administered, was regarded as (to quote the words of St. Paul) "a translation from the kingdom of darkness." They felt that if it could be accomplished, either by fair means or foul, the power of Thor and Odin—a power they did not attempt to despise—was at once broken ; and so they believed with all sincerity, that no matter how it was brought about, whether by persuasion or torture, if the people could be baptized the battle was practically won.

In a sense this was true, because those who had been baptized had at any rate their faith shaken in the power of the gods their fathers worshipped. Might was the thing which appealed most strongly to the heathen Norsemen, and when they saw that their gods were not able to give them the victory over their Christian antagonists, they were ready to fall in with the creed of Harald Haarfagre, and to believe in the God that was the strongest.

Then, again, with many of the heathen, who were of a very superstitious mind, they felt that their baptism, whether

it was done willingly or by yielding to force, was an act which
cut them off entirely from the old gods, and made a return
to the former state of things an impossibility.   It was a
Rubicon which when once crossed, retreat was out of the
question.   There were, it is true, heathen of a sterner mould,
like Haakon Jarl, who almost immediately after his baptism,
put his priests ashore and at once proceeded to sacrifice
to the gods; but with the majority it was not so, and
their baptism left the ground cleared, as it were, for the
reception of real Christianity.

The wholesale destruction of temples and idols by Olaf
Trygvessøn (and before his time, by Erik's sons, for the
purpose of plunder) was an object-lesson for the Northmen
of precisely the same kind as that afforded by Gideon to
the people of Orphra* in connection with the worship of
Baal.   If Thor and Odin were the powerful gods they had
believed them to be, how was it they did not resent the
destruction of the temples and of their images?   It was
clear "the White Christ" was the strongest, and therefore
they would be safe to follow Him.   The early Christian
teachers did not attempt to deny altogether the existence
of the old gods, but they taught the people they were
devils and powers of evil, which Christ came to cast down
and destroy; and our Lord's declaration, "All *power* is
given unto Me in heaven and in earth," was the one which
perhaps impressed the heathen Northman, and led him to
be baptized, much more than any promise to the weary and
heavy laden, which, with other nations and at other times,
has drawn men to the Son of Man.†

* Judges vi., 25–32.

† The work of Olaf Trygvessøn, as compared with that of Olaf
Haraldssøn (the saint), has been admirably summed up by the Icelandic
monk Odd when he says : " Olaf Trygvessøn prepared and laid the
foundation of Christianity, but St. Olaf built the walls ; Olaf Trygvessøn
planted the vineyard, but St. Olaf trained up the vine covered with fair
flowers and much fruit."

Such was, in brief, the religious condition of Norway when Olaf was chosen king; for the interval between the death of Olaf Trygvessøn and the coming of Olaf Haraldssøn was so short that no material change had taken place, and there was not (as in the time of Haakon Jarl) any heathen reaction under the Jarls Erik and Svein.

King Olaf's rule in Norway was guided by two leading principles, which were manifested in all his actions—First, the completion and development of the work which Olaf Trygvessøn had begun in christianizing the country; and, Secondly, the consolidation of his kingdom by the establishment of the rule of a single monarch, making it, what Harald Haarfagre had designed it to be, one kingdom, under one king, and the subjection of the petty kingdoms which that great man in his old age, to the manifest injury of the land, had established. These two principles are to be seen in all the actions which marked the eventful reign of King Olaf. They were so closely connected that, as we read the history of the time, it is hard to say whether the king's journeys through Norway, more nearly resembled an episcopal visitation or a royal progress.

Olaf's chief advisers in all ecclesiastical matters were Bishops Grimkell and Sigurd, and along with them there were of course priests.* Of their names we have no very certain knowledge, though two, Rudolf† and Bernhard, are mentioned, but it is probable that Iceland, and not Norway, was the scene of their labours. There seems no doubt whatever that both Grimkell and Sigurd belonged

---

* Adam of Bremen, Book II., Chap. lv., says: "He (Olaf) had with him many bishops and priests from England, by whose admonition and doctrine he himself prepared his heart for God, and intrusted his people to be guided by them. Amongst these Sigafrid, Grimkell, Rudolf, and Bernhard were renowned for their teaching and virtues."

† This Rudolf seems to have returned to England in 1050, and to have become abbot of the Monastery of Abingdon.

to the English Church, and were either Englishmen by birth or bringing-up. In any case their connection and inclinations lay in the way of Anglo-Saxon, and not German, Christianity. In England at that time there were of course, in the eastern counties, a large number of clergy of Norse extraction, and naturally Olaf would have selected them to accompany him to Norway, on account of their knowledge of the language and customs of the Northmen. Political reasons also, at the time of Olaf's adventurous journey to Norway, would have prevented his applying to Bremen, the metropolitan see of the North of Europe, for it was in close connection with Denmark, where Knut the Great ruled, and whose authority over Norway, Olaf went to dispute. Later on in Olaf's reign, it is true, he had to apply to Bremen for help in his work, but the reason for that was again political, and not ecclesiastical. His enemy Knut was in power in England, and supplies from that country were, to a certain extent at any rate, practically stopped, as the English bishops would not have wished to consecrate or ordain men, for service under the rule of the antagonist of such a powerful king as Knut the Great.

It is best perhaps at this point to speak of the work of Olaf as a Church lawgiver. We have no certain information as to the exact period in which he drew up his Christian code, but it was doubtless within the first ten years of his reign. He was too wise and far-seeing to have postponed it longer than was absolutely necessary, but he had first to establish his power in the land before he began the great work of his life. Olaf saw clearly from the commencement of his reign, that if heathenism was to be entirely eradicated from among his people, it was necessary that the laws of the land should be brought into conformity with Christian usages and customs. He therefore set to work to draw up a Christian code. Snorre tells

us that he had often read to him the laws which Haakon
the Good had given to Trøndelagen, but these had not
any direct reference to Christianity. Then he decided that
a new code should be drawn up, which would embody all
those points in which Christianity affected the life of the
people. It would seem likely that for this purpose Olaf
called together an assembly of his bishops, clergy, and
other learned men at Moster, a spot sacred as the place
where his great predecessor, Olaf Trygvessøn, had landed,
and where he had built a church. This gathering does not
appear to have been an ordinary *Thing*, but partook somewhat of the nature of a synod, at which the laity were
represented equally with the clergy. The code there
agreed upon was known as Olaf's *Kristenret*, and it is
always spoken of as the joint work of Olaf and Bishop
Grimkell. This *Kristenret* Olaf seems to have taken round
the country with him, and, having been read and explained,
it was adopted by the great *Things*, and thus became a
part of the law of the land. The original form of this
law has not survived. What we now possess dates from
the time of Magnus Erlingssøn (1155—1184), though
possibly it may belong to the reign of Eystein (1103—
1123). There can be no doubt, however, that it embodies,
with but little deviation, the original law which Olaf promulgated, which had been preserved both orally and in
written form.

The scope of this law we give below, but it is interesting
to note that it always claims the name and authority of
the royal saint and his famous adviser, and the phrase is
reiterated throughout " as King Olaf and Bishop Grimkell
appointed at the Moster *Thing*."

Much of this law was in accordance with the principles
of the canon law, with which the king's English-bred
bishops and priests must have been familiar, and in dealing
with heathen practices the advice given by Gregory the

Great to the Abbot Mellitus * was followed and heathen customs as far as possible christianized.

It is important to note carefully the lines upon which this ecclesiastical legislation of Olaf proceeded, as in later times much controversy arose between the kings and the Church in connection with the *Kristenret,* and the former, at the commencement of their reigns, swore to observe the *Kristenret* " as given by Olaf the Saint."

The new law did not aim at making any change in the methods of government or civil duties, except in so far as they were heathen.

We may note them under different heads—

I. *Purely ecclesiastical matters.*

(*a*) The building and maintenance of churches.
(*b*) Church officials : their rights and duties.
(*c*) The observance of the Holy days and Fast days.

---

* Quoted by Bede, " Eccles. Hist." :—" I have upon mature deliberation determined that the temples of the idols in that nation should not be destroyed, but let the idols that are in them be destroyed. Let holy water be prepared and sprinkled in the said temple, let altars be erected and relics placed, for if these temples are well built it is requisite that they be converted from the worship of devils to the service of the true God. That the nation seeing that their temples are not destroyed, may remove error from their hearts, and knowing and adoring the true God may the more familiarly resort to the places to which they have been accustomed. And because they have been used to slaughter many oxen in sacrifice to devils, some solemnity must be exchanged for them on this account, as that on the day of dedication, on the nativities of holy martyrs whose relics are there deposited, they may build themselves huts of the boughs of trees about those churches which have been turned to that use from temples, and celebrate the solemnity with religious feasting and no more offer beasts to the devil, but kill cattle to the praise of God in their eating, and return thanks to the Giver of all things for their sustenance ; to the end that while some gratifications are outwardly permitted them they may more easily consent to the inward consolations of the grace of God." (Bk. 1, c. 30.)

It is not a little remarkable that nearly 500 years after the above we

From a Photograph by]   **THE CHURCH OF MOSTER.**   *[T. Olaf Willson.*

This Building replaced the original Church erected by Olaf Trygvessön in 995.

[To face p. 72.

(d) Holy Baptism and the bringing up of Children. Exposing infants forbidden, except in case of monstrosities, who were to be brought to the church and *primsigned*, and then either killed or left outside the church to die.

(e) Burials. All except outlaws and suicides were to be buried in the churchyard.

(f) Marriage, and the forbidden degrees.

II. *Heathenism: the worship of the gods and witchcraft, or Troldom.*

All this forbidden under the severest penalties.

III. *Heathen social customs.*

The reforms in this respect dwelt largely with the assemblies known as *Ølgerdir*, social gatherings at which beer was solemnly drunk in honour of the gods. In former days these took place in the heathen temples after the great *blots*, when the presiding chief, or whoever conducted the ceremonial, gave the *skaal* or toast in honour of Thor, Freya, &c. In accordance with the guiding principle of the English mission, it was decided not to suppress these social events, but to give them the sanction and approval of the Church. The law provided for their continuance, and directed that where three families could meet together and have a common feast, *skaals* were to be drunk (the beer having been first blessed) "in honour of Christ and the Blessed Virgin for good years and peace." Fines were imposed for a breach of these regulations. The *Ølgerdir* were usually held at stated times, but it is not certain whether they were held exactly at the same time as the

find the custom of building booths survived in the north of England. In the "Boldon Book" it is mentioned that villeins near Auckland were bound as part of their services to their Lord (the bishop) to erect eighteen booths (*bothas*) at the fair of St. Cuthbert.

old heathen *blots*, or, according to some authorities, on All Saints' day, Christmas, and St. John the Baptist's day.

IV. *Abolition of slavery.*

In the olden days it was the custom to offer up thralls as sacrifices to the gods before the *Thing* began, and there was doubtless a great deal of cruelty practised towards the slaves. But the coming of Christianity to Norway, as elsewhere, soon made a change in this respect. Instead of sacrificing a thrall at the *Thing*, the law provided that one should be set free. This was to take place on the first Sunday during the meeting of the *Thing*. It was also provided that one should be liberated every Christmas.

Such is an outline of the legislation which Olaf and his advisers introduced in order to make the laws in harmony with Christianity. We must not think that exactly the same law was accepted over the whole land. Modifications were made in different districts, as, for example, in the south-eastern part of Norway, in Viken, where we do not find the laws respecting the *Ølgerdir*, or the liberation of thralls. The reason for this very possibly is, that in that part of the country the work of the earliest missionaries had rendered such legislation unnecessary.*

We are now able to resume the history of Olaf's work after this long, but necessary, digression.

Having thus made preparations for bringing the law of the land into conformity with Christianity, Olaf determined to carry out his work in a thoroughly systematic manner,

---

* A remarkable collection of the ancient laws of Norway is now to be found in the *Norges Gamle Love*, in five large volumes, published by the Norwegian Government at intervals between 1846 and 1895. They contain all that now remains of the laws of the early part of the middle ages, including the law of older Gula, Frosta, Eidsiva, and Borgar *Things* and various *Kristenretter;* and also a vast variety of documents relating to both Church and State.

and to leave no part of Norway, from Haalogaland to Lindesnæs, without the knowledge of the Christian faith, without a church and without a teaching priest.

To give a detailed account of all these journeys, and the way in which he often coerced his unwilling people, would occupy too great a space, as it is a subject on which the writers of the Sagas have given most abundant information. It is impossible, however, to pass it over, as the history of his reign is essentially the history of the foundation and organization of the Church of Norway. But as there is so much similarity between the incidents recorded in the struggle against heathenism, it will be sufficient only to describe the most striking scenes in the conflict.

After being formally accepted as king, he began his systematic work in Viken, the same district where his famous namesake wisely made his first attempt. Little or no opposition was encountered in this part, as the inhabitants had, for a very considerable period, been more or less under Christian influences.

At the close of the year 1017 he passed from his newly-founded town of Borg (Sarpsborg) to the district known as the Oplands, that part of Norway lying around the Miøsen, the largest lake in the country. Here he found abundant scope for his labours, for those parts of Norway which lay away from the coast line, had been but little affected by the efforts of Olaf Trygvessøn, and the Oplands, Gudbrandsdal and Valders were the last to receive Christianity.

In the Oplands, Olaf acted with extreme severity, and indeed barbarity, against those who refused to be baptized—death or horrible mutilations awaited those who resisted the king. The same treatment was bestowed on all, high and low alike.

While this was going on a dangerous conspiracy was hatched against the king. In the Oplands there still remained five petty kings or chiefs, and they quickly saw that it was the intention of Ólaf to get rid of all royal power except his own. They had consented to Olaf's accession to the overlordship, and hoped to have been left in peace. The chief conspirator was Rørek, who had his home at Ringsaker, on the Miøsen. The plot was betrayed to the king, who, by a rapid move, secured the five kings. Rørek was blinded, another had his tongue cut out, and the other three were banished. The only remaining petty king in Norway was now the harmless Sigurd Syr, Olaf's stepfather; but in the winter of 1018 he died, and from that time onwards there were no more of these kings. Sigurd Syr had by his marriage with Olaf's mother, a son who was afterwards to play an important part in the history of Norway, and we shall meet with him again as Harald Haardraade.

King Olaf remained in the south for a considerable time, as the state of affairs with Sweden demanded his attention. The Swedish king had become so unpopular with his subjects that he was forced to accept his young son, Aanund Jacob, as under-king. After prolonged negotiations a permanent peace was arranged between Norway and Sweden, and the former country received back again the provinces which had fallen to Olaf of Sweden's share, after the division of Norway between Svein Tjugeskjæg and the two jarls, which was his reward for the help given at the battle of Svolder. The peace with Sweden was further cemented by the marriage of Olaf to Astrid, the daughter of the Swedish king. These matters interrupted for a time King Olaf's crusade against heathenism, and it was the summer of 1019 before he was able to go north to Nidaros. That year and the one following were devoted to the districts north of Trondhjem, Namdalen, and Haalogaland, where he made systematic investigations, built churches, and appointed priests to minister to the people, and at the various *Things* which he called, he had the *Kristenret* accepted.

The harvests in these years had been very bad, and the king had reason to suspect that the bønder, seeing in their misfortunes the wrath of the old gods (as they had formerly noticed in the days when Harald Graafell and his brothers destroyed the temples for their spoils), had begun again to offer sacrifices at the old appointed times. In this he was not wrong, and the evil was not far off. At the northern end of the Trondhjem Fjord was the place of the great heathen gathering (Mæren), where Olaf Trygvessøn had destroyed the image of Thor and where Jernskjægge had been slain. The chief man in that part was now Ølve of Egg, and Olaf sent for him demanding an explanation of the rumours which had reached him. Ølve was a very astute man, and contrived to satisfy the king with a plausible explanation as to the gatherings at Mæren. This was in October of 1020, and again after the January feast he seems to have been able to give reasons which at any rate the king listened to, and took no further steps. It was, however, quite true that the old heathen rites had been revived and sacrifices offered. Olaf was by no means satisfied that all was well, and kept a careful watch, and when the time of the *sommer blot* (which was held in April) came round, he made a sudden descent on Mæren and caught the crafty Ølve and a large number of the bønder in the very act of sacrificing. Ølve was promptly put to death, along with others, and his property confiscated, and the rest were severely punished and afterwards feared to resist the king's will.

Olaf now resumed his work in the central parts of Norway. He sailed from Nidaros, and leaving his ships at the entrance to the Romsdal, went over into the great Gudbrandsdal, which at that time was ruled with almost royal authority, by the famous chief, Dale Gudbrand, whose family had given the name to the valley. At Hundthorp the chief resided, and it was a centre of heathen worship.

A long and picturesque account is given in the Sagas of the way in which Olaf and his men destroyed the image of Thor and conquered the antagonism of the bønder, but it is unnecessary to give it in detail. The result was the same as in other places—they were all baptized and a church was built, and a priest left to teach the people.

From Gudbrandsdal he went south and east, everywhere spreading the faith and laying the foundation for future work.

It would seem likely that it is about this period that we must place Olaf's application to Archbishop Unwan of Bremen for help in his work, by sending to him clergy to minister to his people. The reasons which led Olaf to take this step we have already noted. All, or nearly all, of his first clerical helpers came from England ; but at this time the authority of Knut the Great was firmly established, and as that monarch regarded Olaf as an intruder who declined to recognize his overlordship, it was practically impossible for the Norwegian monarch to receive any longer the help which he had at the beginning. Under these circumstances the king had to look elsewhere, and the nearest and most convenient place was the great Metropolitan see of the North at Bremen. It is curious that the Norwegian authorities at this time are silent on this point, and it is to Adam of Bremen alone that we are indebted for the information. There seems no reason to doubt the fact, which is so plainly stated by Adam, especially when we know that there was practically no other course open to Olaf, but to apply to Bremen.

Just about the time of Olaf's expedition to Norway, Archbishop Libentius died (1013), and his successor was Unwan, who held the see from 1013 to 1029. He was a monk of Paderborn, and was much liked, especially by his clergy. It was to this man that Olaf turned for help. Adam, without clearly indicating the date, says : " He (Olaf) sent also ambassadors to our Archbishop (Unwan) with gifts, praying that he should receive these bishops kindly, and would send some of his own bishops to him, who should strengthen and confirm the rude Norwegians in the faith." How far the petition of King Olaf was answered by the Bremen Archbishop we have no certain means of knowing, and it would appear that not long after it was preferred, Olaf himself was a fugitive from his native land, and only returned to meet his death on the fatal field of Stiklestad. In 1023 we find him in the south and west, from whence he passed to the districts of Sogn and Valders. The last named was a region more isolated than other parts of Norway, as the vast mountain district, now known as the Jotunheim, cut it off from the north, and wild mountain ranges from the west and south. With his customary rapidity Olaf reached the Lille Miøsen lake, and called a *Thing* where his proposals with regard to Christianity were very unfavourably received, but the king with great skill managed to avert an outbreak and set the bønder quarrelling among themselves. Then at night he seized their boats and began to attack and burn the farms, each man rushed off to save his own, and when their forces were divided, the king was able to bring them to terms. Then he followed the long chain of lakes which extends through the district, not being strong enough in men, to risk the land journey, but everywhere carrying out the purpose he had in hand, and providing Christian teachers to carry on the work.

The next year, 1024, may be said to have witnessed the completion of Olaf's great work. Norway, from one end to the other, was at any rate nominally Christian; the laws had been brought into conformity with the new faith, and only in secret could sacrifices be offered to Odin and Thor. "There was no remote valley or outlying island in his kingdom," says the Saga, "where a heathen man could be found."

We must now turn to the events which led up to the fall of Olaf's power in Norway, his expulsion and subsequent return and martyrdom. It was not to be expected that such a powerful and ambitious monarch as Knut the Great, would be content to lose the supremacy which he claimed over Norway without an effort to regain it. In the earlier years of Olaf's reign, however, Knut was too much occupied in consolidating his authority in England, though he did not forget his claim on Norway. In the year 1025 he sent a messenger to Olaf ordering him to appear before him in England and receiving back Norway as a fief from the Danish king, to render the tribute which the jarls had paid to Svein. We can well imagine how such a message would have filled Olaf with rage, for, next to the spread of Christianity, the consolidation and independence of his kingdom was the great object of his life. He heard the ambassadors to the end, and then dismissed them with his answer to the mighty Knut. "Bring him my words," he said ; "I will defend Norway hill and dale as long as life is granted to me, and I will pay *skat* to no man for my kingdom."

After this Olaf saw that he must prepare to defend his crown, and he knew well the mighty power which Knut could wield. He accordingly formed a defensive alliance with his brother-in-law, Aanund Jacob of Sweden, and got his fleet together.

Knut the Great was in Rome, on his pilgrimage, in 1026, so just then they felt safe from attack. The allies decided to strike the first blow, and with their united fleets they made a descent on Denmark. On the approach of Knut they retired, and a fierce but indecisive battle was fought at Helgeaaen, in Skaane. The Swedish fleet dispersed, and Olaf, not finding himself strong enough to resist Knut alone, left his ships in Skaane, and went overland to Viken. Knut had been at work for some time in endeavouring to

seduce the great chiefs in Norway from their allegiance to
Olaf. In the north Haarek of Thjotta, Einar Thamberskjelver, Thore Hund, and Kalv Arnessøn were all ready
to take part against their king; the latter had received
from Olaf the land of the heathen Ølve of Egg, and was
a very powerful chief, who owed much to the king. In
the south, the great Erling Skjalgssøn of Sole was also
ready to join with the king's enemies. Thus we see all
the most prominent men in the country, who had felt the
severity with which Olaf ruled, and who knew that in his
justice he had the same law for rich and poor, were all
united against him, and ready to sacrifice their national
independence for the hope of personal gain and power.

There was also at this time in the land, among the
people generally, a feeling of hostility against the king.
The extreme severity of the way in which he had treated
those who resisted his efforts in spreading Christianity had
raised up enemies on all sides, and many of the bønder
thought that a change might let them have their own
way a little more. Indeed, a very decided reaction had
set in. Olaf's early popularity was on the wane, but
the feeling of hostility was not directed, as we might
have supposed, so much against Christianity, as against
the king personally.

When, then, Knut, with a great fleet, sailed for Nidaros
in 1028, there was no one to stand against him, and Olaf
did not dare to resist. Knut was recognized as overlord,
and Haakon Erikssøn (the last of the great jarls of Hlade),
in spite of his oath to Olaf in 1016, became governor
under Knut. Then the conqueror sailed to Borg, and
meeting with no resistance, thus "won Norway without
a sword stroke." While this was happening in the summer
of 1028 Olaf, with a few men and ships, lay at Drammen,
but Knut did not apparently think it politic to attack him.
When Knut had left the country, and the winter came on,

Olaf emerged from his retreat and sailed round the coast. As he went along, he had the good fortune to capture in Bukken Fjord, the old chief Erling Skjalgssøn, and intended to hold him as a hostage, but one of the king's men, most unfortunately for Olaf, slew the captured chief. This act raised all that part in arms against the king, and he sailed further north, and had reached Søndmøre when he learned of the approach of a superior force from Nidaros. Seeing he could neither advance nor retreat, the king sailed up the Slyngs Fjord as far as Sylte, and there left his ships, and with a handful of devoted followers started in the depth of winter over the mountains. After great hardships he came at last to Einabu, in the Gudbrandsdal, and from thence to Hedemarken. He had now no alternative but to leave Norway, and taking his wife and two children with him, and his faithful friend Bishop Grimkell, he went to his brother-in-law in Sweden, where he spent the winter. When the spring of 1029 came, he left his family in Sweden, and proceeded to his other brother-in-law, Jaroslav, who was king in Gardarike, and there remained for some time.

Meanwhile the government of Norway seems to have gone on quietly enough under Haakon Jarl, as Knut's representative. In the summer of 1029 he went to England, where he was married, and in the autumn set sail on his return home ; but nothing more was ever heard of him or the ship, and it is supposed that he perished in a storm. Thus ended the male line of the great jarls of Hlade, who, for close upon a hundred years, had played such an important part in the history of their country. The death of the jarl under such peculiar circumstances, was regarded by many of the people as a judgment of Heaven upon him, for the breach of the oath which he had taken, never to oppose the right of King Olaf to the throne of Norway.

After the death of Haakon, Einar Thamberskjelver was
now the greatest chief in the land, and he had been
allowed by Knut to cherish hopes of being ruler of the
country under the king. When the loss of Haakon and
his ship became known, Einar at once sailed for England,
and, to his intense chagrin, learned that he was not to be
jarl in Norway, for Knut intended to place his son Svein
there as governor.

While these events were happening, the fugitive, King
Olaf, remained at the court of Jaroslav in Gardarike. He
seems at first to have made up his mind to abandon all
thought of returning to Norway, and to have contemplated
a pilgrimage to the Holy Land, to be followed by retirement to a religious life. There is no doubt that during
the time he spent in Russia the natural religious bent of
his mind was much deepened, and the enforced period of
inactivity enabled him to learn something more of the true
spirit of the faith, for the outward establishment of which
he had been so zealous. He must have regretted the many
acts of cruelty of which he had been guilty towards the
heathen, and have seen that there was a better way than
the sword and mutilation, of advancing the cause which he
had so much at heart. That a real change in him took
place in this respect, is most evident by his actions in his
last campaign.

Notwithstanding his wish for a pilgrimage, he could not
forget Norway : ever and anon his thoughts went back to
his much-loved native land. In a dream he seemed to see
his great predecessor Olaf Trygvessøn, who urged him not
to abandon the work which he had undertaken, and a
longing seized him to return to it. At this time the
tidings came that Haakon Jarl was lost, and Norway was
again without a ruler. In the spring of 1030 he decided
to make an effort to regain his crown. Leaving Gardarike,
he returned to Sweden to Aanund Jacob, who allowed him

to collect men for the purpose of the invasion. He went to Jæmtland, in the northern part of Sweden, and was joined by a number of men (some of them were outlaws), who were attracted by the hope of plunder; which, however, was not realized. Crossing the mountains, he descended towards the Værdal, a wide and open valley which goes from the neighbourhood of the present town of Levanger towards the Swedish frontier. On his way he was joined by his young half-brother Harald, the son of Sigurd Syr, who brought a welcome reinforcement of some five hundred men from Viken.

The last few weeks of Olaf's life are related with much minuteness by the writers of the Sagas, and are full of episodes which are probably inaccurate, and added in later times to enhance the glories of the national saint; but there is undoubtedly in the romantic story, a very large element of truth as well, and which coincides with what we know of the king's character. We are told that good Bishop Sigurd came to him and foretold his approaching death, but Olaf's purpose was not to be shaken. In a dream on the day of the battle, he saw a ladder set up on earth and the top reaching to heaven, and he himself just on the point of gaining the highest rung, when he was awakened. He seems clearly to have foreseen that the struggle in which he was now engaged was to be the last of his life.

When the forces of the king had crossed the mountains he set himself to number his army, and found he had with him about 3,600 men. Further investigation revealed the fact that of these, no less than 900 were heathen. Olaf at once made it clear that all under his banner must be Christians—he offered them the alternative of being baptized or leaving his host. " We will," said he, "not rely on our numbers, but place our trust in God, who by His power and mercy can give us the victory, but I will not mix heathen folk with my men." Of the nine hundred, four hundred were at once baptized and confirmed, and the others left the king's force.

Olaf's adherents at once urged on him the importance of harrying the country around them in the customary way, in order to strike terror into the land, but the king sternly forbade them. He pointed out that where he had done this before, it was because they had resisted the true faith. "We had then," he said, "God's law to defend, but now they have broken faith with me and acted treasonably against me, and that deserves much slighter punishment. . . . There is much greater reason to show leniency towards those who wronged me, than to those who showed their hatred of God."

Meanwhile the supporters of Knut had not been idle. Tidings of the projected invasion had reached Norway, but it was not at first known from what point the attack would be made, and preparations were begun in the south, in case hostilities should commence in that direction. When, however, it was discovered that Olaf was approaching from the north-east, at once all the chiefs who supported Knut, went with their men to Trøndelagen. The principal leaders of the rebels against Olaf, were Thore Hund, Kalv Arnessøn and Haarek of Thjotta,* and they got together a very considerable body of men (largely out-numbering the king's force), and estimated at no less than 14,400. It seems, however, that this total must have been largely in excess of the actual figure.

It must not be imagined that the coming battle was one entirely between Christians and heathen, for as we have already seen, Olaf had almost altogether expelled heathenism from the land, at least the open profession of it.

But those who opposed the king were in the main the survivors of the old heathen party; the chiefs hostile to Olaf had, however, on their side an ecclesiastic in the person

* Einar Thamberskjelver prudently held aloof at this critical time.

of Bishop Sigurd, who had officially been attached by Knut to the retinue of his son, as court bishop. He was a man of most violent temper, and with the most bitter invective urged on the bønder to attack the king, painting Olaf and his men as monsters of iniquity, and wound up with telling them that "the only thing to be done is to advance against these inhuman monsters, and to slay them, casting them forth for the eagles and the wolves, leaving them where they have fallen, unless you drag away their bodies into remote corners of the woods, and let no man dare to carry them to the church, for they are all Vikings and men of evil deeds."

This atrocious advice was happily not carried out after the battle, though at the time it was given, it was greeted with applause by the bønder.

The rebels now held a conference of their chiefs to select a leader to command their army, and it was first proposed that Haarek of Thjotta should lead the host, but he declined, and finally the choice fell on Kalv Arnessøn.

The armies of the king and the rebellious bønder drew near to each other, at a spot called Stiklestad, in the Værdal, not very far from the place where the river, which flows through the valley, enters the Trondhjem Fjord. Olaf's army seems now to have numbered somewhat over 3,000 men, but the forces of the rebels were much more numerous. The king divided his men into three divisions—he himself commanded the centre, the Swedish contingent was on the right, and the rest, under Dag Hringssøn, on the left. The forces of the bønder were similarly arranged—Kalv Arnessøn and Thore Hund in the centre, the men from Rogaland, Horda-land and Sogn on the left, and those of Romsdal, Namdal, and Mæren on the right.

Olaf did not forget that he came as a champion of the faith, and not merely a king striving to recover his temporal power. He chose as the battle-cry of his army, "Christ's men! Cross men! King's men!"; while the rebels' cry was, "Fram, fram (onward, onward), bønder!" In the early morning all Olaf's army made their confession and received the Communion. It is said that the king at this time gave a sum of money in order that, after the battle, prayers should be offered for the souls of his enemies who might fall in the fray.

Before the actual conflict began, and when the armies stood facing one another, Olaf made a final but ineffectual appeal to the leaders of the bønder who had sworn allegiance to him, to return to their duty. We are also told that he made the offer to his own men, that if they had relations in the rebel army against whom they desired not to fight, they could, even then, leave the ranks. No one accepted this generous offer, though one man on the king's side had two sons in the opposite army.

Then the battle joined and raged fiercely. The royal army was, as we have seen, greatly out-numbered, and to add to their misfortunes, a large part of the men under Dag Hringssøn's command did not come into action until the issue was practically decided. The king fought with his usual courage in the thickest of the fray, and his men fell all around him. In the ranks of his foes was a man named Thorstein, who had sworn to be avenged on the king for the capture of a trading vessel which he had owned. Pressing forward he struck Olaf a severe blow on the knee. Unable to stand, the king leaned against a rock and prayed to God for help. Then his foes closed around him. Kalv Arnessøn is supposed to have given the next blow, which fell upon the king's neck, and then Thore Hund thrust his spear into Olaf, inflicting a mortal wound from which he almost at once expired.

When the king fell, the battle practically ended. The remains of the king's army sought refuge in the woods, whence they escaped. A remarkable change seems to have come over the victors. Their previous intense animosity suddenly died down, they refrained even from plundering the slain, and gave them Christian burial.

Thus fell Olaf, king and martyr, on a day long to be remembered in his native land. With his death his passing unpopularity ended, and his memory was ever after held in grateful remembrance in the country for which he had done so much.

Strange as it may seem, the exact date of the battle is rather difficult to determine. The Sagas appear to be unanimous that it was fought on Wednesday, July 29th, 1030, and the 29th of July was kept as the festival of the sainted king, from within a very short time of his death. But there is, before accepting this implicitly, an important point to be considered. The same authorities which fix July 29th as the date of the battle, are equally clear in stating that the sun (which when the battle began had been shining in a cloudless sky) became darkened, and a blackness as of night, for a time prevailed. This of course betokened an eclipse of the sun, and we know for a certainty, that a total eclipse of the sun took place on Monday, August 31st, 1030, which was *visible in Vœrdalen*.

It is clear, therefore, that if the eclipse took place during the battle, the date of it must be August 31st, and not July 29th. But then how was it possible that an error of a whole month took place, and the date fixed as July 29th by the very men who had taken part in the struggle? There seems, however, a possibility of reconciling these two statements. It may be taken that the traditional date of July 29th is the correct one, not August 31st, and for this reason. We shall see later that the saintship of Olaf very rapidly seized hold of the popular imagination, and that, for political purposes, it was encouraged to the utmost, by the chiefs like Einar Thamberskjelver, and therefore the writers of the life of the saint, and of the narrative of his death or

martyrdom, would not be likely to omit what (to a superstitious, and only half-Christian people) would be such a
manifest sign of Divine displeasure as an eclipse. They
therefore incorporated into the narrative of the battle, the
mysterious darkness of the total eclipse which fell over the
north of Norway, just a month after the king had been
slain. This may very possibly be the explanation, and it
seems the only way by which the traditional, and by the
Church universally accepted, date can be vindicated.

Meanwhile Thore Hund and the leaders of the rebel
army, had pursued after the scattered remnants of the king's
forces, which were retreating as rapidly as possible to the
forests. It was their intention on their return to secure
the body of Olaf, and either to burn it or cast it into the
fjord.

When evening fell, a bonde of Stiklestad named Thorgil
and his son Grim, found the body of the king and determined
to save it from indignity. They carried it away and hid it
under some fuel in a barn ; before concealing the corpse they
washed it, and were struck with its extraordinary life-like
appearance. Having hidden it, they returned to their house
hard by. Meanwhile a blind man, who was seeking shelter
for the night, crept into the barn and accidentally wet his
hands with the water on the floor, where the corpse had
been washed, and touched his eyes with his hands. Finding the place too small and damp he came out, and
discovered that his sight was restored to him again. Going
to the house he told the story, which filled all with wonder
as to what could be in the barn. Thorgil and his son were
alarmed lest the body should be found, and hurriedly took
it away into another place.

Thore Hund on his return sought everywhere for the
king, but being unsuccessful left the place. The faithful
Thorgil and his son now resolved that the king's body
should be conveyed to Nidaros, but knowing the danger

which attended such a course, they went to work warily. Two coffins were made; in one he placed the king, and in the other stones and sand of the weight of a man. Then with the aid of friends on whom they could rely, they hid the coffin containing the royal body under the boards of the boat, but placed the other coffin where all men could see it. Then they rowed down the fjord to Nidaros.

On reaching the town Thorgil sent word at once to Bishop Sigurd, that he had brought the body of Olaf. This unlovable prelate was delighted to hear the news. He at once dispatched his men in a boat to meet them, and when they had got the coffin with the stones and sand in it, they rowed out into the fjord and threw it overboard, and returned to their master with the information that their errand had been accomplished. Then Thorgil and his friends rowed their boat a short way up the Nid, and in the night-time secretly conveyed the coffin with the body of the king to land, and hid it in a hut on the river bank. Here it remained for a short time, but knowing well it would not be safe, and finding no one who would dare to take charge of it, they dug a hole in the sand on the river bank, and in it they placed the body. Carefully marking the spot, they started again before daybreak, and quickly made their way back to Stiklestad.

CHAPTER VIII.

MAGNUS THE GOOD AND HARALD HAARDRAADE—THE CONFLICT WITH THE SEE OF BREMEN.

Svein and Ælfgifu as Knut's Representatives—Discontent in Norway—
King Olaf's Body Disinterred—His Saintship Proclaimed—Growth
of the Cult—Magnus brought to Norway—Independence secured
again—Reign of Magnus—His Death—Harald Haardraade—
Murder of Einar—Foundation of Oslo—St. Halvard—Conflict with
the See of Bremen—Letter of Pope Alexander II.

WITH the fall of Olaf at the battle of Stiklestad, it seemed
as if the forces of disintegration had triumphed, and the
cause for which the king had worked so laboriously during
the eventful years of his reign had come to nought. Once
more Norway was to become subservient to Denmark, and
both Church and State were deprived of the strong hand
which had built up the one, and guided the destinies of the
other. But it was not so. Of Olaf the Saint it might well
be said that "the dead which he slew at his death were
more than they which he slew in his life," and far from the
destruction of the cause for which his life was given, it
gained in a very short time a fresh power and impetus,
and the name and fame of the royal martyr was carried far
beyond the limits of the northern kingdom, even, it is said,
to the capital of the Eastern Empire.

Knut the Great had sent his young son Svein as Governor
to Norway, in the place of the last jarl of Hlade. As
Svein was but a lad, he was accompanied by his mother,
Alfiva or Ælfgifu, an imperious and overbearing English-
woman, who but little understood the independent spirit
which actuated the Norwegian bønder. They landed in
Viken about the time of the battle of Stiklestad, and shortly

after arrived at Nidaros, where Svein was accepted as
king.   The rule which the young prince instituted, under
the direction of his mother and the Danish chiefs who accompanied him, was at once very distasteful to the people,
and the imposition of new taxes made them very unpopular.
If there was one thing more than another to which the
Norwegians clung, it was the laws which had been passed
by the great assemblies at Frosta and other places, and the
bønder found that if Olaf had ruled with a strong arm, he
had, at any rate, ruled them under their own laws and
customs, and not according to Danish law and usages,
and they soon began bitterly to repent of their rebellion
against him.   The great chiefs, like Einar Thamberskjelver,
Kalv Arnessøn and others, found also that the change had
done them no good, and their privileges were no more than,
and indeed in some ways not so great as, they had been
under their native king.   Discontent spread everywhere,
but none of the chiefs were ready to risk an open rebellion.
The man who seemed the natural leader was Einar, who,
as has been mentioned, took no part in the battle of Stiklestad, and who, in his early days, had been a devoted
adherent of the race of Haarfagre.

The discontented chiefs, however, thought it prudent to
attain their ends by religious and not political means.   The
Danish court bishop Sigurd had done his best to bring the
Norwegian Church into close connection with Denmark,
and therefore with the see of Bremen, and it was probably
during the short time that he was at Nidaros, that the
Benedictine Monastery at Nidarholm (a small island in the
Trondhjem Fjord, close to the town, now called Munkholmen)
was first established.   Sigurd, however, was so unpopular,
that by the influence of Einar Thamberskjelver, he was
obliged to leave Norway, and Bishop Grimkell, the com-
panion and fellow-worker with Olaf, was brought back
again.   The National party, as we may term them, now

decided that the time had come to declare King Olaf to be a saint and martyr, and for this purpose they obtained formal permission from Knut to re-inter the body of the king. We have seen how Thorgil of Stiklestad had managed to convey it safely to Nidaros, and had secretly buried it in the sand on the bank of the Nid, the exact place being of course, carefully noted.

On August 3rd, 1031, the principal men, including Bishop Grimkell and Einar, in the presence of the young prince and his mother Alfiva, had the body disinterred. On the coffin being opened the body of Olaf was found to be perfectly preserved; his hair and nails had grown, his colour was lifelike, and a beautiful odour pervaded the air. All these things were clear proofs of saintship, and the on-lookers were filled with wonder and amazement. The only sceptic was Alfiva, who maintained that a body buried in sand would not decay. The bishop, however, offered to test the matter by cutting off some of Olaf's hair and placing it in the fire, where, if it remained unconsumed, there could then be no doubt of the saintship. This was done with con-secrated fire, and, surviving the test, all were forced to admit that the late monarch must indeed be a saint. Then the body was carried with great state into the church of St. Clement, which Olaf Trygvessøn had built, and there buried before the altar.

The cult of St. Olaf then proceeded with amazing rapidity, helped on as far as possible by Einar and others for political purposes, and the young king and his mother dared not openly oppose it, as the disinterment and reburial after the proved sanctity, had been done with their formal consent. The usual miracles were soon everywhere reported; the blind saw, the lame walked, and the sick were healed.

Thore Hund, who had given the king his death blow in the battle, was struck with contrition for his heinous offence, and endeavoured to expiate his crime by going on a

pilgrimage to the Holy Land, from whence he never returned.
Olaf was declared to be a saint by Bishop Grimkell, and the
verdict of the Church was formally ratified by the law of
the land. Two days were set apart in St. Olaf's honour—
July 29th as the day of the martyrdom, and August 3rd
as, what we may call, the Translation of St. Olaf, being the
day on which the body was disinterred from the sand and
brought for burial to the church of St. Clement. It may be
well to mention here the curious number of changes which
were made in a short period, before the final resting-place in
the Dom Kirke was reached. From St. Clement's it was
moved to a church dedicated to Olaf by his son Magnus,
which was built on the spot where the body of the saint lay
for one night on its arrival in Nidaros. In the next reign,
that of the saint's half-brother, Harald, it was moved to a
church dedicated to the Blessed Virgin, built by that king on
the bank of the Nid, where Olaf had been buried for a year.
Then Olaf Kyrre built another church, known as Christ
Church (close to the Maria Kirke of Harald), and the body
was taken to it. Finally, when the present cathedral was
built, during the time of Archbishop Eystein (1157—87),
both of the latter churches were incorporated in it, and the
body was placed in a magnificent shrine at the high altar,
and there it remained until the time of the Reformation.
The actual spot of the year-long burial is supposed to be
where St. Olaf's well is now shown in the cathedral of
Trondhjem.

After the formal acknowledgment of Olaf's claim to be
regarded as a saint, things went on in about the same way
for a couple of years ; but the hatred of Danish rule deepened
in the minds of the people, and all their love for the race of
Harald Haarfagre returned in greater force, when they saw
how badly they had treated one, who was not merely a king
of his line, but also one of the saints of God. Still, however,
Einar and the other chiefs played a waiting game, and felt

that the time had not come to make a move. In 1033 a passing disturbance was caused by an adventurer who claimed to be a son of Olaf Trygvessøn, and who raised the standard of rebellion in the south, but he was soon defeated and slain in a battle fought in Søndhordland. Shortly after this, a violent altercation between the Danish party and Einar, which broke out at a *Thing* held at Nidaros, led to the departure of Svein and Alfiva to the south, as they felt it was unsafe for them to remain in Trøndelagen. Then Einar, who had rightly gauged the popular feeling, called the people together to a *Thing* and proposed that Magnus, the young son of St. Olaf, should be chosen as king. This was unanimously agreed upon, and Einar and Kalv Arncssøn were deputed to go to Gardarike to the Court of King Jaroslav and bring back the young prince to Norway. Their mission was successful, and they returned through Sweden, where Olaf's widowed queen was then residing with her brother. Young Magnus was at this time only eleven years old, but he was everywhere received with open arms by the delighted people. Svein and his mother first intended to resist the newcomer, but finding that the country was entirely hostile to them, they took refuge in Denmark, and thus in 1034 the Danish supremacy was once more swept away.

Knut the Great died in England in 1035, and was succeeded by his son Harald; Svein died in Denmark in 1036, and for a time the rule of Magnus over Norway was undisputed.

The early years of King Magnus's reign passed quietly under the wise guidance of Einar and Kalv Arnessøn, and the abolition of the harsh laws and exactions of the Danish king made the people contented. Meanwhile Hardeknut had succeeded his father Knut as king of Denmark, and made an effort to regain the lost power over Norway. Before matters went very far, the leading men

on both the Danish and Norwegian side arranged, after a
conference held at the Gøtha river, that whichever of the
two kings survived, should have the two kingdoms.   This
dangerous compact might have made the subservience of
Norway to Denmark again an accomplished fact, but the
death of Hardeknut in 1042 changed the situation, and
Norway and not Denmark became the sovereign State.
The political result of this was unfortunate for Norway, as
it meant a great waste of blood and treasure, and though
for a time it exalted the position of the northern State
among the nations of Europe, it was but a drawback to the
prosperity of the country.   When Magnus took the government into his own hands he embarked on the very unwise
course, of attempting to be avenged on those who had
taken part in the rebellion against St. Olaf.   The old chief,
Haarek of Thjotta was killed, and Kalv Arnessøn, who by
his zeal for Magnus's succession might have been thought
to have atoned for his share in Stiklestad, was obliged to
fly to the Orkneys.   But after a time Magnus had the
sense to see how unwise and unfair his action was, and
abandoned his thoughts of revenge.   By his just and
kindly rule he became more beloved by his people than
any king since the days of Haakon, and the epithet "The
Good," which the former had won, was everywhere accorded
to Magnus.

One very important work was accomplished in his time.
He reduced the laws of the Frosta *Thing* to writing.
Formerly it would seem, that these laws were more of the
nature of customs, and were preserved orally, but Magnus
had them written out, and his compilation or code, under
the curious name of "The Grey Goose," remained in use in
Trøndelagen for close upon 200 years.

The Danish sovereignty, though it was in many ways a
danger to Norway, brought the king much renown, especially
after his great defeat of the Vends in 1044, which effectually

stemmed the tide of Sclavonic invasion in that part of Europe, and spread the fame of the young king and his sainted father, far and wide.

The year that followed the victory over the Vends nearly witnessed another of the many dynastic struggles which had before rent the kingdom. Harald, the son of Sigurd Syr, and the king's half-uncle, had after the battle of Stiklestad, gone to Constantinople and taken service under the Eastern Emperor, where he won a great reputation as a warrior. He returned to Norway, and demanded half of the kingdom. This was refused, and Harald retired to Sweden, and later joined Svein Ulfssøn, the new claimant for the Danish Crown. The year after, however, Magnus agreed to Harald's demand, but stipulated that the kingdom was not to be divided; there were to be no more under-kings in Norway, but they were to reign jointly. How this unwise plan would have worked, there was no opportunity of judging, for Magnus the Good died suddenly in 1047, and Harald reigned as sole king. Denmark was now separated, and Svein Ulfssøn reigned there.

The short reign of Magnus was not remarkable for any important ecclesiastical events, beyond of course the growth of the cult of St. Olaf, and the building of churches in different parts of the country. In his reign a magnificent silver shrine for the body of St. Olaf was made ; the king kept the keys of this, and every year is said to have cut the hair and nails of his father. After Magnus's death Harald Haardraade did the same thing, but on his departure for the great expedition against his English namesake, he threw the keys of the shrine into the sea, and two centuries then elapsed before it was again opened.

The unexpected death of Magnus the Good removed the probability of disputes between the kings in Norway, and there was no one to contest the claims of Harald. The new monarch possessed many of the characteristics of the race of Haarfagre, and his near relationship to the royal saint made him at first very popular with his people. But along with great personal courage and skill in war, he had a very strong will, and was often guilty of great cruelty in the prosecution of his ends, and his subjects had soon to learn that he was no light and easy ruler of either chief or people. The name by which he was known, *Haardraade*, the hard or stern ruler, was well deserved by the king, and his power was felt in all parts of the land.

The political history of his reign need not long detain us, though it was an exciting time, and the death of the king at the hard-fought battle of Stamford bridge is well known to all readers of English history. A great part of the king's reign was taken up with his constant warfare against Svein Ulfssøn, king of Denmark.* Harald could not forget that his predecessor Magnus was king both of Norway and Denmark, and although success often attended his arms, he was finally obliged to make peace with Svein in 1064.

His hard rule in Norway naturally aroused the resentment of the great chiefs, who had had an easy time under the mild rule of Magnus. Foremost in the opposition to the king was the old chief Einar Thamberskjelver, who, along with his son Eindride, was treacherously murdered by the king's command at Nidaros. "Hard bites the king's dogs," said the old chief as he fell by the spears of Harald's servants. The death of Einar removed the most prominent figure in the history of Norway for nearly sixty years; as a youth and far-famed archer, he had fought beside Olaf Trygvessøn in the battle of Svolder, and had witnessed all the strange vicissitudes which had befallen his royal race for more than half a century. One could have wished that

---

* The fierceness of his attacks on Denmark is well described by Adam of Bremen, who was, however, in this matter, not an impartial witness: "Nunquam quietus fuit a bellis, fulmen septentrionis, fatale malum omnibus Danorum insulis."—Book III., Chap. xvi.

he had met with a more honourable death after his many services to his country.

This murderous act aroused a deep feeling of hostility against King Harald, and the people of Trøndelagen rose in arms to avenge the death of their beloved chief; but the king was too strong for them, and the insurrection was soon suppressed.

In 1066 he joined with Earl Tostig (brother of Harold of England) in his attempt to regain his power there, and with a great fleet set sail for England, where he fell in battle against Harold at Stamford bridge near York on September 25th, 1066.

Before we advert to the ecclesiastical politics of the reign of Harald Haardraade, there is one event which must be mentioned, and which, indeed, had both political and ecclesiastical importance. This was the founding of the town of Oslo, which is now the capital of Norway, and bears the name of its second founder, Christian IV., who in 1624, after a fire at Oslo, built the new town close by. Harald, as we know, was closely connected by birth and friendship with that part of Norway, and he probably saw that the Trøndelagen district had an undue share of political importance in the land. To counteract this, and to balance the growing power of Nidaros (which after the saintship of Olaf had been established had received a constantly increasing number of pilgrims) he determined to found in the south, a town which might rival Nidaros. Furthermore, he provided the town with a saint as well, who was afterwards regarded as one of the three patrons of Norway, Halvard of Huseby, who was his own and St. Olaf's first cousin. It is a little difficult to see where Halvard's claim to saintship comes in. He was the son of a wealthy bonde named Vebjørn who lived at Lier, a spot but a few miles from the present town of Drammen. His father married Thorny, the sister of Aasta, wife of Sigurd Syr, and mother, by her

first husband, Harald Grenske, of St. Olaf, and by her
second, Sigurd, of Harald Haardraade.   Halvard seems to
have been a very estimable man and to have carried on a
considerable business as a Baltic merchant.   One day he
chivalrously rescued a woman from some men who were
attacking her, and brought her over the Drammen river.
He was, however, followed, and killed along with the woman
he had saved for the time.   His murderers tied a stone to
his neck and threw his body into the fjord.   It, however,
refused to sink, and this circumstance, with the other usual
signs, proclaimed Halvard to be a saint, and his claim was
soon acknowledged by the Church.   When Harald founded
Oslo he had his kinsman's body brought thither, and buried
in a church which bore his name, and Halvard became, to
the people of the south of Norway, a saint second only in
rank, to his royal cousin at Nidaros.

Harald was not merely a hard ruler in the affairs of State,
but he showed himself none the less stark in ecclesiastical
matters.   He decided in his mind that he was to be the head
of the Church, as well as of the State.   Early in his reign
the assertion of this principle brought him into conflict
with Bishop Bernhard, and the consequence was, that the
bishop was obliged to leave Norway and go to Iceland,
where he remained during the whole of Harald's reign.

A vastly more important conflict, however, arose with the
see of Bremen, which was held, during the greater part of
Harald's reign, by a prelate of as strong and unbending a
will as that of the king himself.

We have already seen that the connection of Norway
with the archiepiscopal see of Bremen (notwithstanding
the fact that it had received papal authority over all the
Scandinavian lands) was not a very close one.   It depended
largely on political considerations, and also it must be
borne in mind that the ecclesiastics whom the two Olafs
brought with them were nearly all Englishmen, either by

birth or education, and looked to Canterbury, and not Bremen, as the see to which they owed allegiance. The application of St. Olaf to Unwan of Bremen, for help in his work, was made at a time when he could not expect any substantial aid from England. The early bishops in Norway were not diocesan officials, but were merely men in episcopal orders, who went with the kings into a heathen land to spread the faith, and the priests who accompanied them were, until St. Olaf's day at any rate, not as a rule fixed in one place, but accompanied the king and the bishops on their journeys. These men were not likely to let the claims of a metropolitan make any very great impression upon them, even when backed by papal authority, and they always retained the sturdy English dislike to foreign ecclesiastical rule, which was so often manifested in the history of the English Church.

In 1043 the see of Bremen was filled by the appointment of Adalbert, who held it for a period of twenty-nine years. He was a strong and worldly-minded man, not specially renowned for his sanctity, and with an ambition equal to that of a Hildebrand. He entertained very lofty projects for enlarging the power and authority of the see of Bremen, and, it is said, hoped to have made it a sort of patriarchate of the North. He found, however, that he was not able to carry out all that his personal ambition suggested, and it was not long before he crossed swords with Haardraade.* The king had been accustomed to have his bishops consecrated in different places, but chiefly in England. These bishops had no love for Adalbert, and it was their refusal to attend

---

* For the details of this controversy between Harald and the see of Bremen, we have only the testimony of Adam of Bremen and his scholiast. It must be borne in mind that there was a not unnatural prejudice against the Norwegian Church, which manifests itself here and there, in spite of the general reliability of this famous historian of the North. See the "Gesta Hammaburgensis Ecclesiæ Pontificum."—Book III., Chap. xvi., and Scholiast, 69.

which caused the failure of an ambitious project of the archbishop, for a great synod of the North to be held at Slesvig. These bishops naturally declined to acknowledge the authority of the see of Bremen, and Adalbert was equally determined on his part to assert it. During the constant war with Denmark in Harald's reign, his bishops were consecrated in various places—in England, in Aquitaine—by the Pope, and even by the Eastern Church at Constantinople, where Harald had many friends. Adalbert, however, watched his opportunities, and as the bishops who were returning to Norway, had, as a rule, to pass through his diocese, he caught and imprisoned them until they were ready to swear obedience to the see of Bremen. It is said that Asgaut, nephew of Grimkell, when returning from Rome, was one who suffered in this way. Adalbert did not hesitate to accuse Harald of plundering the shrine of St. Olaf, and taking the gifts which were offered there, for the purpose of carrying on his wars—a charge probably true; but Harald was not quite as black as Adam paints him in his Chronicle.

Adalbert now decided to take another line. He found that imprisoning bishops who had just come from being consecrated at Rome, might possibly entail unpleasant consequences later, and also that promises of allegiance extorted by imprisonment, were not likely to be much regarded when once the bishop was safe in the kingdom of Norway. He therefore took the more regular course of sending messengers to Harald with a formal claim to exercise the rights of a metropolitan over the Norwegian bishops. In making this claim it cannot be said that Adalbert was exceeding his lawful powers; for when the archiepiscopal see of Hamburg was founded in 834 (?) for Ansgar, and transferred, as we have seen, to Bremen in 849, it was expressly intended by the Kaiser to be the head of a new province, to include the three Scandinavian kingdoms, and this was confirmed by Pope Nicholas I. in 858.*   But, on the other hand, it must be remembered that Norway never formed any part of the Roman Empire, and therefore the Kaiser had no special claim upon it, or authority to enforce his will there, and also that the christianizing of Norway was the work of English, and not German, missionaries, except to a limited and uncertain extent in Viken.   Adalbert, however, was, from his point of view, quite in order in making a demand, for which he could claim the authority both of Pope and Kaiser.

The archbishop's ambassadors were the bearers of a letter to the king, which was worded in a manner little calculated to conciliate such a man as Harald Haardraade.   In it Adalbert lectured the king on his iniquities in appropriating for his own uses the treasury of the shrine of St. Olaf, and, further, with not having his bishops consecrated in Bremen, and thereby acknowledging the metropolitan authority of that see.

This letter filled Harald with fury, and he sent Adalbert's messengers back to their master with the scornful words : " I know of no archbishop or ruler in Norway save myself, Harald, alone."

Having received this response to his demand, Adalbert decided to invoke the papal aid, and laid his case before Alexander II.   The Pope supported his metropolitan, and despatched a letter to King Harald.   In this he reminded the king and his people of his apostolic authority.   He pointed out to them, that they in Norway, were as yet but comparatively unlearned in the faith and in all matters of Church discipline, and ended up with an exhortation, or rather command, that they should submit themselves to the Archbishop of Bremen, and yield the same obedience to him as they should show to the chair of St. Peter.†

* This again was confirmed by Pope Victor II. (1055) in a bull which recognized the right of the Bremen archbishops to consecrate bishops in Sweden, Denmark, *Norway*, Iceland, and Greenland.

† Adam.—Book III., Chap. xvi., and Scholiast, 70.

This letter is a notable document as being the first papal brief sent to Norway. It, however, met with no more consideration than Harald had shown to the messages of Adalbert, and the Norwegian king was equally indifferent to the threats and thunderings of Bremen or Rome. While he lived, affairs remained in the same state; but this was not long, and his successor, Olaf Kyrre, was ready to admit the authority of Bremen without any question. Shortly after his death the claims of Bremen were no longer in existence, as Lund, in Skaane, at that time a part of the kingdom of Denmark (1104), was made the metropolitan see of the North.

CHAPTER IX.

OLAF KYRRE, TO THE DEATH OF SIGURD JORSALFARER.

Olaf the Peaceable and his Character—Development of the Country—Viking Expeditions come to an End—Gilds Established—Magnus Bærføtte—Lund made a Metropolitan See—Three Kings in Norway—The Crusade of Sigurd—Harald Gille—Last Years of Sigurd—Bishop Magnus—Death of Sigurd.

WHEN Harald Haardraade fell at Stamford bridge, he left behind him two sons, Magnus and Olaf, and they divided between them the royal power. Happily for Norway this state of things did not long continue, for Magnus died in the year 1069, and Olaf became sole king. Magnus left one son, but as he was only a little child, his claim was not then brought forward.

The reign of Olaf, who is known as Olaf Kyrre, or the Peaceable, was a period of much peace and quietness for the land, which was sorely needed after the constant warfare of Harald's reign. Olaf was a man of a most gentle and loveable disposition, and seems to have in every way deserved the name he bore. He devoted the whole of his reign to improving the condition of his people. We are told that his motto was, "The freedom and happiness of my people is my joy and pleasure."

The Church in Norway found in Olaf Kyrre a true "nursing father," and it advanced much in power and authority during his reign. We find an interesting account of the king in the Chronicles of Symeon or Simon of Durham, a Benedictine monk, who died in 1143. He tells us of a monk named Turgot, who having been imprisoned in Lincoln, effected his escape, and concealed himself on a Norwegian vessel and reached the court of Olaf Kyrre. "He attained" (says the Chronicle) "to the acquaintance of King Olaf, who, as he was of a very religious turn, was accustomed to the use of the sacred writings, and cultivated learning amid the cares of his kingdom. He was wont also to assist the priest at the altar, and when the latter was putting on the sacred vestments he would pour water on his hands and devoutly perform other offices of this kind. Hearing, therefore, that a clerk had come from England (which at that time was reckoned an important event), he took him as his master in learning psalmody." *

The reign of Olaf Kyrre was a time during which Norway was practically at peace with all other nations, and therefore there is but little to chronicle in the political history of his reign. It was not, however, a time which passed by without leaving its impress on subsequent events. To it we owe the beginnings of two very important cities. Olaf Trygvessøn had founded Nidaros, afterwards known as Trondhjem; Harald Haardraade established Oslo, the future Christiania; and now Olaf, his son, added two more towns, which are well known at the present day—Bergen and Stavanger. The former was originally known as Bjørgvin, and the site was well chosen for purposes of trade, the deep watera nd well-sheltered position making it easy of access for shipping. The town soon grew to be a place of importance, to which the comparative nearness of Evenvik (where the great Gula *Thing,* which legislated for the south-west of Norway, met), probably helped not a little. Stavanger, lying a hundred miles further south, was a good centre for

---

* Symeon of Durham's "History of the Kings," translated by the Rev. J. Stevenson. Turgot after his return to England, was subsequently prior of Durham and bishop of St. Andrew's; he died at Durham in 1115. Selden and others believe that Turgot was the real author of the history, which bears the name of Symeon of Durham.

trade, and was at that time the nearest port to England and the possessions of the kings of Norway beyond the seas.

Olaf did all in his power to encourage trade and to induce his people to adopt a more settled mode of life than had formerly been their custom ; and his reign is usually fixed as the time when we note the practical ending of the famous Viking cruises, which for more than three hundred years had made the Northmen the terror of the coasts of Europe. The political results of these famous expeditions are " writ large" upon the history of nearly every country of modern Europe; and it fills us with wonder that such a small nation as Norway, even when aided by like adventurous spirits from Denmark and Sweden, should have been the means of effecting changes, the results of which are still visible in Europe.

The increase of trade which the foundation of new towns called forth, naturally led also to an increase of civilization, and to a decided improvement in the mode of life of the people, who gradually, especially in the retinues of the king and the greater chiefs, adopted the customs and habits of the more civilized peoples of Europe, and the semi-barbarous life of the early days began to pass away.

In the king's own household changes are noted from the old fashion of a fireplace in the middle of the room, with a hole in the roof for the escape of the smoke, to a regular chimney in the corner, and windows were placed to give light in the room. Costly drinking-cups of silver began also to replace the horns and bowls from which, in ruder times, the king and his men drank their beer.

Olaf increased the royal retinue, which had formerly been small, to one hundred and twenty men, sixty of whom were huskarls; and we can also note the beginning of a body of what might be called, high court officials.

Olaf was a great builder of churches, and the most important of these were Christ Church, in Nidaros, to which the body of St. Olaf was removed, and which was afterwards incorporated in the cathedral; and another Christ Church in his new town of Bergen, which was later on, the cathedral, but which was ruthlessly destroyed in the sixteenth century.

From an ecclesiastical point of view, two very important things date from Olaf Kyrre's reign, namely, the division of the country into dioceses—of which we shall speak presently—and the establishment of Gilds among the people, the members of which were bound by very strict obligations to help one another; and the gild brothers were expected to set a good example in the matter of " temperance, soberness, and chastity."

The king saw that it would be a wise step in the direction of softening the manners of the people and promoting social union, to establish in the towns these associations, which were known among the other branches of the Teutonic nations.* It would not appear that at first these Gilds were especially connected with any one trade or calling, as was afterwards the case, but were open to all. They were held in buildings called *gilderstuer,* or gild rooms, and, though not directly religious, were closely connected with the Church. A short office was often said at the commencement of the gatherings, and the members were expected to live decent and sober lives. The associating together of people for purposes partly social and partly religious was, as we have seen, of very ancient origin among the Norsemen, and the *Ølgirdir,* originally heathen gatherings, where *skaals* were drunk in honour of the gods, were maintained under Olaf's *Kristenret,* and the names of our Lord and the Blessed Virgin substituted for Thor, Odin, &c. The name Gild was not an unknown one in the form *gild* for a feast, which, in heathen days, had always some religious observances connected with it. Thus it was at a *gild* at

---

* See Lujo Brentano's article, on the " History and Development of Gilds," in *English Gilds* (Early English Text Society), London, 1870.

Hlade that Olaf Trygvessøn announced to the astonished bønder his intention of offering six of their chief men, as a sacrifice at the great winter *blot*.*

It was during the reign of Olaf Kyrre that the great struggle between Pope Gregory VII. and the Kaiser Henry IV. was carried on. Norway was not involved in this, though the metropolitan, Archbishop Liemar of Bremen, was the warm and faithful friend of the latter; but Olaf remained neutral. The Pope was naturally anxious to have as many as possible of the sovereigns of Europe on his side during the conflict. He wrote in 1078 to the king in very friendly terms, expressing the great interest he felt in the Church there. But recognizing the difficulties attendant on sending him teachers, who were not conversant with the language of the country, he suggested that the king should send a number of young men to Rome, to be trained up in Canon law and Roman usages, who, on their return, might instruct the people. It is difficult to say if this idea was ever carried out, though we know that, after Breakspeare's mission, the intercourse with Rome was, considering the great distance, very frequent.

Olaf died at Haukby, in Ranrike, in 1093. His body was conveyed to Nidaros, where it was interred in the church which he had built, and where his sainted predecessor then reposed.

The short reign of Olaf's son and successor, Magnus, who at the age of twenty years became king, need not detain us long. At his father's death he had to share the kingdom with his cousin Haakon the son of Magnus, his father's brother. As usual, it seemed likely that a conflict would arise between the two, especially as Haakon was much loved by the people and Magnus was unpopular; but Haakon only lived for two years, and died in 1095 without leaving any son, and Magnus was therefore the sole king. Most of

* See p. 50.

his short reign was spent in warlike expeditions, and the
cost of these provoked much discontent among the bønder,
who, during the peaceful time of Olaf Kyrre's reign, had
escaped contributions for such purposes. Magnus was known
among his people as the "fighting Magnus," but the surname
which has been given to him in history is that of Barfot, or
Bærføtte, from the fact that he was so pleased with the
freedom which the Scottish kilt afforded to the Gaelic
warriors, that he and his men adopted it ; and so he was
nicknamed Barelegs, or Bærføtte.

His battles in Scotland belong to the history of that
country, and the king finally met his death in conflict with
one of the Irish chiefs in Ulster in 1103.

The same year in which the King was slain, saw the
erection of the see of Lund, in Skaane, to metropolitan
dignity, and therefore the close of the long controversy
with Bremen ; and from that time for nearly fifty years
(until the first archbishop of Nidaros), the Primates of
Lund were the metropolitans of Norway.

The death of Magnus, and the operation of the unwise law
of succession, saw now not merely two, but *three* persons
entitled to the royal dignity. The late king left three sons,
Eystein, Sigurd, and Olaf, who were at his death of the ages
of fourteen, thirteen, and four years respectively. The two
elder, being of legal age to rule, became joint kings, and
acted as guardians of their young brother, who, however,
died at the age of eighteen, leaving no issue.

The first few years of the joint reign of the two lads
Eystein and Sigurd were peaceful and orderly times.
Eystein inherited the disposition of his grandfather Olaf,
while Sigurd desired to emulate the warlike deeds of his
father. When he reached the age of seventeen his opportunity came. It was the time which succeeded the first
Crusade, and the religious fervour of these extraordinary
enterprises quickly reached Norway. The old Viking

expeditions had been abandoned, but now an opportunity presented itself of warfare of the same kind, only it was directed against the enemies of God and the Holy Church, and for the purpose of delivering the holy places from the grasp of the infidels. King Eystein elected to remain behind, and Sigurd joyfully equipped a great fleet and army, with which to proceed to the Holy Land. Both kings shared the cost, and the people, without any compulsion, eagerly offered themselves for service. In sixty ships, and with about 10,000 men, Sigurd left Norway in 1107.

As it was late in the season when they sailed, the winter was, by permission of Henry I., spent in England. "After expending vast sums upon the churches, as soon as the western breeze opened the gates of spring to soothe the ocean he regained his vessels," * and set sail in the early part of 1108. Proceeding slowly along the coast of France, the winter of 1109 was spent in Galicia. As they passed through the Straits of Gibraltar they had an opportunity of slaying the infidels, as they encountered and defeated a large Moorish fleet. Thence they made for the Balearic Isles and Sicily, where a considerable time was spent, and in the summer of 1110 they came at last to Palestine, where Sigurd was received at Jerusalem with great honour by King Baldwin and the Patriarch.

Sigurd then visited many sacred spots, and the Holy City, and received a portion of the true Cross, which he duly carried back to Norway. After leaving Jerusalem, he assisted Baldwin in the attack on Sidon, which was captured, a result largely due to the Norwegian fleet. Snorre tells us that during his visit to Jerusalem Sigurd vowed to introduce into Norway the payment of tithes, which promise he did not forget on his return home.

From Sidon, Sigurd sailed for Myklegaard (Constantinople), where he was welcomed by the Emperor Alexius I.,

* William of Malmesbury.—Book V.

and received many splendid gifts, and in return presented " a ship beaked with golden dragons" to the Church of St. Sophia.* Leaving the whole of his fleet at Constantinople, he travelled overland to Denmark, *viâ* Hungary and Bavaria, and reached home in 1111, crowned with glory from his successful expedition. From his having undertaken this crusade, he was henceforth known as Sigurd "Jorsalfarer," the traveller to Jerusalem.

This participation in the Crusades produced results in Norway similar to those in England, and other countries of the north of Europe. It brought a large number of the people into direct communication, with the civilization and luxury of the south of Europe, and the products of "the gorgeous East," and was therefore of educational value to a people who had seldom, if at all, come in contact with the more polished Latin races. We can well understand with what wonder the men who had only been accustomed to rough wooden churches, or very bare and simple stone ones, such as we now find at Moster or on Kinn, must have gazed on the stupendous pile of St. Sophia, or the wealth of gilding and colour of many buildings which they met with during the Crusades. It seems not at all improbable that they brought back from their stay in the East, many ideas which were afterwards put into practice in their own land. Witness, for example, the *klokketaarn*, which we find built alongside some of the *stavkirker* of Norway, such as Ringebu, in Gudbrandsdal, and Borgund, in Lærdal, and there we will find the way in which the Norwegians reproduced the Campanile.†

* Snorre says it was to St. Peter's.

† It seems likely, also, that the curious *laxetrapper* (ladders or stages) erected along the shore for the purpose of watching the salmon nets, which are to be found in Norway, were brought from the shores of Greece, where similar structures for watching the movements of the fish have been in use since classical times. It would seem that these are only found in Norway and the Mediterranean.

During the long absence of Sigurd, his brother Eystein had devoted himself to the development of his kingdom, and had ruled wisely and well. He did much to improve the greatest source of the wealth of Norway—the fisheries— and also looked closely after the inland parts of the country as well. The roads were improved, and in places where no regular road existed, but only an accustomed track, he caused *varder* or cairns to be erected to indicate the way. On one of the land routes to Nidaros, frequented by pilgrims to the shrine of St. Olaf, that over the bare and inhospitable Dovre Fjeld, he erected *fjeldstuer*, or houses of refuge ; and travellers in our own day have often had cause to thank good King Eystein for the shelter which Hjærkin, Fogstuen, or Drivstuen afforded them as they cross the Dovre.* The stay-at-home king also enlarged the borders of the kingdom by including within them the district of Jæmtland, now incorporated in Sweden.

The applause which Sigurd had everywhere won by his famous crusade, made him inclined to be not a little vain and boastful on his return home, and several times it seemed as if a breach must ensue in the relations between the two royal brothers ; but prudent counsels prevailed, and the death of Eystein in 1123, without any male issue, left Sigurd in undisturbed possession of the kingdom.

In 1123, on the invitation of the Danish King Nicholas, he went on a crusade against the inhabitants of Smaaland, in Sweden, who were at that time still heathen, but of the details of this expedition we know little or nothing.

* Eystein was the founder of the great monastery of Munkeliv, in Bergen, dedicated to St. Michael, the archangel, and for centuries in the possession of the Benedictines, but in later days transferred to the Birgitta order.

In 1126 a claimant to the throne appeared in a very
unexpected way. A man named Halkel Huk, of Blindheim,
in Søndmøre, met, in the western isles of Scotland, an
Irishman calling himself Harald Gille-Krist,* who professed
to be a son of Magnus Barfot, the king's father. Though
admittedly an illegitimate son, he would, nevertheless, by
the Norwegian law, be entitled to a share of his father's
kingdom. He, accompanied by his mother, went to
Norway to King Sigurd and repeated his story, and
offered to prove his claim by trial by ordeal. To this
Sigurd agreed, on the understanding that, if successful,
Harald was to make no claim to the kingdom during his
life, or that of his son Magnus. On these conditions
Harald Gille submitted to the ordeal of walking barefoot
over hot irons, and having accomplished this successfully,
was recognized as the king's brother. This strange proceeding was strictly in accordance with the law. It was
the first instance in which trial by ordeal was employed to
determine such an important question, but, unhappily for
Norway, it was not the last.

The concluding years of the reign of Sigurd the Crusader
were sad and inglorious, and only redeemed by the brave
stand made in the cause of morality by the bishop of
Bergen. The king was much struck with the beauty of a
woman named Cecilia, the daughter of one of his chiefs,
and in order to marry her, he determined to put away his
wife, Malmfrid, a Russian princess. This he intended to
do during a stay in Bergen, where he proposed to celebrate
this scandalous marriage. But he reckoned without his
host. To the honour of Magnus, bishop of Bergen, such
an act was not to pass unnoticed. When he learned the
king's purpose the bishop at once went boldly to him
and demanded an interview. The king came to him

* He is also known as Harald Gille. Gille-Krist is the gille, or
servant, of Christ.

with his sword in his hand, and invited the bishop to join in the feast which was then in progress. But the bishop, in the true spirit of St. John the Baptist, declined to do so.

"I come on a different errand," said the fearless prelate. "Is it true, O King, that you intend to put away your queen and marry another?"

Sigurd reluctantly admitted that it was so. Then, with stern countenance, the bishop demanded how the king dared to transgress the commandments of God and the holy Church, and degrade his royal office.

"In the name of God, and the holy King Olaf, and the Apostle Peter, and all the saints, I forbid this crime."

The dauntless bishop stood with bent head, expecting every moment to be his last; but the king merely glared at him and said nothing, and the bishop went his way rejoicing in having done his duty.

The protest of Magnus was for the time effectual, and Sigurd left Bergen, without having accomplished his purpose, and proceeded to Stavanger. There, alas! he found a bishop of less scrupulous conscience than Magnus of Bergen.

The first bishop of Stavanger was Reinald, who was an Englishman from Winchester; he was a capable man, but grasping and avaricious, and in him King Sigurd found a tool to work his evil purpose. By means of large gifts the king induced the bishop to agree to his wishes, and Sigurd was married to Cecilia. It is sad to think that a bishop could be found in Norway to consent to such a crime, but he did not long enjoy his ill-gotten gains, and a shameful death befell him under Sigurd's successor.

The closing days of the far-famed "Jorsalfarer" were rendered still more sad by the attacks of insanity to which he seems to have been subject, and in his lucid intervals he was filled with gloomy anticipations as to the future of his native land. In 1130 he died at Oslo, at the comparatively early age of forty years. He left behind him an only son, Magnus. He was illegitimate; but this was no bar to his succession to the throne, and Harald, the king's "accepted-by-ordeal" brother, was in the same case.

CHAPTER X.

CHURCH ORGANIZATION IN THE EARLIEST TIMES, AND THE COMING OF THE MONASTIC ORDERS.

The Early Missionary Bishops—No Diocesan Episcopacy at First—Its Establishment at the Four Centres—The Cathedral Churches—Parochial Organization—Patronage—The Churches of the *Fylker* and *Herred*—*Høgendes* Churches—Ecclesiastical Incomes—Duties of the Clergy, &c.—Adam of Bremen's Testimony as to the State of Religion in Norway—Tithe and its Apportionment—The Coming of the Monastic Orders.

The death of Sigurd Jorsalfarer seems a suitable point at which to review the condition of the Norwegian Church during the century which had elapsed since the martyr king fell at Stiklestad. For Olaf the Saint, by his ecclesiastical legislation, left his impress on the Church for a long period, and at this time we are enabled to estimate it better than fifty years later, when the result of the mission of Cardinal Nicholas Breakspeare, and the firm establishment of the monastic orders, led to changes in several respects, and Norway fell into line with the other Churches of Europe which owned allegiance to the Roman see.

The earlier chapters have shown to us the thorough and systematic manner in which St. Olaf carried out his work, and the way in which he saw that, if heathenism was to be eradicated, it was necessary that the people should receive systematic instruction in the faith from resident priests, and that they should be in their turn, superintended by the bishops whom he, in the first instance, brought with him from England.

Although the methods of St. Olaf would not always commend themselves to us, there can be no manner of doubt that the results which followed were very wonderful, and showed the extraordinary power of Christianity in transforming a rude, fierce nation of heathen into Christian men and women, whose lives were, in many respects, a pattern and example to those whose Christian ancestry exceeded by centuries that of the Norwegians.

It will be well for us to consider the condition of the Church in Norway at the end of the first century of its existence under two heads—(1) The external organization of the Church ; and (2) the manner in which Christianity affected the life of the people.*

It must be borne in mind that from the period of the introduction of Christianity into Norway, down to the time of King Olaf Kyrre, there was no diocesan organization in the land. All the early bishops, the Sigurds and the Grimkells, were merely what we would call missionary bishops. They were consecrated in England and elsewhere to carry out the work of christianizing the North, and they followed the king in his journeys throughout the land, consecrating churches as they were built or adapted from the old temples, and along with their priests helping to baptize the multitudes who were so often obliged by force to receive the ordinance. Then, when heathenism was expelled, they had to confirm the people, and to ordain the natives, who had been prepared for holy orders by the priests who were placed in charge of the various churches, and to perform the duties which appertained to the episcopal office. Gradually, however, when things had settled down, it became necessary that the bishops should have assigned

---

* Most of the details of ecclesiastical legislation referring to this early period will be found in the laws of the Gula, Frosta, Borgar, and Eidsiva *Things* ; chiefly in Vol. I. of the *Norges Gamle Love.* The reader is also referred to the very full details given by Keyser in Vol. I., Chap. xx., of his *Kirkes Historie,* and to Chap. iii. of Bishop Bang's *Udsigt over den Norske Kirkes Historie,* &c.

to them fixed parts of the country—in other words, to establish diocesan episcopacy. The political condition of the country helped to facilitate this. We have noted that for legislative purposes, there were three centres where *Things* were held and the laws promulgated. These were Frosta (for Trøndelagen), close to the city of Nidaros ; the district under the Gula *Thing*, held at Evenvik, a little to the south of the Sogne Fjord, and not far from the newly-founded town of Bergen ; and Eidsiva, or Eidsvold, a little to the north of Harald Haardraade's town of Oslo.

These local *Things* came gradually to consider themselves as entitled to a bishop in their immediate neighbourhood, and as it was a part of the episcopal duties to preach before the *Thing*, the towns of Nidaros, Bergen, and Oslo were naturally selected as the seat of the bishop, and the part of the country which met at the Frosta, Gula, and Eidsiva *Things* to form his diocese. But there was another and a very strong reason for the selection of those towns as the residence of the bishop. Norway, in the early days of its Christianity, was not rich in native saints, but the three towns were each closely identified with a national saint.

Nidaros ranked first of all as the guardian of the body of the royal saint of Norway, whose cult was now spreading rapidly over the North ; then Oslo, where the shrine of St. Olaf's cousin, the sainted Halvard, had been placed by Harald Haardraade ; and lastly, Bergen, to which the relics of St. Sunniva were brought by Bishop Paul in 1170. For about one hundred years before Bergen became a cathedral city, it was the little island of Selje, which lay to the north of the Nordfjord, which was the seat of the bishop, and the ecclesiastical centre of the Gula *Thing* district. It was felt, however, after the founding of Bergen that that town was much better adapted for the residence of the bishop, than the small island of Selje, lying as it did off a part of the coast particularly exposed to the force of the northern ocean, and close to the always dreaded passage round the peninsula of Stadt.

The three original dioceses of Norway were therefore, for political and religious reasons, formed from the districts attached to the principal *Things*, and hallowed by associations connected with the three patron saints of Norway, St. Olaf, St. Sunniva, and St. Halvard.* The dioceses of Stavanger and Hamar were of later foundation; the former town owed its origin to Olaf Kyrre, but it was not made the seat of a bishop until the reign of Sigurd Jorsalfarer. The erection of the Hamar bishopric was the result of the mission of Cardinal Nicholas in 1152. From the fourteenth century onwards Hamar, instead of Eidsiva, was the place where the meetings of the *Thing* were held.

The cathedral churches of the three original sees, and, later, of Stavanger, seem all to have been dedicated to the Holy Trinity, but in two instances *called* Christ Church.† Bang says, as an explanation of this, "when these Trinity churches are more often called Christ Church, it is because Christ was, to the mind of the people at that time, the most prominent of the three Persons of the Godhead." On the other hand, it is said that this form of dedication is a trace of the English influence, and the example is quoted of the Cathedral of Canterbury, usually called Christ Church, but called in Domesday Book *Ecclesia Sanctæ Trinitatis.*‡

---

* It is a curious coincidence that Norway and Ireland, which were so closely connected in those days, had each three patron saints; for the latter, the *insula sanctorum*, had St. Patrick, St. Bridget, and St. Columba as its patrons. Further, it may be noted that both countries had as patrons, two men and one woman.

† *Udsigt over den Norske Kirkes Historie*, p. 57.

‡ Taranger's *Den Angelsaksiske Kirkes Inflydelse, &c.*, p. 220. This writer quotes also the instance of Christ Church Cathedral, Dublin, which is really dedicated to the Holy Trinity. It is interesting, however, to note that it was founded by the Northmen, and was not the cathedral of the Keltic Church.

The Christ Church in Nidaros was the original cathedral, afterwards incorporated in Eystein's great Dom Kirke. This church, we know, was built by Olaf Kyrre over the spot where St. Olaf's body had been buried for a year in the sand beside the river Nid. The great Christ Church in Bergen (there was the little Christ Church as well) was the work of the same monarch. The Cathedral of Oslo was known as Halvard's Kirke, from the fact that the relics of the saint were there deposited, and, though probable, it is not certain that its original dedication was to the Holy Trinity. The same remark applies to Stavanger Cathedral, commonly known as St. Swithin's Church. It was probably so named by its first bishop, Reinald (who was a Benedictine monk from Winchester) in honour of the famous saint.*

Such seems to have been the diocesan organization of Norway, which only became fixed about the close of the eleventh century. What we might call the parochial organization was more ancient, and was practically an adaptation of the system of heathen temples. We have already seen that the temples were of two kinds, the *fylke hov* and the *herreds hov*, and in the latter division there were also private temples belonging to the wealthier bønder.

This arrangement remained practically unchanged on the introduction of Christianity, and so from the earliest times we meet with three classes of churches—the church of the *fylke*, of the *herred*, and what were called *høgendes kirker;* the last named might most correctly be rendered chapels-of-ease. It would appear that at the very beginning the most that the missionary kings could do, was to convert the *fylke hov* into a Christian Church, and make it a centre for the evangelization of the district. These *fylker* were many of them of very great extent, but, roughly

---

* The observance of St. Swithin's Eve can still be traced in West Norway.

speaking, they were the original parishes of Norway. The *fylke* churches were usually built on the site of the heathen temples, or the actual buildings were purified and made to serve for Christian worship. Gradually, however, when Christianity spread more widely through the land, it was found difficult, if not impossible, owing to the great distances, for the people to attend at the *fylke* church, and so the second kind of heathen temples were made into Christian churches. The *herreds* into which the *fylker* were divided offered a solution of the difficulty, and *herreds kirker* began to spring up over the country. These smaller parishes were practically independent of the *fylke* church, though at first certain rights were reserved for the church of the *fylke* with respect to baptisms and burials; and its priest occupied the position of the rector of a very large parish, containing many churches, ministered to by priests having practically sole charge of them. Then by degrees these *herreds* churches became entirely independent of the *fylke* church.* The *høgendes kirker* were, as the name implies, chapels-of-ease, and were practically private chapels, erected by chiefs and others for their own convenience; there were a considerable number of these scattered throughout the country. These chapels had not, as a rule, any burying ground attached to them.

We are thus enabled to see what was the organization of the Church in the times which followed the introduction of Christianity. We now come to the question of patronage, around which in later times so much controversy raged. In the early days the matter was much more simple. The kings were the embodiment of power, not merely in the State, but in the Church as well; and Harald Haardraade's boast was not far from the truth when in answer to Adalbert's envoys

---

* In some parts of the country slightly different arrangements prevailed—*e.g.*, in Trøndelagen, where the *fylker* were not so large, there were sometimes two *fylke* churches, and that sufficed for the district.

he exclaimed, "I know not who is archbishop or ruler in Norway except I alone."

The earliest bishops were the friends, counsellors, and court chaplains of the kings, who ordered the clergy from place to place as seemed best to them. We therefore find that the appointment to the bishoprics was the prerogative of the kings, and jealously guarded by them. Subsequent history will show us how tenaciously they held to that right, and how unwillingly and grudgingly they finally allowed the chapters to make the election.

With respect to the clergy generally, we find various kinds of patronage. To the *fylke* church the king in the early days presented, but gradually the bishops acquired the right. Even at first this was not the universal rule, for in the Gula *Thing* district the bishops seem always to have presented to these churches.

The appointment to the *herreds* church partook of the nature of an arrangement between the bishop and the parishioners. The old law provided that the bishop was to nominate a priest to these parishes for a period of twelve months. If at the end of this time the priest had carried out the duties of his office in a manner satisfactory to the parishioners, then he obtained what we might call a freehold benefice, and could not be removed from his parish by the bishop except for some canonical reason. In later times it would seem that the privileges of the parishioners became disregarded, and they only had a right to make a protest against the episcopal nominee.

The *høgendes* churches, or private chapels, were naturally in the patronage of those who built and maintained them, and the bishop had no direct voice in the appointment.

The incomes of the bishops and clergy in the time of which we are treating, were derived from various sources. It must be remembered that tithes in Norway only dated from the reign of Sigurd Jorsalfarer, who instituted them on his return from his famous Crusade. Before their establishment the episcopal income was mainly derived from what was called the *biskopsrede*, or bishops' tax. This was a poll tax on all males in his diocese. In addition to it he had a share in the fines which were levied for various ecclesiastical offences, and also the fees, sanctioned by law, for the performance of episcopal functions, such as the consecration of churches, &c. When tithes were introduced the old *biskopsrede* gradually ceased.

The clergy of the *fylke* churches were in a somewhat better position than the rest of their brethren. In the heathen times there were frequently endowments given to the maintenance of the *fylke hov*, and these passed over to the Christian priests. The early Christian kings had also, in many instances, given grants of land for the support of the *fylke* churches.

The provision for the clergy of the *herreds* churches was of a more uncertain nature, and it mainly consisted of voluntary contributions, and also of the legally-enforced fees for marriages, baptisms, burials, &c. The rest of the income was usually a matter of arrangement between the priest and his parishioners. The introduction of tithes, however, put an end to this. The income of the private chapels was of course provided by those for whose convenience they existed.

The duties of the bishops and clergy were mainly the same as in other places, but care was taken by the various *Kristenretter* that they should be effectively carried out: the bishop was obliged to visit every parish in his diocese once a year, and to remain in it for three or four days. During his visitation tours he was brought on his way free of charge by the bønder, and maintained during his stay by the priest and people. If the bishop failed to visit a parish he forfeited his claim on the *biskopsrede* from that parish for a year.

The duties of the parish priests were prescribed with much minuteness in the old laws, and a list of the holy days upon which service was to be performed was drawn up. The keeping of these days, as well as Sundays, was strictly enforced, and fines appointed for any failure in this respect. The priest was obliged to keep his people informed as to the holy days, and a curious expedient was adopted for the purpose. The Gula *Things* law ordained that he should cut a cross before each holy day and send it round to every house in his parish " where smoke smoked." The man to whose house it came, had to forward it to his neighbour, and so the scattered inhabitants of the large parishes were warned when the holy day would come, and were obliged to observe it strictly. A rigid observance of these days often caused much loss and inconvenience to the people, and we shall find later on that they obtained a special dispensation to continue the work of harvesting and fishing on them when necessity so required. In connection with funerals there were some curious customs. The priest had, before the funeral, to go to the house of the deceased and to sing a dirge over the body, as well as saying the appointed service in the churchyard. A few days after the burial a feast known as the *Arveøl* (lit. the inheritance beer) was held, at which the heir of the deceased entered upon his inheritance. At this ceremony the priest had to be present, and to bless the beer, and he, *with his wife*, sat in the high seat. This festivity was also known as the *sjæleøl*, because the beer was drunk in memory of the *sjæl* or soul of the departed.

The position of the parochial clergy in the early times was not always an easy one. Later on when the power of the Church, under the guidance of the archbishops, had vastly increased, they formed a part of the well-drilled army of the Church in Europe, which often defied the power of kaisers and kings. But in Norway before the twelfth and thirteenth centuries they were very much in the hands of their parishioners, and episcopal control was not very effective. The clergy were in the closest connection with the bønder, whose sons they were, and, being a married priesthood, they were more liable to local influences. The people who were ready, if need be, to support them against the bishop were also quite prepared to hold them in bondage to themselves. The *Kristenret* of the Borgar *Thing* laid down that the priest was not to be absent from his parish, except he obtained permission from his congregation the Sunday before. The only exception to this being, if he was going to attend a *presta motz*, or clerical meeting.

The first priests in Norway were doubtless men who came from England or Germany, to work under the bishops who accompanied the two Olafs, and were almost altogether foreigners, though of course speaking the language of the people. But the next generation of priests were largely natives whom the first priests had trained, and who had been admitted to the inferior orders. They were unlearned men with just sufficient instruction to enable them to perform the Divine service. When after the year 1100 monastic life was firmly established, there were greater opportunities for learning, and there was a corresponding improvement in the education of the Norwegian priests.

In spite of the difficulties which the Church in Norway had to contend against in the first century of its existence, it already ranked high among the Churches of Western Europe for the zeal and piety of its members. We possess a very remarkable piece of evidence with respect to this, in the writings of Adam of Bremen with regard to several points connected with the early history of Norwegian Christianity. It is all the more valuable, as the Church of Bremen was not particularly inclined to look with favour on the work of the English bishops and priests in Norway, who were not the emissaries of the great North German see, and who had accomplished what the Bremen missionaries had more or less failed to effect; but though praising the people, he cannot refrain from attacking the English priests.

In Adam's description of Norway[*] he thus writes, contrasting the condition of the country, in the old heathen and Viking days and the time which followed the introduction of Christianity:—

"After they received Christianity, being imbued with fuller knowledge, they have now learned to love peace and truth, and to be content in their poverty; yea, to distribute what they have stored up, and not, as aforetime, to gather up what was scattered. And, although they had from the beginning all been enslaved by the evil arts of wizards, now with the apostle they in simplicity 'confess Christ and Him crucified.'

"Of all men they are the most temperate, both in food and in their habits, loving above all things thrift and modesty. In addition to this, so great is their veneration for priests and churches, that there is scarcely a Christian to be found who does not on every occasion that he hears Mass make an offering. Baptism, however, and confirmation, the dedication of altars, and the blessing of Holy Orders, with them, as well as with the Danes, are all highly paid for. This, I consider, springs from the avarice of the priests, because up to now the barbarians are either ignorant of, or unwilling to pay, tithes, and therefore they are compelled to pay for what should be offered free—for everything there costs money, even the visitation of the sick and the burial of the dead. Their morals are of such a high character that I am convinced that it is only by the avarice of their priests that they are corrupted. In many places in

---

[*] "Descriptio insularum Aquilonis," Chap. xxx. Adam lived in the middle and end of the eleventh century, and was therefore a contemporary of Olaf Kyrre.

Norway and Sweden the tenders of the flocks are men
even of the most noble rank, who, after the manner of the
patriarchs, live by the work of their hands.   But all who
dwell in Norway are most devout Christians (*Christian-
issimi*), with the exception of those who are far off beside
the seas of the Arctic regions."

The period which ends with the reign of Sigurd
Jorsalfarer is remarkable also for the introduction of
tithes and for the establishment of monasticism in Norway
on a firm basis.

In the early days the incomes of the bishops and clergy
were mainly dependent on the voluntary offerings of the
people and the smaller, law-appointed *biskopsrede* and
payments to the *fylke* churches.   But under Sigurd an
important change took place.   It is said that when on his
memorable Crusade, he made a vow that if he returned
home in safety, he would introduce tithes into Norway.
This he did, and from his time we find that they gradually
superseded the older system of payments, to the great
advantage of the Church.

The apportionment of tithe in Norway was four-fold—
(1) To the support of the parish church; (2) to the bishop;
(3) to the parish priest; (4) to the poor of the parish.
This was by no means a popular move, as the people
regarded it in the light of a new tax on the necessities of
life, tithe being levied not merely on agriculture, but on
the harvest of the sea and on the cattle.   Its introduction
was apparently gradual, but there were parts of Norway
(such as the Telemark) where it was resisted, and, with
more or less success, down to the time of the Reformation,
when all the property of the Church was seized by the
State.

The establishment of tithe was naturally a very important thing for the Church, as it rendered the clergy much
more independent of their people, and they were no longer

liable to be starved out, if they acted in a way displeasing to the majority of their parishioners, which was quite possible under the old system.

The close of the eleventh century, and the beginning of the twelfth, saw also, among other important developments in the organization of the Church, the firm establishment of monasticism in Norway.* It was hardly to be expected that at first this form of religious life would commend itself to the national character. A people accustomed to a life of adventure, and among whom warlike expeditions and constant civil war, continued almost without intermission for the first century after they had embraced Christianity, would not willingly adopt the quiet and regular life of a religious community.

The earliest monastic establishment, however, seems to have been the one which Knut the Great, shortly before the defeat and death of St. Olaf, founded on the little island of Nidarholm (afterwards called Munkholm), which lay in the fjord close to the town of Nidaros. Knut's bishop, Sigurd, who did all in his power to incite the people against St. Olaf, seems to have been mainly instrumental in this, and the Benedictines were the first of the monastic orders who thus obtained a footing in the land.

The movement, however, did not spread, and the country remained for some time longer without any other monasteries. When, however, a long period of peaceful progress ensued, during the reigns of Olaf Kyrre and the sons of Magnus Barfot, we begin to find the religious orders in different parts of the country. The Crusade of Sigurd Jorsalfarer taught the Norsemen many things, and the hardy band of the Northern Crusaders could not have failed to be impressed by the great monasteries

* For the history of monasticism in Norway the great authority is Lange's important work, " *De Norske Klostres Historie.*"

which they must have seen in the southern countries of Europe.

The earliest monks, like the earliest of the secular priests, were undoubtedly Englishmen, who, leaving their great establishments in England, settled down among the Norsemen and began to teach them the arts, which at that time, were only to be learned in such communities.

The Benedictines were the first comers, as we have seen, and in addition to Nidarholm they were duly established on the little island of Selje, where the shrine of St. Sunniva was kept until its transference to Bergen. The monastery on that island was dedicated to St. Alban, probably the English proto-martyr.

Next after the Benedictines came the Cistercians and Augustinians; the former were, in Norway, closely associated with the Benedictines. The latter had, as their earliest establishments, Elgesæter, close to Nidaros, the Jons Kloster at Bergen and the great monastery at Halsnø, in Søndhordland. The Cistercians had, as the earliest of their monasteries, the one at Lyse,* about twenty miles from Bergen, which was first served by English monks from Fountains Abbey, in Yorkshire. They came on the invitation of Bishop Sigurd of Bergen (who had been on a visit to Fountains) under Ranulf as their first abbot. Monks from Lincoln, the year after the foundation of Lyse, established another monastery of the same order on Hovedø, an island close to Oslo.

These were the earliest of the monastic orders in Norway, and later on came the Premonstratensians. The Dominicans and Franciscans arrived in the following century. The only

---

* This place is remarkable as being " the only Norse monastery the history of whose foundation is preserved, and that by means of a document published in England."—Metcalfe's Introduction to the " Passio et Miracula Beati Olaui " of Archbishop Eystein. Clarendon Press, Oxford, 1887.

northern order, that of St. Birgitta, we shall meet with at the end of the fourteenth century.

It is only necessary for our purpose to indicate as above what orders established themselves in Norway; the history of these various foundations is beyond the scope of our present inquiry.

CHAPTER XI.

THE MISSION OF CARDINAL NICHOLAS BREAKSPEARE. MAGNUS ERLINGSSØN AND ARCHBISHOP EYSTEIN.

Civil War—Sigurd, Eystein, and Inge, joint Kings—Reidar, the First Archbishop of Nidaros—The Mission of Cardinal Nicholas, 1152—The New Province of Nidaros—The Results which followed the Mission of Cardinal Nicholas—Civil War again—Erling Skakke—Archbishop Eystein—His Policy—Erling's compact with Eystein—The Coronation of Magnus Erlingssøn—The Triumph of the Church over the State—The Rise of the Birkebeiner—Magnus victorious at Re.

THE sad forebodings which filled the mind of Sigurd Jorsalfarer in the closing days of his life, were but too fully realized in the events which followed. His and his brother's reign had been a time of peaceful progress for Norway ; and, saved from foreign invasion and internal strife, the country had made great strides in material prosperity and social advancement. But all this was now to receive a check, and for close upon a century civil war raged almost without intermission, and the progress which had been so marked, absolutely ceased for a time. The period was, however, characterized by a very great increase in the power and authority of the Church, which profited by the weakness of the rival kings to advance her claims ; for none of them dared to speak with the tones of Haardraade and declare that he was the sole ruler in the Church as well as the State.

Sigurd was no sooner dead than Harald Gille (disregarding his oath which he had taken before proving his claim by ordeal) had himself chosen as king, by a gathering at Tønsberg. At the same time Magnus's adherents proclaimed

ST. ANDREAS KIRKE—BORGUND, LÆRDAL.

Erected about 1150. An excellent example of the Norwegian
Stavkirke. See Appendix II.

[To face p. 132.

him king in Oslo. Harald justified himself for this breach
of his oath by maintaining that he only took it under compulsion. An immediate outbreak was averted by the chiefs
on both sides, and the two divided the kingdom. This,
however, only lasted for about four years, and in 1134
Magnus attacked Harald, who was obliged to fly the country.
Early in January, 1135, Harald, having got help, came
back and surprised Magnus in Bergen, and cruelly blinded
and mutilated him, and the miserable man sought refuge in
a monastery in Nidaros, and left the country to Harald.

The latter, however, did not profit by his cruel deed, and
much indignation was felt throughout the country. This
was increased by a further atrocity. Harald, who had tried
in vain to extract from Magnus the secret of the place
where his treasure was hidden, had reason to believe that
Reinald, the bishop of Stavanger, was in the ex-king's
confidence. On his refusal to assist Harald he was ordered
to pay a heavy fine, and when he declined to do so, on
the ground of its impoverishing the revenues of the see,
Harald, in his rage and fury, condemned him to be hung.
This atrocious sentence was carried out on January 18th,
1135.

This savage king was not long left to rule alone. We
have seen what a dangerous precedent was established when
Harald was allowed to prove his claim by ordeal. He had
now to permit another to do the same thing. The new
claimant was a man named Sigurd, who alleged that he,
like Harald, was a son of Magnus Barfot. This claimant
had, it seems, been trained up for holy orders, and had
actually been ordained deacon, hence the name by which he
became known of Slembediakn, the bad deacon, or, as it is
usually shortened, Slembe. He arrived in Bergen in 1136,
and Harald was most reluctantly obliged to admit his
claim; this Sigurd repaid by having Harald treacherously
murdered in his bed. Sigurd then thought that, having

removed his brother, he would have the kingdom to himself; but he was quickly told that, as his brother's murderer, they would have none of him, and if Harald was not his brother he would have no claim to the throne.

A wearisome strife followed. The chiefs took as kings Harald's two sons, Sigurd and Inge, who were but little children, and prepared to defend them against the fratricide, Sigurd Slembe. Then Sigurd, to strengthen his cause, went to Nidaros and took the poor blind Magnus out of his monastery and forced him to follow his army. The civil war raged with varying fortune until 1139, when the unfortunate Magnus was killed and Sigurd Slembe taken prisoner in a battle at Holmengraa, near Strømstad. The war had aroused the worst passions of both parties, and the wretched Slembe was put to death after horrible cruelties had been inflicted on him, which he seems to have met bravely, and we are told that he sang the psalms until death ended his tortures.

Two kings having now been disposed of, there remained but Sigurd and Inge. The former was known as Sigurd Mund, Sigurd of the Mouth, as that was the most prominent feature of his face; and the latter as Inge Krokryg, or the Humpback, the hardships of his early days, and his having been carried about to all the battles of the civil war, having caused the deformity. But they were not to be left to rule alone, for in 1142 their brother Eystein arrived in Norway from Scotland, and claimed and received his share of the kingdom. There were now no less than three kings of Norway, and this situation contained all the elements of future disturbance, but for the time, as all the kings were so young, there was a short interval of peace, and the country began to recover itself a little from the desolations of the previous civil war.

It was at this time that the famous mission of Cardinal Nicholas Breakspeare took place, which led to such important

results in the future development of the Church ; but here
we must retrace our steps.

It will be remembered that it was in the first year of the
joint reign of Eystein and Sigurd Jorsalfarer (1104) that
the jurisdiction of the see of Bremen over the three
northern kingdoms ended by the elevation of the see of
Lund, in Sweden, but politically in Denmark, to metropolitan dignity.   This step finally terminated the disputes
which had been carried on between the bishops in Norway
from the earliest times of the introduction of Christianity
under Olaf Trygvessøn, and the archbishops of Bremen.
The change of the metropolitan see from Bremen to Lund
was chiefly due to the initiative of the Danish kings, who
found the archbishops of Bremen much too ready to interfere in the internal affairs of Denmark.   Svein Ulfssøn
seems to have opened negotiations with the Pope for this
purpose, but nothing definite was settled.   Later, Erik the
Good, of Denmark, applied to Urban II., who was favourable
to the project of a Danish metropolitan, but it was not until
the time of Pope Paschal II. that the plan was carried out.
Liemar, the archbishop of Bremen who had been the friend
of the Kaiser Henry II., died in 1101, and was succeeded
by Archbishop Hubert.

In 1103 the Pope sent a cardinal legate to Denmark for
the purpose of carrying out the wishes of the king.   He
chose Lund as the most suitable place, and invested the
bishop there with the pallium.   Thus Denmark, Norway,
and Sweden ceased to be any longer under the metropolitan
jurisdiction of the archbishops of Bremen.

From this time, down to the middle of the century,
Norway was officially under the authority of the see of
Lund, and most of the bishops were consecrated there, but
notwithstanding this, the old connection with the English
Church was closely maintained.   Most of the monasteries
which sprang up in Norway at that time were filled with

monks and priors from England. Stavanger diocese seems
to have been closely allied to Winchester, and the cathedral,
as we have already noted, bore, and still bears, the honoured
name of the great prelate of Winchester, St. Swithin.
The monastery of Lyse, which was situated only a few
miles from Bergen, was the foundation of monks from
Fountains Abbey, in Yorkshire.*

No difficulties, however, seem to have arisen between the
Norwegian Church and the see of Lund in the fifty odd
years during which its authority extended over Norway. It
was felt, however, that as Norway had now a fully
recognized place among the nations of Europe her claim
to a separate ecclesiastical province could not be denied,
especially after the famous exploits of the Norwegian King
Sigurd in his Crusade. That monarch during his stay in
Jerusalem is said to have announced his intention of establishing a metropolitan see in Norway, but no formal steps
in this direction appear to have been taken.

Thus matters remained until the period which we have
now reached in the history of the Church, when the country
found itself under the weak rule of the three joint kings,
Eystein, Sigurd, and Inge, the sons of Harald Gille.

That negotiations must have been carried on with Rome,
and the see of Nidaros selected as the one for metropolitan
dignity is clear, but there are no records of them. We
learn, however, that in 1151 Bishop Reidar of Nidaros was
invested with the pallium in Rome as archbishop. He,
however, died very soon after his appointment, and before
he had time to return to Norway.

The year after, the Pope (Eugenius III.) took the necessary steps for selecting the metropolitan see for Norway, and,
following the precedent of his predecessor (Paschal II.) in
1103, he dispatched a cardinal legate to the North. For
this purpose the Pope selected the famous Englishman

* See p. 130.

Nicholas Breakspeare, at that time cardinal archbishop of Albano. There are few more striking stories than that of the life of this famous prelate, who, from being a poor lad begging for bread at St. Albans, rose at last to the chair of St. Peter, and was the only Englishman who ever filled that exalted post. It was to his own great talents and power that he owed his elevation. After leaving England he went to the monastery of St. Rufus, in Provence, where his great learning and ability gained him, after some time, the post of prior. Though he had been unanimously chosen by the monks, his stern rule made him unpopular with them, and they appealed to the Pope, who, at once seeing what a strong man Nicholas was, determined to exalt him to higher rank, and, appointing another prior to St. Rufus, made Breakspeare a cardinal, and archbishop of Albano.

A wiser selection than this astute Churchman to bring the Norwegian Church fully under Roman obedience could not possibly have been made. With all his firmness of purpose the legate was a man of the most winning disposition, and secured for ever a firm place in the affections of the Norwegian people.

When he arrived in Norway he found the three kings on indifferent terms with one another, and he skilfully availed himself of this, in order to advance and confirm the authority of the Church. Of the three brothers, the best was undoubtedly the delicate Inge Krokryg, for whom the legate seems to have entertained a warm feeling of regard.

In July, 1152, the cardinal came from England to Norway, where he was received with great honour. Steps were immediately taken to call together a representative assembly of the whole kingdom. This seems undoubtedly to have been held at Nidaros (though, curiously, we have no actual record of the exact place), for no other town was as likely to have been selected as that where the body of the national saint reposed, and whose bishop was now to be advanced to metropolitan dignity.

At this gathering the three kings were all present. The bishops of Bergen, Stavanger, and Oslo, along with twelve representative men from each diocese, gave the meeting the character of a national assembly. The see of Nidaros was vacant at the time, as Reidar was only a few months dead, and the vacancy still remained, the kings having probably purposely abstained from appointing his successor until the visit of the cardinal.

It was decided that Nidaros should be chosen as the metropolitan see, and the vacancy was filled up by the translation from Bergen of the bishop Jon Byrgessøn, who was forthwith invested with the pallium by Cardinal Nicholas at a function marked with great solemnity. The province for the new archbishop was a widespread one, embracing not only Norway, but all those other lands which had been either colonized, or conquered by the Norwegians. It was decided that the diocese of Oslo must be divided, and Hamar, on the Miøsen Lake, was selected as the most suitable centre of the new diocese, which was to consist chiefly of the Oplands and surrounding districts.

The new metropolitan of Nidaros had therefore under his jurisdiction the following sees :—

NORWAY—Bergen, Stavanger, Oslo, and Hamar.

ICELAND—Skaalholt and Hole.

GREENLAND—Garde.*

FÆRØERNE (Færoe Islands, p. 57)—Kirkebø in Straumø.

ORKNEYS—Kirkevaag.

SODOR (*Suderøerne*) and MAN.

---

* An interesting point connected with this see lies in the fact that the Norwegian colony founded in North America about the year 1000, and which lingered on for a considerable time (much longer than is usually supposed), lay in the diocese of Garde.

It will thus be seen that, including Nidaros itself, eleven sees made up the province, and when we remember the immense distance which separated some of the suffragan bishops from their archbishop, such as Garde and Man, it was not likely that, except in Norway and Iceland, any very effective control could easily be maintained over these far-distant dioceses. The bishops who ruled over the Norwegian Church in Ireland in former years had at this time come practically under the control of the Irish metropolitans.

The stay of Cardinal Nicholas was marked by several very important changes in the constitution of the Church in Norway, into which we must enter in detail; but here we may say that his mission was entirely successful, and he left the country having won the honour and love of all the people. From Norway he went to Sweden for a short time, and then returned to Rome. Two years afterwards, on the death of Anastasius IV. in 1154, he was chosen as his successor, and assumed the tiara with the title of Adrian IV. During his short reign as Pope (1154—1159) he never forgot his friends in the North, and it is told of him "that no matter what important business he might have on hands, he would always give an audience first to the Northmen when they sought it," and, though never canonized, they reverenced him as a saint.

We must now sum up the results which followed from this important mission.

From what we have learned of the state of the Church in Norway from the days of St. Olaf to the coming of Nicholas, it is quite clear that there was a great deal which would not at all commend itself to the papal theories of government, which were fully established in the middle of the twelfth century. The bishops and clergy were very far from being the well-drilled and disciplined ecclesiastical force which the papacy had organized in other parts of

Europe. They were ready enough to conform in matters
of doctrine, but there was amongst them a very strong
feeling of dislike to any kind of foreign interference, which
was most characteristic of the national spirit, and which
was often manifested in England as well, from which
country, the clergy were largely recruited. The stronger
kings, we know, fiercely resented the claims of the archbishops of Bremen, and it was the same spirit of aversion
to the rule of prelates outside Norway which led to the
establishment of the Nidaros archbishopric. But the time
was propitious for the assertion of the power of the Church,
and three weak kings made easy what would have formerly
been an impossible task.

It was not likely that cardinals who had recently seen the
triumph of the papacy over the very greatest of the kaisers,
would have been inclined to regard with patience the claims
of a few small kinglets in half-civilized Norway. Trained
up in such a school, the cardinal archbishop of Albano was
not likely to look with favour on a Church organization
in which the king alone chose the bishops, and the people,
if they did not directly appoint the parochial clergy,
had them, at any rate, very largely under their control.
Then again, although the Pope was willingly recognized as
the head of Western Christendom, the recognition did not
proceed as far as the popes (now at the summit of their
temporal power) desired, for it brought them no tribute.
The freedom-loving Norseman, who only grudgingly paid
skat to his king, had no desire to swell the papal treasury
by his share of Peter's pence.

The ecclesiastical revolution—for it was nothing less than
a revolution—may be summed up under the following
heads :—

1. The transference of the choice of bishops from the
king to the cathedral chapters. Originally, as we have
noted, the bishops were but missionaries in episcopal orders,

and they had not for over one hundred and fifty years after the days of Olaf Trygvessøn, any fixed dioceses or regular cathedral churches; and when they gained these, the "sacred circlet of the presbytery" assembled in chapter, was wanting. These were supplied by the reforms of Cardinal Nicholas, and to them was given the choice of the bishop. This choice, however, was to be subject to the royal approval, and naturally led to frequent conflicts in future years. The argument of the astute Churchman who succeeded in thus weakening the royal control over the Church in such a striking way, was a very reasonable one, and based on the very unwise law of succession to the throne which prevailed in Norway. Given three kings with equal powers, what was to happen if they could not agree on a suitable man—how much better it would be for the cathedral chapters to choose a man subject to the royal approval.

2. The appointment to parishes. This was now given to the bishops. This was also an infringement on the royal power, for the kings exercised a good deal of patronage, but by no means exclusively, for the bishops appointed largely to many parishes, especially to the *herreds kirker*, in which their patronage was to a certain extent shared by the people.

3. A change in the law of the land with respect to bequests. This power was formerly very limited, but through the cardinal's influence it was permitted to every one to give a tithe of inherited property, and one-fourth of personal earnings to any one they desired. The presumption of the old law was practically that all property belonged more to the family than to the individual, including what we would call personal as well as real property. Under the old laws there was recognized the custom of giving what was called a *hovedtiende*, or chief tithe. This custom prevailed before the introduction of ordinary tithes under Sigurd Jorsalfarer, and it was only given *once* in a man's

life, usually on his death-bed. If paid by the heir it was
known as a *sjælegave*, or a gift for the soul of the
deceased. The object of the cardinal's change in the law,
was of course to enrich the Church, which it eventually did
to a very considerable extent after some years. It was
necessary that this change in the law of inheritance should
receive the sanction of the *Things*. This was granted at
once by the Frosta *Thing* for the north, and the Gula *Thing*
for the west, but it was not until about the year 1224 that
the Eidsiva and Borgar *Things* accepted the new proposal.

4. The payment of Peter's pence. If Norway was to
receive the benefits of papal supervision, it was only natural
that the country should pay its share of the contributions
of Western Christendom to the papal see. This new
ecclesiastical tax was known as the *Roma skat*, and was
fixed as a Norwegian " penny " to be paid by all who
owned not less than three marks, besides weapons and
clothing.

All these important results appear to have followed from
the visit of Cardinal Nicholas, and though they did not all
at once come into operation, yet we may safely ascribe them
to the influence of this far-seeing prelate. There was one
point, however, in which he failed. The papal power at
this time tried everywhere to enforce the new doctrine of
the celibacy of the clergy, and it was only to be expected
that the cardinal would attempt to do the same in Norway.
We have no clear information as to what was done by him
in this direction, but later on, when the bishops sought to
enforce it on the parish priests, as part of the discipline of the
Church, it was resisted by the clergy, on the ground that
Nicholas had attempted it, and finding the opposition too
great, he had then given them permission to marry. It is
hardly likely that the cardinal had given any formal permission, for what was so entirely contrary to the designs of
the papacy at the time ; but it is probable that, perceiving

the clergy were very determined on the point, and being a very far-seeing and prudent man, he did not wish to risk the success of the other great results which he had achieved, by insisting on the celibacy of the priests, and his acquiescence in this was taken by them as a formal permission. The cardinal doubtless saw, and saw rightly, that the celibacy of the clergy would follow, when the authority of the bishops, who were directly under the papal power, began to make itself felt.

To Nicholas has also been ascribed the drawing up of a catechism for the instruction of the young, but for this we have no positive authority.   He doubtless impressed upon the clergy the extreme importance of attending to catechetical instruction, and indicated the lines upon which it should proceed.   It is very probably true, as has been stated, that in addition to the Creed and *Paternoster* which formed the foundation of the earliest Christian teaching in Norway, he added the *Ave Maria.**

Thus was Norway brought fully under the dominion of the Apostolic see and its metropolitans invested by Rome with the pallium, the outward sign of their authority.   The old semi-independent days were now over, and a new era dawned upon the Church.   Hitherto the struggles which had raged so fiercely in other lands between the Church and the State were unknown, but the time was not far distant when Norway was to be the scene of many similar conflicts.

It cannot be denied that the closer connection between Norway and Rome was of very great benefit to the cause

* It may also be noticed that a change was made in the form in which the laws began.   The oldest form which we have of the Gula *Things* law, began thus : "It is the foundation of our law that we should bow to the East and pray to the Holy Christ for a good season and peace," &c.   In 1274 we find the same laws (under Magnus Lagabøter) opening with these words : "The peace and blessing of our Lord Jesus Christ, and of our Lady the Holy Mary, and the prayers of the holy King Olaf and all the saints be with us, and all the Gula *Things* men."

of religion and learning, whilst the old Norse love of independence and freedom, prevented the growth of that
spirit of servility manifested in other lands under the
Roman supremacy.   The learned and pious men who
from time to time filled the highest offices in the Church,
used their influence in spreading civilization, and the
true spirit of Christianity amongst the rough, and in
many cases still even half-barbarous, inhabitants of the
wild mountain valleys of Norway.   When we remember
how, even in our own day, many districts are still remote
and inaccessible, we can see how difficult it must have
been in the middle ages to minister to the higher needs
of the people, and to teach them the doctrines of the
Christian faith.

After the mission of Cardinal Nicholas was over, the
smouldering antagonism between the three kings of
Norway broke into a flame, and once more civil war began.
The two brothers, Eystein and Sigurd, had no love for each
other, but—probably from feelings of jealousy towards their
brother, whose kindly nature had won the love of the great
cardinal—they decided to join in an attempt to exclude
him from his share in the kingdom, on the ground that his
feeble health rendered him unfit to rule.   Inge had, however, a strong following in the land, led by Gregorius
Dagssøn, of Bratsberg, and the famous Erling Skakke, of
Stødle, in Søndhordland.   Civil war raged again, and in
1155 Sigurd was killed in battle at Bergen, and Eystein,
in 1157, met the same fate at Viken.   Inge was thus left
the sole king, though the opposite faction took Sigurd's son,
Haakon Herdebred, and made him king in Nidaros (1159),
though little progress was made in his cause as long as
Dagssøn lived to champion the side of Inge.   In 1161,
however, Gregorius Dagssøn was slain, and a few weeks
later Inge was also killed in a battle fought on the ice at
Oslo, on the 3rd of February in the same year.

There was no king now left to contest the throne with Haakon Herdebred, and it might have been thought that peace would have been restored to the distracted land. This, however, was not to be. The great chief Erling Skakke was determined to try and secure the royal authority to one of his own family. He had married a daughter of Sigurd Jorsalfarer, and by her he had a son named Magnus, who at this time was but a child of five years old. It was quite an unheard-of thing that any one should lay claim to the throne by right of his mother; and all the previous kings—even those whose paternity was, to say the least, doubtful, like Harald Gille and Sigurd Slembe—never ventured on such a step. There were many who might have traced a direct descent, through females, from the great Haarfagre, but none had ever claimed the throne on such grounds.

Erling, however, decided on making an effort on behalf of the youthful Magnus, relying on his own great popularity and power, and also on the fact that Magnus was the grandson of the great Crusader, and, it might be hoped, that one so nearly related to him, would bring back again the long-lost prosperity which the land had enjoyed in the reign of Sigurd. A few months after the death of Inge, Erling had Magnus chosen as king, at a *Thing* held in Bergen. Thus again there were two kings — Haakon now accepted in Trøndelagen as sovereign of the whole country, formerly only of his father's share, and Magnus also claiming the entire land.

Erling sought help from Denmark, on his son's behalf, and promised to hand over once more to the Danish king's authority, the old district of Viken. Then he returned to Norway, and shortly after, in 1162, defeated and slew Haakon Herdebred in a sea-fight in the Romsdals Fjord; and now there seemed to be no rival to his son's throne. After the battle Erling sailed on to Nidaros, and at a *Thing* held there extracted a rather unwilling acceptance of Magnus as king of Norway.

We now come to a period in the history of Norway, when the Church (the foundation of whose power had been so carefully laid by the famous cardinal) was about to enter upon a long conflict with the State, which continued with varying fortunes for over one hundred years. It was but an incident in the great struggle which was experienced in almost every country of Europe, and in which the greatest of the Hohenstaufen Kaisers had to bend before the imperious pontiff, and the great Plantagenet to humble himself at the tomb of his martyred prelate.

The preliminary victory of the ecclesiastical over the civil power in Norway was, however, a much easier one than that which fell to the lot of the Church in other lands, and was the result of a bargain between an ambitious chief, on behalf of a child king, and an ecclesiastic of the highest rank in power and wisdom.

Jon Byrgessøn, who had been invested with the dignity of a metropolitan by Cardinal Nicholas, only lived for a few years after his translation to Nidaros, and died in the year 1157. Not much about him is known, but he seems to have been a kindly and tolerant archbishop. Inge was, at the time of his death, the sole king, and, in spite of the newly-made agreement that the chapters were to have the choice of the bishops, he nominated as archbishop his chaplain and chancellor, Eystein Erlendssøn, a man who belonged to one of the most ancient and influential families in Trøndelagen, and who was related to the royal line of Norway.

Eystein was, perhaps, the most remarkable man in the long list of the archbishops of Nidaros. He was a man of great power and ability; learned, pious, eloquent, and possessed of an iron will which would brook no resistance;

he was filled with the loftiest ideas as to the power and authority of the Church. In some points he resembled his great contemporary Thomas à Becket, though he had not to climb from low estate to the highest office in the Church of his native land. Eystein was the equal or superior in birth, to most of those with whom he came in contact, nor had he to serve a master so strong and powerful as the English Henry II. He escaped the martyrdom which fell to the lot of the great prelate of Canterbury, but he had to endure, at any rate, three years of exile from the Church over which he had been called to rule. Though he was nominated as archbishop by the king in 1157, he was not consecrated in that year, and he seems to have spent some time in wisely endeavouring to conciliate his cathedral chapter, and to make them acquiesce in the manner of his selection. He does not appear to have reached Italy until 1159—the same year, and about the same time, as Adrian IV. (Cardinal Nicholas Breakspeare) died.

The death of Adrian IV. was followed, as is known, by the choice of two popes, Alexander III. and Victor IV. The struggle between the two, does not concern us here, but Eystein threw in his lot with the one who eventually triumphed, Alexander III., and was by him consecrated and received the pallium (probably in France) in the year 1161. He returned to Norway at once, to find his friend and patron Inge, slain in the battle at Oslo, and Erling Skakke, on behalf of his son Magnus, contesting the kingdom with Haakon Herdebred.

On his arrival at Nidaros he probably saw that the time was ripe for asserting the claims of the Church, and for putting into practice the lessons which had doubtless been impressed upon him by the haughty Pope Alexander III. In order to strengthen himself for the fray, he decided that the first step to be taken was to increase the revenues of his see. These were, as we know, very largely

augmented by the fines (*sagøre* or *bøder*), which were
levied and sanctioned by the State, for breaches of
ecclesiastical discipline under the *Kristenret*. The archbishop set to work with great astuteness to accomplish
this. At a meeting of the Frosta *Thing* he put it to the
people, that they had now received the great honour of
having a metropolitan and archbishop in Nidaros, and
that if they were to enjoy so great an honour and dignity
above all the other dioceses of Norway, they must be
ready on their part, to provide a suitable income for the
see. The bønder, much as they might appreciate the
honour of belonging to the archiepiscopal diocese, were not
enthusiastic over the suggestion, which would entail the
payment of a larger sum in fines than had hitherto
been levied on them; but the great local influence of
Eystein and his persuasive eloquence, induced them to
assent to the archbishop's proposal. What Eystein carried
through was a very simple and effective reform. The fines
had been customarily paid according to an old standard
of coinage called the *lagøre*, which was worth only one
half of the current silver coinage or *sølvøre*. The *Thing*
agreed that in future the fines should be paid in *sølvøre*,
and thus the archbishop by a single stroke, exactly doubled
his income derived from this important source.

The opportunity which Eystein looked for, of asserting
the power of the Church soon came. In 1162 Erling
Skakke, after having vanquished and slain Haakon
Herdebred in the battle fought off the island of Sekken,
in the Romsdals Fjord, arrived at Nidaros, where he
procured the recognition of Magnus as king of the whole
of Norway.

Erling was far too wise a man not to recognize at once
what a powerful prelate now reigned at Nidaros, and how
important it was for him to secure to his side the growing
power of the Church. He saw plainly enough that his

son's title to the crown was a defective one, and rested
entirely on descent in the female line from the royal race
of Haarfagre, which was contrary to the law and custom
of the whole land, which so strongly insisted on descent
in the male line, that even illegitimacy was no bar to the
succession.

Erling therefore felt that if the legal title of Magnus
was defective, he must support it by the power and
authority of the Church, to gain which, of course, he
must be prepared to make concessions to the Archbishop
and bishops.   In Eystein, Erling saw the very man for
his purpose, and he felt sure that if he could win him over,
his son's claim would be firmly established.

With this end in view, he seems to have held several
secret conferences with the archbishop during the time he
was in Nidaros.   He began with the crafty suggestion
that if the archbishop had got his income practically
doubled, it was only fair that the king should have the
same advantage, many of the fines being divided between
the king and the bishop, and further that the action of
the archbishop was at variance with the *Kristenret* of
St. Olaf.   The archbishop, however, had a ready answer
to this, as he at once pointed out that what he had done,
was done in a perfectly legal manner by the *Thing*, and
that, on the other hand, Magnus had himself no legal right
whatsoever to the crown of Norway.

Erling saw at once the force of this argument, and
suggested that instead of disputing, it would be much the
wisest thing for him and the archbishop to come to terms.
Finally it was agreed that, in return for the support of
Erling and his son in the furtherance of the claims of the
Church, the archbishop and bishops should give the
sanction of " God's law "* to supply the defect in title of

---

* The *Kristenret* was usually known as " God's law," in distinction
from the civil law, or the " land law."

the king according to the "land law," and that this was
to be done by the archbishop crowning and anointing the
young king.

How long exactly the negotiations lasted is not clear,
but it was not until the summer of 1164 that the coronation took place. The archbishop was probably waiting to
make sure of his terms, and also to see whether anything
was likely to arise which might upset the plans of Erling.
In 1163 a papal legate, Stephen, came to Norway (for
what purpose it does not appear), and the presence of the
legate, seemed to Eystein to be the best opportunity for a
great display of the power of the Church. Accordingly, in
1164 a great *rigsmøde*, or parliament, was called to meet
in Bergen in the summer, and at the same time the archbishop gathered around him all his suffragans in Norway,
and one (the bishop of Hole) from Iceland, and the heads
of the religious houses. With great ceremony, and in the
presence of the legate, and all the chiefs and bishops, young
Magnus was solemnly anointed and crowned king in
Christ Church, the cathedral of Bergen, and invested by
the archbishop with all the insignia of royalty.

This was the first king who had been crowned in
Norway, and the ceremony was an entirely new departure
in the land. The older monarchs needed only the choice
by the bønder and chiefs, in the ancient assembly of the
Thing, but now it became apparent to all men that a new
order had come into being, and that the head of the
Norwegian nation was no longer to be only the chosen of
the people, but also "the Lord's anointed," and invested
with a semi-ecclesiastical power from the hands of the
archbishop. The very placing of the crown on the king's
head by the prelate, was in itself a proof that the monarch
derived his authority, not only from the people, but from
the Church as well.

Thus publicly the Church proclaimed her power, and

showed what a change had come from the time when the
bishops, like Sigurd and Grimkell of the days of the two
Olafs, were content to be members of the royal household
and to accompany the kings in their journeys through
the land.

It was not all at once that the terms of the compact
between the Church, as represented by Eystein, and
Erling, as the guardian of the young king, became known.
It is most probable that, had the people generally become
aware of them at the time, a flood of national anger
would have swept away the young king and his crafty
father. It was only little by little that they became
known and were tolerated. We are told that the conditions respecting the Church's prerogatives, were embodied
in a letter written later on by Magnus, when he came of
age, to Archbishop Eystein*; but this has been regarded by
many as unauthentic, though in one very important
particular the truth of the conditions is confirmed in the
laws of the Gula *Thing*, which are undoubtedly authentic,
and in which are set forth clearly the changes that had
been made with regard to the succession to the crown.

The compact between Magnus (or more properly
speaking his father, Erling) and the archbishop was of a
kind which, if fully carried out, would effect a complete
revolution in the constitution of Norway. The principal
points were as follows :—

The king undertook to surrender his kingdom to God
and St. Olaf, and to hold the kingdom as the vicar and
vassal of the saint. As a sign and token of this, at every
king's death his crown was to be offered on the altar in
Nidaros, and the new monarch to receive it there. Norway
was to be a fief held from St. Olaf, who was to be the real
but invisible king.

* This letter will be found in Latin, in *Norges Gamle Love*, I.,
p. 442.

The election of bishops and the appointment to parishes was to be entirely free from royal control.

The special privileges of the metropolitan see were fully confirmed.

There were other clauses which provided for the protection of all pilgrims to the shrine of St. Olaf, and severe laws were to be enforced against sacrilege.

It will at once be seen, that the first of these conditions meant nothing else but the complete ascendency of the Church over the crown, and making the archbishop the real ruler of the land. Nothing could more clearly have set forth the claims which the papacy at this very time laid down for the kings of Europe, and which were so vigorously resisted by the kaiser and others. But perhaps more important still, were the changes which were introduced into the law respecting the succession to the crown.

On the death of a king, his successor was to be his *eldest legitimate* son, unless he was considered ineligible from insanity or wickedness. In that case another brother was to be selected by the archbishop, the bishops, and twelve men from each diocese *nominated by the* bishop. If it should happen that the deceased monarch left no legitimate son, then the next-of-kin was to be selected by the same authority. In case of the choice failing to be unanimous, the candidate of the majority was to be king, *provided the bishops were a part of that majority.*

On the death of a king, the bishops, and the twelve episcopal nominees from each diocese, were to assemble at the shrine of St. Olaf within one month, to confer with the archbishop respecting the succession, and the late king's crown was to be offered upon the altar. These terms, of course, meant that the ancient right of the people of Norway to choose their king, was to be entirely swept away and transferred to five episcopal electors.

There was certainly one point in the new proposals which commends itself—namely, the restriction of the succession to the crown, to the legitimate issue of the king ; the old law which made illegitimacy no bar to the succession left the door open to impostors, and was the cause of many of the troubles which arose after the death of Sigurd Jorsalfarer.   The assertion of the right of primogeniture was also a novel one, for although it usually happened that the eldest son was chosen, it was by no means the invariable or legal rule, as we have already seen in several instances.

Such were the terms of the compact between the archbishop and Magnus, and which the latter is said to have put in writing in a letter to Eystein when on Easter day, 1174, he offered his crown upon the altar in Nidaros.

It was hardly to be expected, that such a revolution would be quietly accepted in Norway, and we shall see it was the commencement of a fierce struggle which lasted many years, and in the course of which the nation was divided into two hostile camps—the Church and her nominee striving for the fulfilment of the compact between Magnus and Eystein, and the chosen of the people, in the person of perhaps in one way the greatest king that Norway ever saw, Sverre Sigurdssøn, resisting to the uttermost her claim to set aside the ancient constitution of the land.

We must now turn again to the history of the reign of Magnus.   The years which succeeded the famous coronation were more or less disturbed by various attempts, made by the enemies of Magnus and Erling, to raise the standard of rebellion, but these were suppressed.   The young king was of a kindly and generous disposition, and seems to have inherited many of the good qualities of his famous grandfather, and possibly he might have brought about a time of peaceful progress in Norway.   But very shortly after he came of age and took the government into his own hands, a storm arose which finally swept him away and brought back the

crown to the male line of Harald Haarfagre. This was the
rise of the famous party of the Birkebeiner, to which we
must now turn.

The severities with which Erling had crushed out all
resistance to his son's rule, had produced much discontent,
and a number of men, mostly young, who had been driven
from their homes, gradually gathered themselves together
into a band. They were found mostly in Viken, where they
lived in the woods and on the mountains, where they had
to take refuge after their occasional forays on the bønder.
They were a very ragged and unkempt body of men, and
when their clothing failed them they bound round their
legs and on their feet the birch bark, from whence they got
the name of *Birkebeiner*, or birch legs, and long afterwards
the name was retained and held in honour by the defenders
of the ancient rights of Norway, against the encroachments
of the hierarchy.*

About the year 1174 they took as their chief a young
man named Eystein, said to be a son of King Eystein,
Inge's brother. He was generally known as Eystein Møila,
the surname being probably given in derision, as it means
the " little girl." With him they ranged over the land,
not daring openly to attack Magnus; but in 1177 they
managed to procure some ships, and determined on an
audacious stroke. They came quite unexpectedly on
Nidaros and captured the town. Then, as they found there
was much discontent among the people, they gathered a
Thing and proclaimed Eystein as king. They had, however,
soon to retreat to Viken, whither the young king Magnus
followed them and defeated them in a battle fought at Re,
near Tønsberg, where Eystein Møila was slain and his party
scattered.†

---

* Compare the name Tory in English politics.

† This is the last historical event mentioned by Snorre, and concludes
the Heimskringla.

It seemed now as if the rule of Magnus Erlingssøn was firmly established in the land, and that an end had come, at least for a time, to internal strife, as there was no one to dispute his title to the throne. The remains of the Birkebeiner force sought refuge in Vermland with Cecilia, the daughter of Sigurd Mund (whom Erling had forced, against her will, into a marriage with Folkvid, a Swede), and appeared impotent for harm.

But Magnus was not to reign unchallenged. The Birkebeiner found a new leader in the great man to whose extraordinary history we must now turn—the priest from the Færoe Islands, Sverre Sigurdssøn.

CHAPTER XII.

SVERRE, AND THE GREAT STRUGGLE WITH THE CHURCH.

Sverre's Early Days — Comes to Norway — Forced to Lead the Birkebeiner—His Extraordinary Adventures—Defeats and Slays Magnus Erlingssøn, 1184—Sverre undisputed King—The Conflict with Archbishop Eystein—His Flight to England—Return and Death—Eystein's two Great Works—Sverre and Archbishop Erik —Sverre's *Kristenret*—The Points in Dispute between Erik and Sverre—Erik Flies from Norway—Sverre Excommunicated— Bishop Nicholas of Oslo—Sverre's Coronation—Bishop Nicholas Flies to Denmark—The Formation of the Bagler Party—Civil War—Innocent III. places Norway under an Interdict—Its Effect not great in Norway—Sverre's *Apologia*—Sverre takes Tønsberg, 1202—His Illness and Death in Bergen—His Character.

THE personality of Sverre Sigurdssøn is, perhaps, the most striking which we meet in the history of Norway. He was the illegitimate son of Sigurd Mund, in whose household his mother, Gunhild, had been a servant. The date of his birth is placed at 1151, the year before the visit of Cardinal Nicholas. Whether the future king first saw the light in Norway or the Færoe Islands is doubtful, but it is certain that his early days were spent in the latter place.

His mother, Gunhild, married a man named Unas, who was brother to Bishop Roe, the prelate of these islands. Here Sverre grew up, passing as the son of Unas, and his quickness and intelligence attracted the attention of his supposed uncle, the bishop, who, as he was in need of native clergy, had him educated for the Church's service, and having passed through the minor orders, he was finally ordained priest about the year 1174 or 1175.

Very soon after this, his mother revealed to him the secret of his paternity, and thus changed the whole current of his life. "If I am born to a crown" (said the young priest), "then shall I strive to win it, cost what it may, for without it life has no value for me." Sverre knew full well that illegitimacy was no bar to his claim, and that he alone, according to the old law of Norway, was the rightful king. He quickly made up his mind to claim what he knew to be his lawful inheritance, but he was not the man to do anything rashly or to endanger his chances of success by any premature move. Armed with a letter of introduction from Bishop Roe, to the great Archbishop Eystein, he went to Norway in order to see for himself the position of affairs, but determining for the present to conceal his identity. Arrived in the country, he saw at once that the power of Magnus and Erling was too great to be easily shaken, and that it would be quite useless to make known his claim or to present his letter to the archbishop. Instead, therefore, of going to Nidaros, he made his way to Vermland, to the house of his sister Cecilia, who received him as her brother and made him welcome.

This was in the year 1177, shortly after the battle at Re, near Tønsberg, where Magnus had crushed the Birkebeiner and slain their chief Eystein Møila. The remnants of this faction had taken refuge with Cecilia, and they at once recognized in Sverre the very chief they wanted—namely, a descendant of Harald Haarfagre in the male line. The prudent Sverre, however, was very unwilling to have the leadership of this handful of defeated men thrust upon him, but the Birkebeiners would brook no refusal, and insisted on his becoming their chief. Seeing there was no help for it, he reluctantly agreed to their proposal, and taking his courage à deux mains, embarked on what appeared to be a forlorn hope. At Easter he started northwards with his small band, having obtained what help he could from his sister.   He did not dare to go through the frequented parts of the country, but made his way through the forests, enduring terrible hardships from the fierce cold of the winter.   Having established himself in Jæmtland, where he gathered around him a considerable body of men, he determined on a bold stroke.   Moving into Trøndelagen he encamped for a time on an island in the Selbusjø, not far from Nidaros.   Shortly after, with that wonderful good luck which seldom deserted him, he suddenly attacked and captured the town, and, calling a *Thing*, was proclaimed king by the bønder.   The Trønder were always well disposed towards him, and it was only the armed power of Erling which had forced them into submission to Magnus's claim.

Notwithstanding his unexpected stroke of good fortune in the capture of the town, Sverre at once saw that he was not yet able to meet Magnus and Erling in the field, and on their approach with an army to recapture Nidaros, he at once evacuated the town and betook himself to the south.

The next two years Sverre went through a series of extraordinary adventures whilst he carried on a guerilla war against Magnus.   Often reduced to the greatest extremities, and over and over again almost captured, he always managed to extricate himself and to astonish his foes, by appearing unexpectedly in places where they least looked for him.   Through the wildest mountain districts of the west of Norway, Sverre and his men roamed, and to the present day the memory of his journeys is preserved in such names as Sverre's Skar and Sverre's Stigen, passes and paths over which a goat could scarcely travel, but by which Sverre and his men escaped from the hands of their enemies.

At the end of two years spent in this way, Sverre felt himself strong enough to take the field against Magnus and Erling, and moving north again descended on Nidaros and defeated and slew Erling Skakke in a battle at Kalvskindet, near the town. The death of the great chief was a severe blow to the power of Magnus, but Archbishop Eystein did his best to encourage him and to rally the forces against Sverre. The next year, however, 1180, a decisive battle was fought, again near Nidaros, at Ilevolden, in which Magnus was totally defeated and obliged to fly to Denmark. The archbishop also took refuge in flight and went to England, whence he issued a sentence of excommunication against the now victorious and openly acknowledged king, Sverre—the first time this great weapon of the Church had been directed against a king of Norway.

The struggle against Magnus was not yet, however, at an end. He found support in Denmark and returned again to Norway, and the war was resumed and lasted for some time. Again, however, Magnus was obliged to fly to Denmark in 1183. The year following he made one more effort to wrest the kingdom from Sverre, and this time he very nearly succeeded. Sverre was in the Sogne Fjord with a small fleet and engaged in punishing the Sogninger for their share in the resistance to his power. He had sailed up the narrow Sogndals Fjord, when Magnus, with a fleet which much outnumbered his opponents', came from Bergen, and caught the redoubtable Sverre in a trap from which there was no escape. A fierce battle ensued at Nore, the narrowest part of the fjord, and in spite of his vastly superior force, Magnus was utterly defeated and slain, and now Sverre was undisputed lord of Norway.

We must now turn back to Sverre's other great antagonist, the archbishop. The excommunication which he had issued from England against the king on his arrival in that country, does not seem to have had the effect of injuring Sverre. Indeed, it seems probable it was but little known in Norway, and was certainly unheeded. The archbishop and the clergy generally had from the commencement of the struggle, done their very utmost to inflame the minds of the people against Sverre. He was described as a "recreant priest," a deceiver, a godless sorcerer, who owed his good fortune to the devil; and they promised to those who fell in combat against him an entrance into paradise "before their blood should be cold upon the earth." The archbishop spent three years of exile in England, where he represented his antagonist in a very unfavourable light, to judge by the remarks of some of his English contemporaries.*

Eystein, with all his hostility to King Sverre, was a very prudent man, and when he saw that there was no doubt that the latter would finally win in the struggle, he made peace with the king in Bergen, and removed the ban, and in 1183 (the year before the defeat and death of Magnus) he returned again to his see.

From that time on until his death, five years later, he seems to have had enough of the strife, and to have devoted himself with great assiduity to the care of his

---

* During Archbishop Eystein's three years' stay in England he spent a part of his time at Bury St. Edmunds, and seems to have been there during the famous election of Abbot Samson, of which Jocelin de Brakelond tells us in his chronicle.—See Metcalfe's Introduction to "Passio et Miracula Beati Olaui," p. 52.

William, of Newbury, Book III., Chap. vi., says: "In 1180, Eystein, archbishop of Trondhjem, refusing to crown Sverre, a successful rebel, who had defeated Magnus, king of Norway, was driven into exile and came to England." William further describes Sverre as "famosissimus ille presbyter," who "tempore non modico sub tyranni nomine debacchatus." He also calls him "execrandus" and "nefandus presbyter," "illa virga furoris Domini."

The same writer, however, in spite of the above very choice controversial epithets, adds later on, that the inscription on his seal was "Sverus Rex Magnus, ferus ut leo, mitis ut agnus," inasmuch as he showed clemency to those whom he had subdued and showed reverence to churches and monasteries.

diocese, and did much to atone for his share in the desolating strife of the previous years, in which, however, his actions seem to have been based on worthy motives, and not on the lower ones of self-interest and aggrandise- ment.   In addition to the important part which he played in connection with the advancement of the power of the Church under Magnus, the great archbishop must ever be remembered for his work as a legislator, and as a cathedral builder.

The closing years of his life were devoted to a careful revision of the Frosta *Thing's* law, both on its civil and ecclesiastical side.   In the disorders of the preceding generation, many of the older provisions of the law had been neglected.   These were again enforced, and every effort was made to secure the reign of law and order. The peace of the *Thing*, which was such a prominent feature of ancient days, was again affirmed, and provision was made for the better order of the country generally. The *Kristenret,* which probably dated from St. Olaf's time, was revised on the lines of the famous agreement with Magnus Erlingssøn, so as to secure the privileges of the clergy and the archbishop, but in a fair and statesmanlike manner.   These laws were now carefully written out, and the collection was henceforth known as " The Golden Feather," to distinguish it from the older compilation of Magnus the Good, which was called " The Grey Goose."* The archbishop's collection probably received its name from the fact of its being beautifully illuminated.

Eystein, who loved the people well, endeared himself further to them by procuring from Pope Alexander III. a relaxation of the law with respect to work on holy days. He well knew how essential to the prosperity of the people the harvest of the sea always was, and, further, that it was necessary to secure the herrings whenever they approached

* See p. 96.

M

the coast.   Formerly fishing was forbidden on holy days, but the archbishop had the rule so far relaxed, as to permit the fishing whenever the herring appeared, save only on holy days of the highest rank.

To Eystein we owe also the beginning of the great cathedral of Trondhjem.   He felt, not unnaturally, that, now that Nidaros had become the seat of a metropolitan, it was only right that a cathedral of more imposing proportions should be erected, than that which sheltered the body of Norway's patron saint.   We have seen how two churches at that time stood where the cathedral now stands.   One was the Maria Kirke, built by Harald Haardraade on the place where the saint's body had lain for a year in the sand.   The other was the Church of the Holy Trinity, commonly called Christ Church, the foundation of Olaf Kyrre, which was then the cathedral.   In order to carry out his plan for the new cathedral, Eystein had the Maria Kirke taken down, and the materials carried across the river to the newly-founded monastery at Elgesæter for the Augustinians.   He then began the splendid pile which was completed some fifty years later, and which was the most magnificent ecclesiastical building in the North, and a noble monument of the great archbishop.*

One of the last official acts of his life was to pronounce the dissolution of the marriage of the king's sister Cecilia, who had been forced by Erling into a union with Folkvid, the Swedish chief.   The Church was the natural guardian of the sanctity of this sacrament, and was not inclined, at that time especially, to relax the law of Christian marriage.   But the archbishop, on the facts coming into review before him, declared Cecilia's marriage to be null and void, on the ground that she had acted under

---

* About the same time the cathedral of Christ Church in Bergen was completed, and the relics of St. Sunniva transferred to it from the island of Selje.

compulsion, and was not a consenting party, which the law of the Church naturally required in all cases. After her marriage had been declared void, Cecilia married Baard Guttormssøn, of Rein, a very powerful chief among the bønder of Trøndelagen, and her son by this union, as we shall see later on, was for a time king in Norway.

In the close of 1187 the archbishop lay dying in Nidaros. King Sverre was at that time in the city, and Eystein sent for him. What then occurred we only know from Sverre's account, but there seems no reason to doubt that a full reconciliation took place between the two great men. The old archbishop would hardly have wished to die, with feelings of enmity in his heart, towards the man whom he had so strongly, though conscientiously opposed, but with whom he had lived in outward agreement in the closing years of his life. On both sides there was much to forgive ; the archbishop had denounced Sverre in very harsh language, and preferred charges against him in the heat of the conflict, which in calmer moments he must have regretted and felt to be groundless ; Sverre also had not been free from blame for his share in the strife, and we must hope that this private conference ended, as it ought to have done, in the old archbishop giving his blessing to the man whose bitter opponent he had once been.

Eystein died on January 26th, 1188, and was buried in the sacristy of the new cathedral which he had begun. At his funeral Sverre made a speech in which he declared that the archbishop had admitted, in their last interview, that he was wrong in the course he had taken in so violently opposing him. This statement, of course, only rested on the authority of the king himself.

Thus passed away the famous Archbishop Eystein, a truly great Churchman and great man in every respect, and in the steps which he took to advance the claims of the Church, he only acted in accordance with the spirit of his day, not from unworthy motives of personal ambition and glory. He was long loved and reverenced by the people and clergy, and in 1229 he was declared to be a saint by a provincial synod held at Nidaros, but no formal papal canonization seems ever to have taken place.

It will be seen that Sverre, during the years in which he fought for the throne, never specially attacked the Church, though its whole power was directed against him, as the opponent of her nominee, Magnus Erlingssøn, and that he had lived in peace from 1183 to 1187 (the period we have now reached) with the head and champion of the Church in Norway. This, however, was not to last; the great and fierce struggle was now to begin.

Sverre, when he had at last, after 1184, firmly established his authority over the whole country, set himself to remedy the disordered state of the land, and brought in many wise measures of reform. To improve the administration of the law he appointed eleven *lagmænd* in different parts of the country, who were authorized to judge in all matters of dispute. The people had the choice of having their cases settled by these officers, or by the older court of the *Thing*. He also appointed officials called *sysselmænd*, who held the authority of revenue officers and district judges. The result of these reforms was to check the power of the greater chiefs among the bønder, and to enlist the mass of the people on the king's side.

After the death of Archbishop Eystein the ordinary course (if the new ecclesiastical law had been carried out) would have been for the chapter of Nidaros to proceed to the election of a new metropolitan. Sverre, however, was not prepared to permit this, nor, on the other hand, did he follow his uncle Inge's example and nominate a new archbishop. He adopted a middle course, which showed a desire to conciliate his clerical opponents. A few months after Eystein's death he called a meeting in Bergen of the bishops and principal men, and there brought forward the question of the appointment. The general feeling of the gathering was in favour of Bishop Erik Ivarssøn, of Stavanger, a man of learning who had studied in Paris, and whom the late prelate was supposed to have desired as his successor. Sverre at first raised some objections, but finally gave way, and Erik was chosen and went to Rome, where Pope Clement III. invested him with the pallium, and he returned to Norway in 1189 and took possession of his see.

At first all went smoothly between the king and the archbishop. The latter immediately set to work to correct many of the abuses which had, in spite of the strong rule of Eystein, sprung up in his diocese, and his reforms were all in a good direction. He enforced the canon law, which forbade the clergy to take any part in warfare, a restriction which was much needed, as a number of them had in the civil wars so far forgotten their office, as to join in many of the battles. This prohibition he extended to Iceland, a part of his province, where it seemed to be even more needed than in Norway. With the laity he took steps to stop the spread of immorality and to enforce the Church's law respecting affinity, which had, it seemed, been much relaxed and many marriages contracted within the forbidden degrees.

In these reforms he was fully supported by King Sverre, and it seemed as if the heads of the Church and State were now working well together.

The archbishop held a council in Bergen, in 1190, of the bishops, at which Sverre was present, and at this a number of regulations were made with respect to breaches of the Church's law which were punishable by excommunication. This was actually known as Sverre's *Kristenret*, which clearly indicates that at that time both the king and the bishops were working harmoniously together.

This concord, however, was not likely to last long, when we remember that the king and the archbishop held diametrically opposite views as to the relations between the Church and the State; and the storm, which had only been lulled for a time, soon broke out with redoubled fury.

Archbishop Erik had no sooner returned to Nidaros, than in a sermon preached in his cathedral he made a furious attack on the Birkebeiner, which immediately raised the anger of the king, and the old controversy was at once revived. Most of the points in dispute were not new, but they embodied the rival claims of the king and the Church. We arrive at them most fully in the Bull which the pope subsequently issued, confirming the archbishop's privileges, and we may briefly summarize them as follows:—

1. *The Coronation.*—The king claimed to be crowned by the archbishop as a matter of right, and not of favour.

2. *The question of the Archiepiscopal Income.*—We have seen that Eystein adroitly managed to double that part, which was derived from fines by the substitution of payments in the *sølvøre*, and not the old *lagøre*. Sverre demanded a return to the old method, or, failing this, that the king's share of the fines should be paid in the same way.

3. *The Rights of Patronage.*—The king demanded that the ancient right of the sovereigns to nominate to vacant sees should stand, instead of the election by the chapters. Another and a newer point was with regard to the right of appointment to the *høgendes kirker*, or private chapels. This had customarily been exercised by the founders, royal and other, but the archbishop desired that it should rest with the diocesan.

4. *The Clergy and the Civil Courts.*—This was practically the same dispute as between Becket and Henry II. at the Constitutions of Clarendon—Archbishop Erik desiring that

the ecclesiastical courts alone should judge the clergy for all offences.

5. *The Archbishops' Retinue.*—After gaining the dignity of metropolitans, the archbishops of Nidaros had striven to increase their following, and to surround themselves with a court and state which would rival that of the king. Eystein and Erik added to the archbishops' retinue, and Sverre decided to restrict it to what the law allowed—viz., thirty men, of whom only twelve were to be armed, and no ships of war, such as Eystein had possessed.

These were the chief points in dispute, and they were quite sufficient for a struggle to the death, between the king and the archbishop. The former in all his demands took his stand on the old law of St. Olaf, which his son Magnus the Good had embodied in "The Grey Goose," while the archbishop relied on "The Golden Feather" and the canon law.

Erik, seeing that the king was quite determined, and that his power was too strong for him, sought safety in flight, and in the summer of 1191 he made his way to Denmark, where the Archbishop Absalon of Lund received him with open arms.

From Denmark, Erik probably early in 1192, laid his case before the Pope Celestine III., in which the points of dispute we have just enumerated were fully set forth. In the letter the archbishop seems to have made a very fair statement of his case, without exaggeration or any of the bitter personal attacks on the king which afterwards marked the controversy. It will be seen, however, that the demands on both sides embodied the rival claims of the king and the Church, which were practically as irre-concilable in Norway as in other countries, and as neither party was disposed to give way, there was but little prospect of peace.

It was a question whether the old law of the kingdom

of Norway and the ecclesiastical arrangements of St. Olaf should stand, or whether the recent compact between the feebler kings in the days of Cardinal Nicholas and Archbishop Eystein should supplant them. Sverre was the champion of the ancient rights of the Crown and the early Church, Erik of the new claims of the Church at the time of the greatest papal arrogance. Throughout the whole long controversy Sverre, on his side, dwelt most on those points which affected the relations of the Church and the people—such as the fines, the rights of patronage, &c.—and the archbishop on matters which were more purely ecclesiastical. Soon after Erik arrived in Denmark he unfortunately lost his eyesight, but this did not impair his power of carrying on the dispute.

It is a little difficult here, to explain the delay which followed the appeal to the pope, before any decisive action was taken by the pontiff; but it would seem as if Celestine III. made inquiries of the archbishop, which were sufficiently satisfactory to the former, so that he authorised the archbishop to excommunicate Sverre, which he accordingly did in 1193.

When the information about this duly reached Sverre he treated it with supreme contempt, and in his speeches at the *Things* even went so far as to jest about the archbishop's blindness, and to declare that there was nothing whatever to prevent him returning to his see at Nidaros.

If the flight of Erik had delivered Sverre from one active antagonist in Norway, it left him with a foe much more malignant and treacherous, in Nicholas the bishop of Oslo. This man was of an ancient family in the Nordfjord district, and closely connected with the royal house. His mother having been left a widow by Harald Gille, subsequently married Arne, Nicholas's father. In his early days he fought on the side of Magnus Erlingssøn, and was later ordained priest. When the vacancy in the see of Stavanger occurred, by the translation of Erik to Nidaros, he was chosen for his successor. King Sverre, however, refused to accept him, and being a keen judge of men, he described Nicholas as a man with "a smooth tongue, a hare's heart, and the fidelity of a fox." That he deserved this estimate was abundantly shown by his subsequent history. When Sverre objected to his nomination to the see of Stavanger, Nicholas applied himself to the queen, Margreta, who, after many entreaties, at last induced Sverre to consent, though he foresaw that both he and she would have cause to regret it. Almost immediately afterwards, however, Nicholas was translated to Oslo. This took place probably in the year in which Erik fled to Denmark.

In 1192 a rebellion against Sverre was raised by two of Magnus Erlingssøn's party, Hallkel Jonssøn and Sigurd Erlingssøn. They took as their chief a son of King Magnus, named Sigurd, and gave Sverre much trouble before he was able to crush them, which he did finally at Florevaag, near Bergen, in the early part of 1194, when Jonssøn and the young chief Sigurd were killed. There is no doubt that this rebellion was prompted by Bishop Nicholas, and Sverre was not long before he called him to account.

The king now decided to take a step which he hoped would strengthen his position very much and finally disarm the opposition of the Church, but which unfortunately seems, on the whole, to have had the opposite effect. We have seen how one of his demands to the archbishop was that he should be ready to crown him as a matter of royal right, and that the archbishop had refused. Though the coronation of a king was an entirely new ceremony in Norway, yet Sverre thought that as Magnus was crowned and had received the blessing of the Church, it would be well for him to have the same sanction, which he believed would make a favourable impression on the minds of the people.

After crushing the rebellion of Hallkel Jonssøn, Sverre

felt the time was come for this. There is a story in the
Sverre Saga, that there was, at this time, a papal legate in
Norway, whom Sverre met at Konghelle whom he almost
succeeded in inducing to crown him, but that the clergy
poisoned his mind against the king, and on his refusal,
Sverre ordered him out of the kingdom. This account
seems to be open to considerable doubt, as at this time the
excommunication against Sverre, pronounced by Archbishop
Erik, was a year old, and it was quite impossible for the
legate (if there was one at all in Norway at the time) not
to have known of it.

Sverre, however, decided on being crowned. When in
Oslo he met Bishop Nicholas, and charged him, at an interview, with treason, for his share in the late rising and
sternly threatened him. The " hare-hearted" bishop was
terrified by the king's anger, and begged for mercy and
swore to be faithful in the future. Sverre, keeping Nicholas
with him, and calling upon Nial of Stavanger and Thore of
Hamar to join him, at once set out for Bergen. The see of
that city was just then vacant by the death of Bishop Paul.
Sverre had his chaplain, Martin (an Englishman by birth),
chosen as his successor, and immediately consecrated by the
three bishops. Sverre had now all the bishops of Norway
with him in Bergen, except, of course, the archbishop, and
he was by them crowned with great solemnity in the
cathedral, on the festival of St. Peter and St. Paul, 1194.
Nicholas, we know, and some of the others, afterwards
declared that they had acted under force, a statement which
was, in his case at any rate, perfectly true.*

* We may, however, very reasonably refuse to accept Roger de
Hoveden's account of the matter when he says : "Amongst these [the
bishops who crowned Sverre] was the bishop of Wie [Viken, that is
Oslo], whose name was Nicholas. He declared that he was unwilling
to be present at the Coronation because of the absence of the archbishop.
On hearing which Sverre caused the bishop to be seized and to be bound

Meanwhile an important missive was on its way from Rome. The pope had taken a long time to act officially on the letter of Archbishop Erik, but a few days before the coronation of Sverre, namely on June 15th, 1194, Celestine III. issued a Bull in which he took the see of Nidaros under the protection of himself and St. Peter, and confirmed in every detail the claims of the archbishop as set forth in his letter to the pope in 1192. The bull wound up in the customary manner with threatening excommunication upon any one who resisted the claims of the Church. The tidings of this came to Denmark, and soon after to Norway, but not, of course, until after the coronation of Sverre. When the pope learned that the four bishops had actually crowned the excommunicated king, he was naturally furious, and on November 18th in the same year he solemnly excommunicated the bishops who had taken part in the ceremony for their unheard-of conduct in "anointing an excommunicated priest as king." The archbishop followed this up by ordering his four suffragans at once to appear before him in Denmark, and explain their action. Notwithstanding the thunders of Rome the four bishops stood firm, Nicholas of Oslo, undoubtedly most unwillingly, from fear of Sverre.

Early the following year, 1195, Sverre called a meeting of the bishops and some leading men in Bergen to consider the best course to take. The four excommunicated prelates were present, and also the bishop of Skaalholt, in Iceland, and the bishop of the Orkneys. At this meeting it was decided to send two representatives to Rome to lay the case of the bishops and the king before the pope. The men selected for this delicate mission were Thore,

on the seashore on a small eminence, so that the waves of the sea flowing on, nearly entered his mouth, upon which the bishop, being terrified, consented to the wishes of Sverre Birkebein and consecrated him king in Bergen." Such a proceeding would be very unlike Sverre's usual treatment of his opponents.

bishop of Hamar, and a monk named Richard. Before the conference separated, all the bishops again renewed their assurances of being faithful to the king and then went home. The value of the promises of Bishop Nicholas was shown soon after, for on his return to Oslo he promptly fled from the country, and betook himself to Archbishop Erik, with whom he made his peace.

It was not likely that Sverre's enemies (now that they had got Nicholas over to them) would remain long without attacking him ; and we come now to the formation of the Bagler party, which for a long time carried on a desolating strife in Norway.

The way it came about was a strange one. The Eastern emperor, Alexius III., who had just deposed his brother Isaac, was in need of recruits, and sent a man named Reidar (a Norwegian probably by birth) to Sverre, asking permission to enlist men for the service of the emperor. Just at that time, 1195, Sverre did not see his way to do so, but later on, in 1196, thinking possibly that some of his opponents might join Reidar, gave him leave. The emperor's representative quickly collected a large number of men, chiefly in Viken, and with them crossed over to Denmark. Sverre had, however, made a mistake, which very nearly proved fatal to his cause. As soon as Reidar and his men got to Denmark they found Bishop Nicholas waiting for them, and very soon the emperor was forgotten, and they were ready to fall in with the treacherous bishop's plans.

Nicholas had one of the usual pretenders to the throne of Norway ready. This was a young man named Inge, who was said to be the son of Magnus Erlingssøn, but who was most probably a Dane. The episcopal party which Nicholas had thus got together, were known in Norway as the Baglers, from the word *bagall*, a bishop's crozier. This party, when the strife began in earnest, showed that there was very little of religious spirit among them, though nominally contending for the Church's cause, for they pillaged and destroyed impartially on all sides, and neither churches nor ecclesiastical property escaped their hands.

Before we allude to the struggle between Sverre and the Baglers, we must advert to the strange termination of the bishops' and Sverre's Embassy to the pope. It is not known what actually took place in Rome; but there is no doubt the envoys reached Denmark, on their way home, in the winter of 1196—7, and that there was with them there a Cardinal Fidentius, who had gone to Denmark for the purpose of collecting the papal revenue. After a considerable time some Danes came to Sverre, with the information that both the bishop and Richard had died suddenly, and produced a papal letter, duly sealed, which they said had been left with them as security for a loan. Sverre paid over the money, said to be advanced, and the men departed. Soon after Sverre had the letter, purporting to be from the pope, read out in Nidaros, in which Celestine declared that he was satisfied with the explanations of the embassy, and that he released Sverre from the excommunication.

This seems to have been without much doubt a forgery; but the charge which was subsequently made in some quarters against Sverre, that he first had his men murdered and then forged the letter, is in the highest degree improbable; and although Sverre's enemies, and the pope himself, did not hesitate to denounce him, and to declare the letter to be forged, no responsible authority ever charged him with murder.

There is every reason, however, to believe that Thore of Hamar and Richard *were* poisoned, for the cardinal undoubtedly was; he had made himself most intensely hated, even by the strongest papal adherents, by the way in which he had extorted money in Denmark, and it is thought that the poisoning of Sverre's men (who were with him at the same time) was unintentional. It is quite possible that Sverre, now in great straits, assented to the letter passing as genuine; or it may have been that his ambassadors, when they failed in Rome, procured there (as was easily done at the time) a forged seal, which they attached to the letter which eventually came to Sverre's hands.

It would not be fair to blame Sverre too severely for the use of a forged document, in his contest with the papacy, when we remember in how great a degree the papal claims in Europe, themselves rested on those "*metropolitanis muscipula*," the False Decretals.

The party of the Baglers, with Inge and Nicholas, began their attack on Sverre's power in Norway about the same time as the ambassadors on their journey from Rome died in Denmark. The details of this desperate struggle belong chiefly to the secular history of Norway, and need not occupy us long here. It was a fierce conflict, in which the king had to put forth all his strength, and during which he seemed over and over again on the verge of ruin. The Baglers began in the south, but soon went north and captured Nidaros; from it they were driven by Sverre, and again they seized it. Though defeated several times by the king, they managed to collect fresh forces, and at one time Sverre was left without any fleet, while the Baglers ravaged the coast. During Sverre's absence they attacked Bergen, and when they failed to capture the Borg, Nicholas, who was with them, suggested burning the town. Even the Baglers raised an objection to this, as it would involve the destruction of churches, but the bishop assured them that as Sverre's supporters were all excommunicated, the churches where his clergy ministered, were no more sacred than common houses. In the conflagration which followed, six churches are said to have been destroyed!

Thus matters stood in 1198, when things seemed to go

from bad to worse for Sverre, and a heavy blow fell upon him. After Bishop Thore's death and Nicholas' flight and treachery, there were only two bishops left who were faithful to him, for Thore's successor does not seem to have then come to his see, after his consecration in Denmark. Of these two, Nial of Stavanger fled to Denmark, and Sverre was left with only Martin of Bergen, his former chaplain.

The great weapon of the Church's armoury was now about to be employed against Sverre. The aged Pope Celestine III. died in January, 1198, and immediately after, the conclave unanimously chose as his successor, the famous Cardinal Lothair, of the noble Conti family, who ascended the papal throne with the title of Innocent III. The new occupant of the apostolic see was filled with ideas as to the authority of the papacy over the princes or Europe, loftier perhaps than any of his predecessors, even in the midst of the struggle with the Kaisers. Innocent was not long before he determined to try and crush the " apostate priest," as he termed Sverre, and to force the kings of Norway to hold their royal office as a gift from the Church. As one of the most prominent members of the Curia, it was certain that he knew well the facts of the quarrel between the king and the archbishop, which had been in progress for the previous eight years.

His action towards Sverre was the same which he adopted, a few years later, to a very different kind of monarch, John of England. No sooner had he begun his pontificate than he turned his attention to Norway, and in 1198 despatched no fewer than five papal letters in connection with the case of Sverre and the archbishop. In his letter to Erik he announced his intention to use the most terrible punishment of the Church of the middle ages, the Interdict.

He pointed out to the archbishop that the existence of such a king as Sverre was intended by God as a visitation on the Church in Norway for the sins of the bishops and people ; that Sverre was by his own admission a bastard, who had dared to be admitted to the priesthood, in defiance of the Church's law ; that he was a forger of the bull of Celestine, an oppressor of the Church, and persecutor of the clergy. Then he ordered the archbishop to declare all Sverre's followers excommunicated, to close the churches, and forbid all services and sacraments (save only holy baptism and extreme unction), and to deny to all of Sverre's men Christian burial.

Dealing with Martin, bishop of Bergen, he commanded the archbishop at once to suspend him, and bid him repair immediately to Rome.

Not content with this, the pope sought to secure the aid of the temporal power to drive away Sverre from his kingdom, and wrote urgent letters to the kings of Denmark and Sweden calling upon them, as faithful sons of the Church, to at once invade Norway, and drive out this " monster " and " limb of the devil," so that he would no longer be a persecutor of the Church of God. We may say at once, with reference to this, that both Knut of Denmark and Sverker Karlssøn of Sweden manifested no wish whatever to carry out the amiable designs of Innocent. The Danish king contented himself with giving shelter to Erik, and some of the Bagler from time to time, but on the whole, both monarchs seemed to have had a good deal of sympathy with the Norwegian king.

The Interdict in Norway does not seem to have carried with it any of the terrors which the same weapon, later on, produced in England. It must be remembered that all the bishops, except one, were absent from the country, and there was really no one to enforce its provisions. Also it must have been a very long time before its existence could be known all over the land, and in the parts where Sverre's authority was recognized it was most likely that it made no difference, and the king himself had always priests to

say Mass and to perform all ecclesiastical duties.   On the
whole we may take it that, formidable, nay terrible, as
an Interdict was in other lands, its effect in Norway was,
comparatively speaking, slight, and in Sverre's Saga, at
any rate, there is no notice of any general closing of the
churches.

Then another blow, which Sverre must have personally
felt very much, fell on him.   Martin, bishop of Bergen,
who up to now had to his king, been "faithful found
among the faithless" unable any longer to resist the
pressure which must have been put upon him, fled from
Norway to Denmark to seek reconciliation with the
archbishop.   This took place in 1199.

Sverre was not a man to submit quietly to the charges
which the pope and the archbishop laid against him ; and
he issued, probably at the end of 1197 or in the spring of
1198, a very remarkable document, in which he defended
himself, and which embodied very fully his views of the
relations between the Church and State.   This notable
defence sets forth the lines upon which, the kings and
kaisers fought and struggled, against the popes of the
twelfth and thirteenth centuries, and Sverre's reply was
in its way, worthy to rank with the defence of the Kaiser
Frederick II. in his contest with Gregory IX. not very
long after.

This document was known as the *Tale mod Biskoperne*
(speech against the bishops), which we may best render
Sverre's Apology.   Though not actually written by the
king (he is said to have employed a learned priest who had
studied at Bologna),* it was clearly inspired by him,
and his early studies in the canon law, before his
ordination as priest, must have stood him in good
stead.   This document was widely circulated in Norway

---

* It does not appear what was the name of this Peter de Vinea of
the North ; but it may have been Einar, Sverre's son-in-law.

and read at all the *Things*, and seems to have produced a very great impression upon the people and to have helped the king's cause not a little.

We may briefly summarize Sverre's Apology as follows :—

It begins with the statement that it was necessary that the people should know the true facts of the case respecting the quarrel between the king and the bishops. Then he uses the illustration of the body and the members, and how all should work together. The eyes of the body were the bishops, the tongue the priests, the ears the deacons, the shoulders and back the chiefs and principal men, the legs and feet the bønder, and the heart the king. Then he enters upon a scathing criticism of the actions of the bishops and clergy. The eyes, which should see aright and guide the body, squinted, and did not rightly perform their functions. The bishops forced men to build churches and then drove them from them. The priests were silent and set a bad example to men, and when they were guilty of acts of injustice they sought to evade being tried by the ordinary courts of law. The bishops and clergy together deceived the pope, and prevented him from learning the truth respecting the king and his party.

Then comes a great deal about the royal authority. The king's authority comes from God, and is not given by the Church ; he is the protector of the Church, and should receive the support and obedience of its officers. Our Lord, by His example and by the teaching of the apostles, enjoined submission even to a heathen emperor.

The king, as God's appointed protector of the Church, has a right to appoint men to office in it, and for the exercise of this, he is responsible to God. No king has the right to alienate this power from the Crown. The arrangement with Cardinal Nicholas was only in the case (which then existed) of there being more than one king, and was only a temporary measure, as was shown by the fact that when Inge was sole king, he had nominated Eystein to the archbishopric. Sverre's object was not to bring shame on the bishops and clergy, but rather to set the truth before the people. If they accuse and excommunicate the king for exercising that power which God has given to him, they encroach on his prerogative and sin against God, and their excommunication does not hurt the king, but recoils on those who issue it.[*]

Such is an outline of this remarkable document, by which it will be seen that Sverre regarded the royal power and authority as every bit as sacred a thing as that of the Church, and repudiated entirely the way in which the kings, in the past few years, had alienated the rights of the Crown. He went back to the times of St. Olaf and his immediate successors, and pointed out that he was only following in the steps of those famous men.

It will be seen by this that Sverre was not yet conquered, and had no idea of giving up the position he had taken. Yet now he had practically lost the whole of Norway, except Trøndelagen, where the people, as a body, remained still faithful to him. But at what seemed the very darkest moment of his life—with the greater part of his kingdom in the hands of his enemies, deserted by the bishops and many of the clergy, himself excommunicated, and the land under an Interdict—a change for the better began. Early in 1199 he managed to build a sufficient number of ships to encounter the Baglers at sea, and in June of that year he gained a decisive victory over their forces in Strindsøen, near Nidaros. His arch-enemy Nicholas was present with the Baglers and fled with them ; he seems to have had enough of fighting, as he does not afterwards appear to have taken any active part in the subsequent battles. The next year,

* Sverre's defence exists in a modern edition by Professor Storm, Christiania, 1885.

1200, a determined attempt was made to crush Sverre by a great rising in Viken, but he managed by his own extraordinarily rapid movements to attack the forces of his enemies before they could form a single army, and inflicted on them a crushing defeat. In spite of this the Baglers managed to prolong the struggle. It ended, however, as far as Sverre was concerned, in the capture of Tønsberg, where the Baglers, under Reidar (the man whom Sverre had permitted to enlist followers in 1196), held out for a long time, and only surrendered in January, 1202.

The end of the heroic king was now fast approaching. Worn out by the terrible hardships which he had endured, first in his struggle for the crown with Magnus, and afterwards in the contest against the Baglers, he was in very bad health when the town of Tønsberg fell. He went thence to Bergen, and with a brave heart set himself to prepare for death. Calling his men together he told them that he left no son behind him save Haakon, his other son, Sigurd, having died in the year 1200.

When the end drew near, and he felt his strength fast failing, he sent for the priests who remained faithful to him in Bergen (in spite of interdict and excommunication) to administer the last sacraments of the Church.

Then he had himself placed in his high seat and awaited their coming. "If I die here," he said, "in my high seat, surrounded by my friends, it will be different from what Bishop Nicholas expected, when he said that I should be hewn down for the dogs and the ravens. Praised be God, He has saved me in many dangers from the weapons of my enemies." Then, "houseled and aneled," he awaited the coming of the great conqueror. As his men stood around him, he bade them, when he was dead, to let his face be uncovered, so that his people might see that the excommunication had done him no harm, as his enemies had maintained. Then, before his departing, he summed up the experience of his troubled reign :—

" I have had more trouble and sorrow in my reign than peace and pleasure. I believe I have had many envious men who have let me feel their hatred. May God forgive them for all of it. Now may the Lord judge between me and them, and vindicate my cause."

Thus, on Saturday, the 9th of March, 1202, " passed the strong heroic soul away," in the fifty-second year of his life. His dying wishes were respected, and the people looked, for the last time, on the face of their dead leader, and saw that no change, but the last and great one had come to him. No difficulty seems to have been found as to his burial. He was laid to rest in a niche in the wall between the choir and the south door of Christ Church Cathedral in Bergen, and on a copper plate hung upon the wall was inscribed in letters of gold these words: " Here rests the man who was the glory of kings, the defender of his native land, and the joy and pride of his men."

Friends and foes alike lamented him, and said, truly, " such a man Norway had never before seen."

Sverre Sigurdssøn is perhaps the most striking figure in the history of Norway. In estimating his character we must not forget that all the evil which could be said of him, was remorselessly dragged to light by his inveterate enemies, who represented him as almost a monster in human form, while many of the other great men, especially in the early days of the Church in Norway, had the record of their lives set forth by writers who were to their failings not a little kind, and who softened down their worst actions. But we fortunately possess as well a record of his life in the Sverre's Saga (written by Karl Jonssøn, and probably Styrme, a priest, of Iceland), which sets him forth in another and more favourable light, and we have reason to believe with truth. Had he lived at another time, and been given the opportunities, which he undoubtedly wished for, of healing the wounds which the long period of civil war had inflicted upon Norway, he would have received a unanimous tribute as to his great genius as an organizer and ruler, as well as a warrior. To him, however, fell the task of being the champion of the cause of liberty, against the overwhelming and unlawful claims of the Roman see, and of upholding the authority and independence of Norway against foreign ecclesiastical tyranny. His struggle against the right of the pontiff to depose a national king was one of the same kind as was waged later on in other countries of Europe, and the feeling of indignation which filled his followers, at the attempt of Innocent III. to deprive their king of his power, was akin to that which stirred the barons of England to resist the claims of the same pontiff not many years after.

Sverre was no enemy of the Church in Norway. His antagonism was against those who sought to overturn the settlement of both Church and State, as it had been arranged in the days of his great predecessor Olaf, the king and saint. He represented the spirit of antagonism among the Teutonic races to the encroachments and aggressions of the papal authority, which manifested itself in England in a long series of legislative enactments, calculated to check the usurpations of the Roman see. Had he been allowed, he would have lived and worked harmoniously with the bishops. Even his first antagonist, the great Archbishop Eystein, found that after all Sverre was not such a tyrant as he had imagined, and he was able to spend his last days in peace with the king, and Eystein was, in all respects, a greater man than his successor Erik.

Far from being tyrannical and overbearing, Sverre seems to have erred on the side of moderation, and a desire to yield to the wishes of the bishops. He was a shrewd judge of men, and had he chosen to insist on what he believed to be the right of the Crown (a right universally exercised by all his predecessors, except Magnus Erlingssøn) and refused to assent to the appointments, first of Erik to Nidaros and afterwards Nicholas to Stavanger, all the troubles that followed might have been averted. In those two instances Sverre gave way against his own better judgment, for which he suffered severely afterwards.

With all his skill in war and the desperate battles in which he so often engaged, Sverre was a man of great kindness of heart, and never (except perhaps on one occasion, and under very great provocation) exercised vengeance on his enemies, which was everywhere looked upon as the most natural thing to do in his day. His private life was no more free from blame than that of the sainted Olaf, but he was certainly no worse than many who died in the odour of sanctity, and in the full enjoyment of papal favour and love. His men, the far-famed Birkebeiner, followed him with the most intense devotion, and he was truly, as his epitaph said, "their joy and pride." His genius transformed a band of wild outlaws into a highly-trained and strictly-disciplined body of men, and made their name, once a term of contempt and derision, one coveted and esteemed by brave men.

We are often tempted to speculate what would have been Sverre's life, had he not given up the service of the Altar for the Throne. Would he have risen from the obscurity of the storm-beaten islands of the northern seas to a position of great power and authority in the Church? A man of his genius would most likely have come to the front in those days, when many of the greatest prelates, like Nicholas Breakspeare, often rose step by step until they gained the very highest places in the service of the Church. His life might have been a happier one, and he might not have aroused so much hostility as fell to the lot of the king of Norway. But it is Sverre the king, not Sverre the cardinal or pope, with whom we have had to deal, and that kingship brought to him, in his own sad words, " more trouble and sorrow than peace and pleasure"; and he passed away at any rate comforted with the feeling that he had won the love of his followers, and was to his last day "the defender of his native land."

CHAPTER XIII.

HAAKON SVERRESSØN TO THE DEATH OF HAAKON HAAKONSSØN.

The Truce with the Church—Erik Returns—Haakon Dies Suddenly—
Internal Struggles—Inge Baardssøn—Haakon Haakonssøn cared
for by the Birkebeiner—Proclaimed King—End of the Struggle
between the Birkebeiner and Baglers—Death of Bishop Nicholas of
Oslo—Duke Skule Killed—Cardinal William of Sabina Crowns
Haakon—The Cardinal's Mission—Haakon's Legislation—Union
with Iceland—New Law of Succession—Death of Haakon—
Papal Letters during his Reign.

At the time of Sverre's death, his only surviving, but
illegitimate son Haakon was at Nidaros. Tidings of the
event were conveyed in great haste to him, and he was at
once proclaimed king, and soon after formally accepted by
the *Thing*. Sverre's other son, Sigurd, who died in 1200,
had left a son, who, however, was only an infant, and no
claim on his behalf was then advanced. Haakon was at
this time a young man of great promise, and well beloved
by all the Birkebeiner party ; he was an excellent speaker,
and of most kindly and generous disposition. In person he
was of commanding height, and his skill in war had been
abundantly proved in the many conflicts in which he had
taken part. Like his father, he was a man of education far
beyond the average of the kings of his time, and a translation from the Latin ascribed to him still survives.*

Sverre before his death had written to Haakon with

---

* This was the " Barlaam's and Josafat's Saga," a religious romance,
originally written in Greek about the eighth century (traditionally by
John of Damascus) and afterwards translated into Latin. The Norse
version is ascribed also to Haakon the Younger, a son of Haakon
Haakonssøn, who died in 1257.

reference to the quarrel with the bishops, and urged his son to make peace with them. Accordingly the first step of Haakon, after his succession, was to recall the fugitive bishops, who gladly availed themselves of the offer of peace, and by the summer of 1202, Erik and the others returned to their sees.

It now seemed as if an era of peace and tranquillity was about to dawn once more on the land, for both parties were exhausted by the prolonged conflict and anxious for a settlement. When the prelates had come back, the king issued a letter " to the archbishop, bishops, clergy, and bønder," in which he expressed his willingness to grant to the Church all its rights and privileges ; but with this important reservation added : " My kingdom and my full royal rights unimpaired, in agreement with the arrangement made by Cardinal Nicholas, and agreed to by the three kings, Eystein, Sigurd, and Inge, and which King Eystein's letter witnesses, and King Magnus confirmed, as also my father by his letter . . . whilst the Church and all the clergy agree to pay to me that homage and honour they are bound to offer to their lawful king." It will be seen by this that the peace between the king and the Church, was after all merely an armistice, and that all the critical points in the dispute were practically passed over by a kind of tacit agreement. In other words, both parties were content to let matters stand " as in 1152," and we know that Sverre regarded the burning question of the right of the appointment of the bishops by the Crown, as unimpaired by Cardinal Nicholas's arrangement, when there was only one king in the land. The archbishop now took off the excommunication on Sverre's adherents, and removed any of the restrictions which had followed the Interdict, and all parties in Norway were for the time satisfied.

Not so Innocent III. When information reached him of the death of Sverre, and of the events which we have just

ALTAR PIECE FROM ST. EDMUND'S CHURCH, LURØ (NORDLAND).

Now in Bergen Museum. The figures, from the left hand, are St. Thomas of Canterbury, St. Olaf, St. Edmund (King and Martyr), and St. Magnus.

[To face p. 186.

mentioned, he was extremely angry, though he does not seem to have taken any official notice until January, 1204, when he wrote a very sharp and scathing letter to Archbishop Erik. He began, indeed, by rejoicing that peace had come once more to the land after the death of Sverre. Then he reminded the archbishop that he had dared to take too much upon him, by releasing from the ban those whom he had excommunicated, and compares the archbishop to an ape that imitates the actions of men, and finally ordered him to send some one to Rome to explain his conduct.

By the time this letter reached Norway, however, the condition of affairs was changed, for on January 1st, 1204, Haakon died suddenly in Bergen (said to have been poisoned by Sverre's widow, Margreta), and the hopes which were cherished for peace and prosperity under the wise and prudent rule of Haakon, were dashed to the ground.

The events of the immediately following years need not closely concern us, but it is necessary to state them as briefly as possible.

During the short reign of Haakon the remains of the Bagler party had tried to carry on the strife, chiefly in the Oplands, but they were defeated and their chief, Inge, killed in the close of 1202.

Haakon left no legitimate heir, and his illegitimate son (afterwards the famous King Haakon Haakonssøn) was not then born. There was therefore no direct heir in the male line, except the little four-year-old son of Haakon's brother, Sigurd Guttorm Sigurdssøn, and he was proclaimed king in Bergen immediately after his uncle's death, and Haakon Galin, the son of Cecilia (King Sverre's sister) by her first marriage was named as regent.

There was, however, another person who, through his mother, might have a claim to the throne, and this was Inge Baardssøn, son of Cecilia by her second marriage. The little Guttorm lived only a few months, and died in Nidaros (by poison it was supposed) in the summer of 1204, and then Inge Baardssøn was, with the archbishop's approval, accepted as king.   At this time he was only sixteen years of age.

Now the Baglers started again in the south, and secured a new chief, Erling Steinvæg, whom they announced to be a son of Magnus Erlingssøn.   They very nearly succeeded in capturing King Inge at Nidaros, while he was engaged in celebrating his sister's wedding, but he managed to escape.

The struggle with the Baglers went on with varying fortune for some years longer.   Their chief died in 1207, and then Bishop Nicholas got them to accept his nephew Filippus as their leader, and entered into negotiations with the young king and Haakon Galin, which resulted in his nephew being granted the kingship over Viken and part of the Oplands, and in 1209 he married Kristine, the daughter of King Sverre, and there was peace for a time.

Archbishop Erik, whose blindness unfitted him for the duties of his office, resigned his see in 1205, and Thore, a member of the Oslo chapter, was chosen as his successor and went to Rome, where he was consecrated and received the pallium.   In 1207 he returned again to Norway. Archbishop Erik had held the see of Nidaros for sixteen years, ten of which he lived in exile in Denmark. Thore, his successor, was, in spite of his connection with the see of Oslo, a man well disposed for peace, and did much to help to bring about a better state of feeling between the parties.

King Inge had always a dangerous rival in Haakon Galin, who claimed a share of the kingdom by right of his mother and being Inge's half-brother.   To avoid war the king made (through the mediation of Archbishop Thore and Erik, who still lived) an agreement in 1213 to share the royal dignity with his half-brother, providing that whichever of them survived should have the other's share, and then, after their death, the *legitimate* son of either of them. This was intended to secure the succession to Haakon's family, as Inge had no legitimate heir, and also to exclude the one who, according to the old law, had a better right to the crown than either Inge or Haakon— namely, Haakon Haakonssøn, the illegitimate son of Haakon, the son of Sverre.

Haakon Haakonssøn was the son of Haakon Sverressøn and a woman named Inga, who lived near Sarpsborg; he was not born until after his father's death, and the fact of his birth was for some time kept a secret. Some of the Birkebeiner, however, learned it, and decided that it would be safer for Sverre's grandson to be out of the reach of Bishop Nicholas and his nephew Filippus. Taking the little child with them, two faithful Birkebeiner carried him in their arms in the winter of 1205 to Nidaros, where he was kindly received by Inge and allowed to remain in peace. The old Birkebeiner warriors loved the little boy, and watched over him with the greatest care.

Haakon Galin only lived a year after the compact with Inge, who was himself in bad health and depended much upon his half-brother, Skule Baardssøn,* whom he made a jarl, and who now cherished plans for making himself king after Inge. The old Birkebeiner were determined, if the king should die, that young Haakon should succeed him, and, being suspicious of danger, kept a careful watch over the lad.

Archbishop Thore died in 1214, after having held the see for seven years. He was largely instrumental in carrying out the negotiations between the contending parties in Norway, and always carefully looked after the interests and claims of the Church. During his episcopate the

---

* Skule was the son of Baard, Inge's father, by his second marriage after Cecilia's death.

Cistercian monastery at Tautra, on the Trondhjem Fjord, was founded, probably in 1207. Thore was succeeded by a priest named Guttorm, who was consecrated by the pope in 1215. The year after Bishop Martin, of Bergen, Sverre's old chaplain, died, and Haavard was unanimously chosen as his successor. On his election the new archbishop raised a question about his consecration. Haavard was the son of a priest, and the archbishop declined to consecrate him (on the ground of his being therefore illegitimate) without a dispensation from the pope. Application was made to Innocent for this, but he died in July, 1216, before the matter was considered; his successor, however, Honorius III., granted the dispensation, and Haavard was consecrated by Guttorm. This was the first case of the kind in Norway.

On April 22nd, 1217, King Inge, who had been ill for some time, died at Nidaros. The Birkebeiner at once proclaimed young Haakon as king, and this was approved at the *Thing*. Skule Baardssøn did not dare to oppose this, and had to be content with his jarldom and the regency of the kingdom. Soon after the king and Skule went to Bergen, and in spite of some efforts to stir up opposition to Haakon in that part of the country, he was well received by both clergy and people, and at a Gula *Thing* was accepted as king. The Bagler king in Viken, Filippus, died in the same year as Inge, and the rule of Haakon was extended to that part of the country as well.

When Haakon returned to Nidaros in 1218, after having been to Viken, Archbishop Guttorm received him with great coldness, not to say rudeness, while he treated Skule with marked respect. When called to account for this, he stated that there was yet lacking some sufficient proof of Haakon's parentage. In order that this matter might be set at rest, a *Rigsmøde*, or meeting of all the chief men of the kingdom, was called to meet at Bergen in the summer of the same year. At this, all the bishops, chiefs, and representatives of the bønder were present. It was first proposed that King Haakon should follow the example of Harald Gille and others, and submit to the trial by ordeal; but this was strongly objected to by Haakon's faithful Birkebeiner, and one of them, named Dagfinn, said that if it was to be a trial by iron it would be by cold iron (swords), which they would use against the king's enemies. Finally it was agreed that Inga, the king's mother, should undergo the trial by ordeal, to prove that Haakon was really the son of King Haakon Sverressøn, and this she did successfully at St. Peter's Church, in Nidaros, and all doubt was thus set at rest. This was the last occasion in which this method of trial was used in the matter of royal claims, and soon afterwards trial by ordeal was for all cases stopped by law.

Then, as Haakon's royal birth was undoubted, a sentence of excommunication was pronounced against all who in future questioned it.

The Baglers, however, still gave trouble under a new leader named Bene; but the people in Viken had had enough of them, and called in the king and the Birkebeiner to help them, and defeated the Baglers. After this the old chiefs of the Baglers in Viken finally made peace and swore allegiance to King Haakon, and thus formally ended the great struggle between Baglers and Birkebeiner, which for twenty years had devastated Norway and done an almost irreparable amount of injury to the land.

Jarl Skule did not cease to cherish his ambitious designs of supplanting Haakon, and various different risings took place from time to time, in which both he and the wily Bishop Nicholas, who hated all of Sverre's family, undoubtedly had a share.

Efforts were made to avert the growing hostility between the jarl and the king by an arrangement by which the latter should be betrothed to the jarl's daughter Margreta, then only a child, but even the prospect of having the king for a son-in-law, did not stop the intrigues of Skule.

There were a number of persons who claimed to have a right to, at any rate a share in, the kingdom at that time, and it was decided to hold another *Rigsmøde* in Bergen in the summer of 1223. When this met, Archbishop Guttorm who presided, went in detail through the claims of the different candidates—the jarl Skule, who claimed as Inge's half brother; Guttorm, Inge's illegitimate son; Sigurd Ribbung, who professed to be a son of Magnus Erlingssøn; and Knut, who was son of Haakon Galin. The meeting, however, decided with practical unanimity in favour of Haakon, who was acknowledged as the rightful king, and Skule Jarl was allowed to govern the third part of the kingdom.

This was about the last public act of Archbishop Guttorm, who died the next year, 1224. The chapter chose as his successor Sigurd of Tautra, who was absent from the country at the time; but the king was in favour of another candidate named Peter, and sent him to the pope, who accepted him, and after consecrating him and investing him with the pallium, sent him back to Norway in 1225.

The same year another rebellion (again incited by the indefatigable plotter Bishop Nicholas) broke out under Sigurd, one of the claimants mentioned above, but this was soon put down.

The long life of the remarkable Bishop Nicholas of Oslo was now drawing to a close; and he seems to have suffered some qualms of conscience for the way in which he had acted towards Sverre and his descendants, to almost all of whom he had at one time or another sworn allegiance, and whom notwithstanding, he had opposed in every way, both openly and in secret. Haakon had now undoubted proofs of Nicholas's complicity in the late rising, and intended to bring it home to him. But the bishop was now a dying man, and desired before he left the world, to make tardy amends for his life-long disloyalty. He sent a messenger to Haakon desiring to see him. When the king came, he first reproached the bishop for what he had done, but then the dying man confessed his share in the various rebellions and asked the forgiveness of Haakon. This the king fully and freely granted, and, remaining with the bishop until his death, afterwards gave him a splendid burial. Thus in 1225, in the seventieth year of his age, and the thirty-fifth of his episcopate, Nicholas Arnessøn passed away. There is no doubt that Sverre's estimate of his character was a correct one; smooth-tongued, cowardly and treacherous, he always was to Sverre and his descendants, and though doubtless he had, what he believed to be, the interests of the Church at heart, yet he was the chief cause of all the troubles which had come upon the country, during the thirty-five years of his tenure of the see of Oslo. Very shrewd he was in all his actions, and Haakon was right when he declared that "he never had his equal in worldly wisdom." We might well wish that, as a bishop of the Church, he had merited a better epitaph.

With the death of Bishop Nicholas the spirit of rebellion did not, however, cease. Sigurd Ribbung died, but Knut took his place, until he was vanquished by Haakon and swore allegiance to him, an oath which, in spite of subsequent temptations to the contrary, he faithfully kept.

Archbishop Peter only lived after his consecration for two years, dying in 1226, and was succeeded by Thore, who after a brief episcopate died in 1230. The next archbishop was Sigurd Eindridessøn, who was the son of one of Sverre's Birkebeiner, and was, it might be supposed, naturally inclined to the king's party; but we shall, later on, find him in a somewhat different position during his long episcopate.

It was now becoming clear that, sooner or later, an open rupture between the king and the great Jarl Skule must come about.   The archbishop and others averted it several times, and the king strove to keep peace with his father-in-law, for his marriage with Margreta had been duly solemnized, and Skule was created a duke, the first who bore that title in Norway.

In 1239 the long-expected outbreak took place.   Skule was in Nidaros and the king in Bergen.   The former called a *Thing* and carried to it by force the sacred relics of the cathedral, including the body of St. Olaf, and was there by his adherents proclaimed king.   But he failed to surprise Haakon in Bergen as he had intended.   The struggle took place in the south.   Skule first defeated the king's party in a battle, but was afterwards himself defeated at Oslo.   Then he fled to Nidaros, pursued by the Birkebeiner. He first hid near the town, and then sought refuge in Elgesæter monastery.   This the Birkebeiner set on fire, and Skule and his followers rushed out, but were to a man cut down by the king's men.   Thus fell, on May 23rd, 1240, in his fifty-first year, the great chief Skule Baardssøn, and now Haakon was left in undisputed possession of his kingdom.   He had just before the final rupture with Skule taken the precaution to have his son, by his marriage with Margreta, accepted as a king by the *Thing* in Nidaros and afterwards in Bergen, though he had also an older, but illegitimate son named Sigurd.   Haakon's idea was to secure the succession of his legitimate son, who alone, according to the bishop's theory, should have a right to the throne.

Haakon Haakonssøn, having now delivered himself and his kingdom from all rivals and claimants to the throne, desired to carry out his wish of being formally crowned by the archbishop, as his immediate predecessor had been. He therefore approached the primate, and he referred the matter to the pope (Gregory IX.), who appointed a commission to investigate the king's claim. Nothing, however, was done at the time, or in the short reign of Gregory's successor, Celestine IV., and in 1243 the famous Innocent IV. became pope.

Haakon, who was in favour with Innocent, felt that this was the best time to give effect to his wishes. In 1245 he summoned a meeting of the archbishop and bishops to meet in Bergen, and there brought before them the subject of his coronation. The archbishop and the others expressed themselves quite willing to anoint and crown the king, but they demanded in return for this that Haakon should be ready to grant the same terms as Magnus Erlingssøn in 1164. They found, however, that they had to deal with a very different stamp of man from Erling Skakke's son. To the demands of the bishops the king replied : " The kings have already granted you such great rights that it would be difficult to add to them, and, besides, you have exceeded all lawful bounds. If I swore such an oath as King Magnus swore, it seems to me that my glory would be diminished and not increased, for Magnus did not mind what he did to gain that to which he had no right. By God's help I hope never to be obliged to accept or to buy from you, that to which God has chosen me after my father and my forefathers, and be sure that by God's grace I shall win my crown so freely and unconditionally that I can wear it as securely as other famous kings, or it shall never come upon my head."

These words, in which we have an echo of his grandfather's famous Apology, showed the prelates that they must not endeavour to push their claims too far with Haakon. After this the king broke off the negotiations with the bishops, but did not abandon his design. He took the bolder and, as it proved, the wiser plan of addressing himself directly to Innocent IV. Accordingly he dispatched Laurentius, abbot of Hovedø, and Bjarne, one of the chapter of Nidaros, with a letter to Innocent begging him to send a cardinal legate to Norway to crown him.[*]

Haakon could not possiby have selected a more propitious time for approaching the pope. The pontiff was, as we know, at that very time in the midst of his great quarrel with Kaiser Frederick II., and had been obliged to flee from Rome and take refuge in Lyons. Innocent saw the importance of enlisting on his side as many as possible of the kings of Europe, and as Haakon had now become powerful and was likely to be useful in the struggle, he listened most willingly to his request.

In October, 1246, he wrote to Haakon from Lyons saying that he would grant his request and send to him William, cardinal bishop of Sabina, as legate in order to crown the king, and in the next month he dispatched another letter in which he dispensed his want of legitimacy, so that it should be no bar to his royal title.

Innocent IV. had in view, not merely the securing of an adherent in Haakon, but intended that the legate should make an investigation into the state of the Church both in

[*] Matthew Paris supplies us with some interesting details as to this embassy. He is an authority of great importance in matters relating to Haakon, as he was a personal friend of the king, and had been in Norway himself. From Matthew's chronicle it would appear that Haakon, in order to secure his coronation, had to give in advance a very large sum of money to Innocent to induce him to send Cardinal William of Sabina to Norway. Considering the pope's position at that time this statement seems extremely probable. One of the king's ambassadors, Laurentius, the abbot of Hovedø, was, as Matthew tells us, an Englishman by birth and a professed Cistercian. He (Haakon) received consecration and legitimation from Innocent IV., "having given to the same pope 30,000 marks of silver by the hand of Master Laurence, afterwards abbot of Kirkstead in Lindesey."—Matt. Paris, Vol. V., page 222 (Rolls series).

Norway and Sweden. He chose a very suitable man for his purpose, just as Eugenius III. had in 1152, for Cardinal William of Sabina had been a legate in Prussia and had visited Gotland, and thus had come in contact with many Scandinavians, though he had never been in Norway itself.

Haakon had now gained his point, and had indirectly won a victory over the bishops of Norway. He called together a great meeting of all the bishops, chiefs, and people in Bergen, in the summer of 1247 to receive the cardinal.

We learn from Matthew Paris that William of Sabina passed through England on his journey as legate to the North. He landed at Dover, and obtaining permission from Henry III. to visit the country, greeted that monarch and received substantial presents from him. The cardinal remained at King's Lynn for three months, and during his stay there "he could not restrain his innate Roman cupidity," and succeeded in extracting about 4,000 marks from the clergy in that neighbourhood, and "often preached to the people under pretence of piety." Lynn was a usual port of departure for Norway, and here he had a ship well filled with corn and wine, "where, as we read in the case of Noah's ark, there were passages and decks one above another, chambers and dining-rooms. In this manner, therefore, having become rich, he committed himself to the North Sea with a fair wind blowing, after bestowing his blessing on England and the prodigal English."

The cardinal arrived in Bergen on June 17th, and was received with great honour by the king. The bishops, however, were determined to make one more effort. They did their best in several interviews to inflame the legate against Haakon, and seemed to have got him over to their side. The cardinal then suggested to the king that it might be well to agree to Magnus Erlingssøn's oath. Haakon, however, boldly told him that he knew very well where that suggestion came from, and added, "I will have no crown if it costs me my freedom." The prudent legate saw he had gone too far, and at once withdrew his suggestion. Great preparations were now made for the coronation, which was fixed for St. Olaf's day. Archbishop Sigurd and five of his suffragans, the bishops of Bergen, Stavanger, Oslo, Hamar, and Hole (Iceland), the principal abbots, and all the great chiefs of Norway were then in the city. The coronation procession to Christ Church Cathedral was one of great magnificence. Following the high officials came four *lendermænd*, bearing aloft the coronation robes, after them were borne two silver sceptres, one with a golden cross on it and another with an eagle. Next came the king's son, Haakon, carrying the crown, and Jarl Knut with the coronation sword, and last of all Archbishop Sigurd and King Haakon, with two bishops as his supporters. At the palace door the procession was joined by clergy intoning, "Ecce mitto angelum meum," and thus they went to the cathedral, where they were met at the door by the cardinal and two bishops, who conducted the king to the altar. During the Mass the king was crowned with the usual solemnities.

The coronation banquet was held in the king's boat-house, there being no other building large enough to receive the great company. After the feast the cardinal made a speech, in which he said : "Now is your king crowned and honoured as no king before him in Norway; God be praised that I did not turn back, as I was urged to do, as I was told that I would not see many people, and if I did, they would be more like wild beasts than men in their conduct, but now I see a great company of people all well conducted and many foreigners, and such a multitude of ships as I have never before seen in one harbour."

After the coronation was over the cardinal did not forget the other part of his mission—an inquiry into the state of the Church in Norway. Lengthy conferences were held in Bergen with the king and the bishops, and various abuses were dealt with, and complaints on the part of the people listened to.

It was found that the bishops had been accustomed to appropriate the income of parishes during a vacancy, and this practice was sternly forbidden, as it naturally gave an opening for abuses and might delay the appointment to the parish. It was ordered that when a parish was vacant some one was at once to be appointed to hold the revenue during the vacancy, and to hand it over, with a proper account, to the newly-appointed priest, and specially to guard the one-fourth part of the tithe which belonged to the parish church.

The parish priests complained about the enforced hospitality which they had to offer to the bishop's officials when he did not come himself on a visitation. This was forbidden, except when illness or the king's business prevented the bishop coming. The bønder complained about the fines which were levied on them for fishing and haymaking upon holy days, and asked for some relief. The cardinal recognized the justice of the claim to make hay while the sun shone, and also to secure the herrings, "sent by God," when they approached the shores, and granted this request.*

Another important matter which was decided at this time was the entire abolition of the trial by ordeal, which had been, not long before, used to decide the question of the king's parentage.

So ended this most memorable mission of William of Sabina, one as important in its way as that of Nicholas Breakspeare in 1152.

The cardinal during his stay in Norway contrived to enrich himself considerably at the expense of Church

* Archbishop Eystein had obtained from the pope a similar concession for Trøndelagen in his time, see page 161.

and king, as he had previously done in England. For the pope he is said to have received a sum of 15,000 marks of silver—a welcome contribution to the papal war chest at the time of the great conflict with the kaiser. For himself he got from Haakon 1,500 marks, and 500 marks from the Norwegian Church, in addition to innumerable smaller gifts.

On his way from Norway the cardinal called at Stavanger, Tønsberg, Oslo, and Konghelle, from whence he passed into Sweden. The legate's view of the state of the Church in Norway is contained in a letter of August, 1247, at the close of his mission. In this he mentions that he found it in full peaceable and quiet possession of the right of judging in all ecclesiastical matters between all persons whomsoever, and over all the clergy, in questions both spiritual and temporal, or with regard to any breach of contract. He also found the Norwegian Church exercised free and unfettered rights of patronage over all churches.

The election of the bishops was also free from the interference of the laity.*

How far the legate was strictly correct in his statement seems open to doubt. The *Kristenret* certainly did not then recognize the immunity of the clergy from secular tribunals, nor had the king abandoned his right to have a voice in the choice of the bishops. It seems likely that the cardinal's letter embodied what the Church wished for, and claimed, more than what it actually possessed at the time.

William of Sabina was for a considerable time engaged in the affairs of the Church in Sweden, and did not return to the papal court at Lyons until 1251, where he died suddenly in the same year. Haakon was now in a position of great power and influence, and was an especial favourite

---

* The cardinal's letter will be found in the *Norges Gamle Love,* Vol. I., page 450.

of the pope. Some time before his coronation he had been urged to join in a crusade, and though he had promised to do so, and afterwards (1248) Louis IX. of France had urged him to join in the unfortunate venture in which he was taken prisoner, yet Haakon never fulfilled his promise. As a substitute for a crusade against the Saracens, the pope permitted and approved of one against Haakon's heathen neighbours in the north of Norway—the Finns. Haakon, however, did better than carrying fire and sword amongst them. He made efforts to spread Christianity in those regions in a more legitimate way, and to his zeal was due the foundation of churches in Tromsø and in Ofoten; the former was for a long time the most northern Christian church in the world. He also received a tribe of Finns from Russia, whom the Tartars had driven out, and allowed them to settle in Malangen, where he had them baptized.

The remaining years of the long reign of Haakon were not marked by any very important ecclesiastical events, though there are several points of interest in the dealings between the king and the Church, some of which were in progress before the time of the mission of Cardinal William of Sabina.

Later writers and legislative enactments frequently refer to the *Kristenret* "of King Haakon Haakonssøn, and Archbishop Sigurd." It would seem that this was not a new enactment, but rather a rearrangement and adaptation of the older laws, to bring them into conformity with the alterations agreed upon in the relations of the Church and the State. There were, as we have seen, a number of laws relating to matters ecclesiastical dating from the time of St. Olaf downwards, and the last was the collection known as the " Golden Feather " of Archbishop Eystein. Haakon and the archbishop revised and enlarged these, and they were accepted as a part of the Frosta *Thing's* law. The exact date of this work is uncertain, but its approximate date can be ascertained by the fact that trial by ordeal was still recognized, and we therefore may conclude with certainty that it was prior to 1247, when that method was abolished at the time of William of Sabina's mission.

Another important event, both ecclesiastical and civil, which marked the reign of Haakon was the practical union of Norway and Iceland. That remarkable island had, from the time of its first colonization, from Norway, in the days of Harald Haarfagre, maintained a sturdy independence of the rule of the Norwegian kings, though there was a very close connection between it and the mother country, and the Church there, with the two dioceses of Skaalholt and Hole, formed a part of the province of Nidaros, together with the more distant Greenland.

One of the most famous bishops was Thorlak Thorhallssøn. This man was born in 1133 and ordained priest in 1152, and spent several years in studying abroad—first at Paris and afterwards, from 1158 to 1160, at Lincoln, then famous as a school of learning in theology and canon law. In 1178 he was consecrated at Nidaros as bishop of Skaalholt. He was the great ecclesiastical legislator of Iceland, and compiled a *Kristenret* for that country. After his death in 1193 he was reverenced as a saint by the Icelanders, but was never canonized at Rome. The unhappy state of affairs in Norway during the civil wars reacted upon Iceland, and the island was in a disturbed state. During the reign of Haakon lived the famous Snorre Sturlassøn, the writer of the great "Heimskringla" (a history of the Norwegian race from the earliest times down to the battle of Re, at Tønsberg in 1177), which derived its name from the first word in the book, which means the world's circle. He became by degrees a very wealthy man, and had large possessions in the island. During a visit to Norway, early in Haakon's reign, he promised to use his influence to bring the Icelanders to accept the overlordship of Haakon, but on his return there in 1220 he did nothing to fulfil his promise.

In the conflict between Haakon and Skule, Snorre seems to have sided with the latter, and Haakon, after the death of Skule, determined to punish him. He sent orders to Snorre's enemy, Gissur Thorvaldssøn, to arrest or kill the historian, and Gissur attacked and killed Snorre in his home at Reykjaholt in 1241.

The king and Sigurd felt that it would conduce to the securing of the supremacy of the island, if they were able to bring the Icelandic bishops into more direct obedience to the see of Nidaros, and not leave them in the position which the bishops of Norway occupied during the Bremen metropolitanship.

An opportunity occurred in 1237, when it happened that both of the Icelandic bishoprics were vacant—that of Skaalholt by the death of Magnus Gissurssøn, who was the last married bishop in Iceland.

To the vacancies were nominated two priests named Magnus and Bjørn, and they came to Nidaros to be consecrated by Sigurd. The archbishop, however, on the ground of their election being invalid, refused to do so, and applied to Pope Gregory IX., who in August, 1237, ordered him to suspend both of the bishops-elect. Bjørn went to Rome to plead his cause, but died on the way back; and Magnus went back to Iceland, where he was afterwards drowned. Then the archbishop decided to fill up the vacancies himself, and consecrated two Norwegians, Sigurd of Selje to Skaalholt, and Botolf of Elgesæter to Hole, and sent them to Iceland, where they were accepted. Still Iceland remained independent, but a gradual movement towards acknowledging the authority of the Norwegian king went on. William of Sabina is said to have strongly urged the Icelanders to submit to Haakon. Finally, in 1256, a part of Iceland agreed to pay *skat* to Haakon, and in 1262 the remainder of the island acknowledged Haakon's sovereignty. The country, however, still retained its own self-government and laws. In 1262 Greenland came also under the supremacy of Norway.

Archbishop Sigurd, who had occupied such a prominent place in the history of his time, died in 1252, and was succeeded by Sørle of Hamar, who only lived a year after his consecration and died in 1254, and was followed by Einar Gunnarssøn, a member of a well-known family in Trøndelagen.

The new archbishop urged upon the king the great importance of making provision for the succession of his two sons during his lifetime, so as to avoid disputes, but the king would not take any definite step. In 1257 the king's eldest son, Haakon, died, and one difficulty respecting the succession was removed. The question, however, was not allowed to drop, for experience showed how dangerous to the peace of the country was a doubtful law of succession, as the older one of the days of St. Olaf, and the more recent one which the bishops and Archbishop Eystein in the time of Magnus Erlingssøn and his father, Erling Skakke, were not in agreement. The latter, which we have at the commencement of the older Gula *Thing's* law, decreed that he should be king of Norway who was the *legitimate* son of the king of Norway, except in cases of imbecility or vicious living, when the archbishop, bishops, &c., were to choose another son of the same father,* or the next-of-kin.

This law, as we have seen, was strenuously and successfully contested by Sverre and others, and illegitimacy was not an obstacle to succession.

In 1260 the king and the archbishop again discussed the matter, and finally an agreement was arrived at and a new

---

* Provision was also made for the temporary filling of the throne if the king was absent from the land.

law promulgated at the Frosta *Thing*. There we read that
the king, " with the counsel and consent of his son, King
Magnus, Archbishop Einar, his suffragans, *lendermænd*,
clergy, decreed that he should be king in Norway who was
the king of Norway's eldest legitimate son, but if there is
no legitimate son, then shall the king's son be king although
he be not legitimate ; and if there be none of these, he shall
be king of Norway who is Odel born and next-of-kin and of
the royal race."

This law was finally accepted by the various *Things* of
Norway, and became henceforth recognized as the law of
succession. It will be seen that the arrangement arrived
at, after long years of struggle, was a compromise. The
Church had hitherto insisted that only the legitimate son
should succeed, whereas the old law of succession from
St. Olaf's days did not insist on this as a necessary qualifi-
cation. Henceforth the legitimate son must be king, if
there be one surviving, but failing a legitimate heir, the old
custom was allowed to stand. The absolute claim of the
hierarchy to arrange the succession was thus, to a considerable
extent, restricted ; whilst at the same time their contention
that the legitimate son should be king was recognized.

Haakon was able to induce the bønder of the south
to make a new offering to the maintenance of the Church
in Trondhjem and Oslo. It was agreed that a penny for
each head of cattle on a farm should be contributed, and
thus divided—two-thirds to the support of the *Dom kirke*
at Nidaros this was known as the Olaf's *skat*, and one-
third to Oslo, called the Halvard's *skat*.

In 1261, at the marriage of Haakon's son Magnus, to
Ingeborg, daughter of the Danish king, a very unusual
course was taken. It was suggested that Magnus and his
wife should be crowned; he had already, as we have seen,
been named as king by the *Thing*, but a coronation was an
entirely new departure. After some consideration, Haakon

consented, and the ceremony was performed by Archbishop Einar.

In the summer of 1263 King Haakon sailed with a large fleet and army to Scotland, to enforce his supremacy over the Hebrides. A fierce but indecisive battle was fought at Largs, in the Clyde, and afterwards Haakon and his fleet retired to the Orkneys for the winter. Here Haakon died on December 23rd, 1263, at the age of sixty, having held the throne of Norway for the long period of forty-six years; his body was in the spring brought to Bergen and buried in Christ Church Cathedral, where his famous grandfather was interred. Archbishop Einar died in Norway a few months before the king.

During the reign of Haakon the monastic orders in Norway were reinforced by the introduction of the two recently-founded orders of the Dominicans and Franciscans. The first Dominican in Norway was a monk named Salomon, who was driven there by stress of weather on a voyage to Denmark, and who, in Jarl Skule's time, visited Nidaros, where he was favourably received. The order quickly gained ground in Norway, and in 1240 had monasteries in Nidaros, Bergen, and Oslo.

The Franciscans seem to have come first in 1230, and they soon had monasteries in Konghelle, Tønsberg, and Bergen.

Some very interesting papal letters were sent to Norway during the reign of Haakon and his immediate predecessor, and they throw a curious light on the life of the people, especially in the remoter dioceses in the widespread province of Nidaros. The archbishop in 1205 applied to the pope (Innocent III.) to know whether it was permissible to substitute beer for water as the "matter" in holy baptism. We might naturally imagine that whatever else were wanting in Norway water was always procurable. The pope, however, was quite clear in his reply that nothing but water could be used in the administration of this sacrament. It is curious that this question was more than once submitted to the papal decision, for we find again, in 1241, Gregory IX. writes an almost similar letter to Archbishop Sigurd, and lays down the same rule as his predecessor.

Another question was submitted to Gregory IX. with respect to the elements in the Holy Communion. The archbishop inquired whether, when the Eucharist was wanting (*deficiente eucharistia*), owing to the lack of corn and wine, they might communicate the people with any other sort of bread, along with beer or any other drink. The pope replied that neither one nor the other was to be done under any circumstances (*quod neutrum est penitus faciendum*), but that the form should be "*visibilis panis de frumento et vini de uvis.*" He concludes by saying that, as had become the custom in other places, "*panis simpliciter benedictus*" could be given to the people.[*] The meaning of this suggestion seems to be that the poor faithful in the remote dioceses would have to be contented with the "oblata," or the *pain béni* of France.

With reference to the long-standing question of the celibacy of the clergy, and the supposed permission of Cardinal Nicholas Breakspeare for the priests to contract matrimony, Gregory IX. wrote (in May, 1237) to Archbishop Sigurd to sternly forbid the practice. In his letter he says that they could show no documentary evidence whatever for this, and that his predecessor of blessed memory could not have granted permission for such an enormity. The plea of ancient custom urged by the clergy, instead of improving, made matters worse—"*peccatum non minuat sed augmentet.*"

The reign of Haakon was on the whole a very prosperous time for Norway, and after the death of Duke Skule, in

* The pope's letter will be found in *Norges Gamle Love*, Vol. IV., page 108, and in "Diplomatarium Norvegicum," Vol. I., No. 16.

1240, when his power was fully established, he became a person of great importance in the North. He was in very great favour with the Popes Gregory IX. and Innocent IV., and the latter tried to induce him to join in an attack on Frederick II., and also to be a candidate for the Imperial crown ; but Haakon had no intention of entertaining such a project, and shrewdly declared that "he was ready to fight against the enemies of the *Church,* but not all of the Pope's."* His alliance was esteemed by many of the princes of Europe, and his daughter Christina was married to Prince Philip of Castile, the brother of Alfonso the Wise. It was this marriage which led to the building of a church dedicated to St. Olaf in Spain, as the princess begged her husband to erect a church to the honour of the patron saint of her native land, which it seems he did.

---

* "This, the said king declared to me, Matthew, who wrote this, and attested it with a great oath."—Matthew Paris (Bohn's edition, Vol. II., page 415).

From a Photograph by]   [T. Olaf Willson.
                    ST. OLAF.

From a Wooden Figure (15th Century) originally in Fjeld
      Church, Søndhordland, now in Bergen Museum.

[To face p. 208.

CHAPTER XIV.

MAGNUS LAGABØTER AND THE TØNSBERG CONCORDAT —ERIK PRESTEHADER.

Jon Raude, Archbishop—Magnus's Codification of the Law—The Tønsberg Concordat—Its Terms—Death of Magnus—Erik *Prestehader* Succeeds—Conflict between the Regents and the Archbishop —Jon Flies to Sweden and Dies there—The Pope Appoints, *per provisionem*, Bishop Jørund as Primate—The Provincial Council of Nidaros—Disputes in the Church—Death of Erik.

No more striking proof of the wisdom of Haakon Haakonssøn's legislation respecting the succession to the crown could have been shown, than the peaceable way in which his son Magnus succeeded his father on the throne. The new monarch had been accepted as his father's successor during Haakon's lifetime, and, unlike any former king of Norway, had already received his crown. Magnus was at home when his father died, having been left in charge of the country when the expedition to Scotland started. The new king inherited much of the ability of his race, but was of a more yielding disposition than his father, and above all things wished to live in peace with those around him. His early education, which had proceeded almost on the same lines as if he were intended for holy orders, had made him a man of very considerable learning, and also inclined to listen most favourably to the demands of the Church. Above all things, the desire to promote the welfare of his people and fulfil the responsibilities of his royal office was the ambition of his life. He is known in history as Magnus *Lagabøter* (the improver of the laws), a title of which any king might well be proud.

The death of Einar left the see of Nidaros vacant at the time of Magnus's accession, and the chapter then elected Birger, a monk of the monastery of Tautra, near Nidaros. This man was the son of a priest (a circumstance which was not likely to make him favourably received at Rome), and required, as in the case of Haavard of Bergen,* a papal dispensation before he could be consecrated. Birger went to Rome in 1264, but just at the time he got there Urban IV. died, and the new pope, Clement IV., did not succeed until February, 1265. Strange to say, nothing more is heard of Birger, who probably died at Rome; and we find Urban IV. (possibly to punish the Nidaros chapter for electing Birger) handing over the choice of a new archbishop to the heads of four of the chief monastic orders in Norway. These men selected Haakon, bishop of Oslo, for the metropolitan see. As he was already a bishop it was not necessary for him to go to Rome for consecration, and the pallium did not arrive for him in Norway until 1267, when it was brought there by a member of the Nidaros chapter, Jon Raude (Red John), who came with it in January, 1267. The new archbishop, however, only lived until the August following, and Jon Raude was elected as his successor, and went to Rome for consecration in 1268, and then returned to his see.

The war with Scotland, which the king had inherited from his father, was brought to a conclusion in 1266 by the Treaty of Perth, in which Magnus, in exchange for his nominal rule over the Hebrides and Man, was to receive an annual tribute from the Scottish kings, as well as a sum of money to be paid down. It is remarkable that in this treaty, while the Norwegian rule over the Hebrides ceased, the authority of the see of Nidaros over the diocese of Sodor (Norwegian, *Suderøerne*) and Man still remained.

* See page 190.

After having obtained peace, King Magnus set himself to carry out his great design of having but one law for the whole of Norway. Hitherto, as we have seen, there were practically four parliaments or *Things* which legislated for the land—the Frosta *Thing* for the north, the Gula *Thing* for the west, and the Eidsiva and Borgar *Things* for the central and south-eastern parts, the Oplands and Viken, &c.

The king, in his journeys, explained his project to the different *Things*, and they expressed their willingness to comply with his wishes. But now a difficulty arose. In all the old laws of the four legislative assemblies there were from the time of St. Olaf two divisions, the general civil law and the *Kristenret*, and any attempt on the part of the *Things* to deal with the latter at once aroused the hostility of the Church. The new archbishop, Jon Raude, had not spent his time in Rome, without being well indoctrinated with the papal theories of the relations of the Church to the State, and in him, Magnus found an opponent. The king had secured the adhesion of the southern *Things* to his scheme in the years 1267—8, and the new archbishop arrived back in Norway in time for the meeting of the Frosta *Thing* in 1269. The theory of the archbishop was that while the king could promulgate laws for the State, it was the sole province of the Church to legislate in all ecclesiastical matters. The consequence of the primate's opposition was, that the new code of laws was issued without practically any ecclesiastical section, and only contained a confession of faith, and a recognition of the royal authority to legislate for the State, and of the Church to deal with all things relating to its government. Magnus's new code was finally published and accepted for the whole country about the year 1274. It will be seen that the Church had now gained a very important victory over the State, in the recognition of its power to legislate for all ecclesiastical affairs, and the time was now opportune for insisting on a full recognition of its rights from the king and nation.

The interregnum which followed the death of Pope Clement IV. was terminated by the election of Gregory X. in 1271, and in the following year the new pope issued the summonses for the general council, to be held at Lyons in 1274. To this, of course, the Norwegian primate and his suffragans were called, and the archbishop, like the other metropolitans, was required to report on the state of the Church in his province.

It seemed well to both parties in Norway that some formal agreement, with regard to the relations of the Church to the State, should be arrived at before the council met, and be there submitted to the pope for his approval. With this end in view the archbishop called a provincial council to meet in Bergen in 1273, and the king summoned all the principal men of the kingdom at the same time. After a long discussion a number of articles were agreed upon between the representatives of the Church and State, which were, on the whole, very favourable to the claims of the former.

With this agreement the archbishop and bishops went to the council at Lyons, and at the conclusion of the general business of the assembly, the Bergen agreement was submitted to Gregory X. for his sanction. The pope approved all that had been done, but added some new clauses, which included the offering of the king's crown on the altar at Nidaros and the giving over to the Church (in the case of a minority of the Crown) the government of the country. Magnus, who was most willing to grant great privileges to the Church, was, however, quite firm in rejecting these additions of the pope, and things were now as they had been before the meeting of the general council.

Both parties, however, desired peace, and the archbishop was fully cognizant of the greatness of the concessions he had received, and did not wish to drive matters too far ; and the king was willing to give all he could, without encroaching too much on the royal prerogative.

A new meeting was therefore called at Tønsberg in 1277, at which all the representatives of the Church and State were present, and what is known in history as the "Tønsberg Concordat" was agreed upon. The principal points of this new settlement, which was practically the same as that arrived at in Bergen in 1273, with a few modifications, were as follows :—*

1. The archbishop, on behalf of the Church, abandoned all claim to choose the king, and to insist on the offering of the crown at Nidaros, so long as there was a lawful heir to the throne. But failing such heir, the archbishop and the bishops were to have a preponderating voice in the choice of the king ; but they were, in such case, to make a declaration that they acted solely for the good of the kingdom.

2. The clergy were to be entirely exempt from lay jurisdiction of all kinds, even when there were cases in which a layman was involved. Also all cases of which the Church had any cognizance by canon law—e.g., marriage, wills, patronage, tithes, oaths, Church property, perjury, simony, public morals, &c.—were to come before the ecclesiastical courts.

3. The right of patronage to churches of all kinds was handed over to the bishops.

4. The election of bishops and abbots to be free from all interference. The nominee, however, before his election was confirmed, had to inform the king, who had a right to protest against the candidate.

* The Latin original will be found in the *Norges Gamle Love*, Vol. II., page 462.

5. All ecclesiastical persons were exempted from military service, except in cases of great emergency, approved by the bishop.

Other articles allowed the archbishop a retinue of one hundred men, and the bishops forty. The archbishop's rights to export corn to, and to trade in falcons from, Iceland were confirmed, also his privilege of coining money. Pilgrims were to be protected.

Finally it was agreed that in all disputes arising from this concordat the archbishop and the king should each appoint a man to decide all questions, and if they could not agree a third person was to be called in.

It will at once be seen, when we contrast these terms with the points in dispute since the time of Sverre, what a striking victory the Church had won, and how much the ecclesiastical power had gained from the State. It is true the archbishop was not able to extort from the king the submission which had been demanded from Magnus Erlingssøn. In spite of his gentle and peace-loving nature, he had enough of the spirit of Sverre, and of his father, to refuse to hold his kingdom as a grant from the Church. Nevertheless the Church had received an enormous increase of her power, and gained privileges and control over the laity above that which was enjoyed in almost any other country in Europe. It is not a little remarkable that this concordat was completed and sworn to by both parties, without any consultation with, or sanction of, the pope, and at the same time his additions to the Bergen agreement of 1273, were abandoned by the Church.

The chiefs of Norway agreed very unwillingly to the terms of the concordat, but they did so in the interests of peace, and the hope of finally putting an end to the disputes, which had lasted so long and done so much harm.

It was at this time that King Magnus, probably with a desire to strengthen the power and authority of the chiefs, gave them new titles.   The *lendermænd,* or feudatories, were henceforth called barons, and the *hirdmænd*, or king's special followers, attached to the court, were named knights.   From this time a special caste of nobility began to arise in Norway, different from the ancient days when all bønder were equal, and the chiefs were generally the bønder who owned the greatest possessions.

Magnus, in a well-meant endeavour to conciliate the Church, took the very unpopular step of extending tithe to all kinds of produce, both of land and sea, and he also conferred many extra privileges upon the archbishop and bishops.

These various concessions and privileges, which the Church had obtained through the mediumship of Archbishop Jon, were not likely to remain unused.   The archbishop at once set to work to have his new ecclesiastical law, based on the Concordat, formally promulgated.   With this in view he summoned a provincial council to meet in Bergen in the summer of 1280, and the king called all the chiefs at the same time, with the intention of having his young son Erik crowned there.

King Magnus, in spite of the great concessions he had made, does not seem to have been very hopeful that they would finally settle all disputes.   " Wait until I am three years dead and you will see," were his foreboding words to his followers when they spoke of the matter.

Magnus did not live to see the council.   He had long been ailing, and died in Bergen on the 9th of May, 1280, at the early age of 42 years.   He was hardly a strong enough man for the difficult part he had to play, and his love of peace often led him to give way, when perhaps the interests of his kingdom demanded firmness.   The great work of his reign was his securing one law for the whole kingdom, for which he well deserved to be held in honour by all his people.

It was during this reign that the Hanseatic League gained a footing in Norway, and though it led to an increase of trade, it ended by the foreigners getting it all into their own hands, to the manifest injury of the country, until at last the power of the great league was broken. The trade of Norway with England had considerably increased in the thirteenth century, and from the year 1200 there was free trade between the two countries.

The death of Magnus Lagabøter left the Norwegian Church at the summit of its power. By the Concordat of Tønsberg it had gained a great victory over the State, which the subsequent grants of the king confirmed and strengthened. But the very completeness of the victory contained the elements which led to the subsequent loss of power ; and the grants of the king, especially in the matter of tithes, aroused a very deep feeling of resentment in the minds of the people, which before long made itself felt.

At first, however, the power of the Church appeared to be supreme. The council, and the meeting of the chiefs, assembled in Bergen, where the archbishop arrived on June 16th, 1280. The first business which came before the meeting was, in consequence of Magnus's death, the corona-tion of his son Erik,* who was then a boy of only twelve years of age. The late king had intended to have had his son crowned (following the precedent in his own case) on June 24th, but difficulties arose between the chiefs (or barons as they were now called) and the archbishop respecting the coronation oath. The form in which the archbishop wished it, was very unpalatable to the chiefs ; but they did not feel themselves at the time, strong enough to do more than object to its terms, and the archbishop had

---

* The name *Prestehader* (the priest hater), by which Erik is known, seems to be quite undeserved. The conflicts with the Church were fiercest during his minority, and when he came of age his influence was always on the side of peace and moderation.

his way.   Erik was crowned in the cathedral on July 2nd,
and took the following oath: "To the bishops and clergy
I shall yield all fitting honour, and I shall hold intact what
has been given by the kings to the Church in accordance
with the compact between the Church and the kingdom.
Wrong laws and bad customs—namely, those which are
against the freedom of the holy Church—I shall abolish
and ordain better ones." This oath, by an oversight on
the part of the archbishop, was not, as usual in the case
of a minority, sworn by the chiefs, to whom, along with
the queen mother, Ingeborg, the regency during the king's
minority was committed.

The archbishop now proceeded with his council, which
was attended by all the bishops of Norway, and also those
of Skaalholt and Hole, in Iceland, and the bishops of the
Færoe Islands and Sodor and Man.   The council drew up
a number of regulations with reference to the ban of the
Church, which was to be pronounced against any one who
dared to infringe on the terms of the Tønsberg Concordat,
or who brought the clergy into any civil court of law, &c.
He was also anxious to have his new version of the
Kristenret fully confirmed and adopted.

But already the reaction had begun, and the archbishop
found he had not to deal with a young lad, but with a
number of barons who would pay but little heed to the
threats which he might utter.   The two principal men in the
new council of regency, which managed the affairs of the
kingdom, were Bjarne Erlingssøn and Bjarne Lodinssøn.
The regents now issued an ordinance, in which were
many things directly in conflict with the terms of the
Tønsberg Concordat, and which was plainly intended as a
challenge to the archbishop and the Church.   Jon at first
tried to get the regents to withdraw from the position they
had taken up, and threatened excommunication, but found
that they were quite indifferent to this.   Then, as a

compromise, both parties agreed to lay the case before the pope, and the archbishop left Bergen and returned to Nidaros. Matters remained for some time longer without any very serious move on either side, and the popular feeling against the claims of the Church, especially in the matter of tithes, increased.

In 1281 the regents negotiated the marriage of the young king, with Margaret the daughter of Alexander III. of Scotland, without consulting the primate. The princess arrived in Bergen in the August of that year, where the wedding was solemnized by the archbishop. In the midst of the festivities, however, the quarrel broke out afresh, the archbishop objecting to the presence of one of the chiefs whom he had excommunicated; and very soon after left for Nidaros, having excommunicated Bjarne Erlingssøn and Andres Plytt, for the crime of procuring from the young king a revocation of his privilege of coining money.

Very soon after Jon left Bergen, Andres Plytt died, and then followed a curious incident. The clergy refused to permit the bells of the churches to be rung at the funeral, as Andres was under the ban, but the regents' men broke open the doors of the church towers and had them rung in spite of them. They then turned on the Bergen clergy, and gave them the choice of ignoring the excommunications or of leaving the country, and the priests in Bergen preferred the former.

The regents now took stronger measures. They ordered the new system of tithes to be given up and the old system again to be universal, and further, in defiance of the council of Bergen and the Tønsberg agreement, decreed that the lay judges should have the power to try, as in former days, all cases which came under the ancient *Kristenret*. The appeal to the pope, on which both parties were agreed, did not lead to anything. Martin IV. was at that time on the papal throne. When the case came on the representatives of the regents demanded that the pope should send a legate to Norway to abrogate the Tønsberg Concordat, and on this being, very naturally, refused, they left Rome, and the matter practically ended.

The king's council now proceeded further against the clergy, and arrested several who stood by the archbishop and confiscated their property. The strife grew so great that at last Archbishop Jon and Bishops Andreas of Oslo and Thorfinn of Hamar, were obliged to leave the country, the archbishop taking refuge in Sweden.

The regents then sent Jon Brynjulfssøn to Nidaros. He seized the property of the archbishop and the chapter, and took up his abode in the archbishop's palace, where, to the great scandal of the faithful, he actually dared to sleep in the archbishop's own bed.

Jon did not long survive his exile. He died at Skara, in Sweden, on December 21st, 1282, and was buried there, as the regents would not permit his body to be brought to Nidaros ; but a year afterwards the permission was given, and it was disinterred and conveyed to his own cathedral.

Jon Raude was much beloved by his friends, who gave him the name of "The Steadfast." That he was steadfast in the maintenance of the claims of the Church there can be no doubt, but he does not seem to have been at all as great a man as his famous predecessors, Eystein and Erik, or to have known how best to use the great victory he had won. With a little more tact and discretion he might have kept the peace and avoided the fresh outbreak between the Church and State. The two other bishops went to Rome first, and then Thorfinn of Hamar went to Doest, in Flanders, where he died,* and Andreas of Oslo made peace and returned to his see. At this time it would seem that a

* Daae "*Norges Helgener*," page 177.

very general attack was made on Church property in different places, especially in those dioceses which were left without bishops, and many of the chiefs or barons were guilty in this respect.

The king, who had now, of course, attained his legal majority (though guided largely by the counsel of Bjarne Erlingssøn and others), found it necessary to intervene for the protection of the Church's property. In 1283 he, along with his brother, Duke Haakon, issued a proclamation taking the see of Nidaros under his protection, and ordering that all the tithes and fines should be paid which were due, but they were to be computed according to the old *Kristenret*, and not after the recent arrangement with King Magnus. It was felt by many that the regents had gone too far in the strife against the archbishop, and this feeling was intensified by the troubles which came upon the country at this time. There was much sickness among men and animals; the harvests had been very bad, almost producing famine in places. The young Queen Margaret died in 1283, and several of the chief men; and the king had a very narrow escape from death through an accident when out riding. In all these calamities, the mass of the people saw an evidence of the anger of Heaven at the way the Church had been treated. The see of Nidaros had been some time vacant, and no one seemed to very much desire such a dangerous post. In 1284 the chapter at last chose Bishop Narve of Bergen, but the pope raised objections against him. Then another attempt was made, and a member of the chapter, Eindride, was chosen, and an embassy was sent to Rome to procure the papal sanction.

The ambassadors on arriving at Rome had interviews with Honorius IV., and the result was that he set aside the nominee of the chapter, and appointed, *per provisionem*, Jørund, bishop of Hamar, in February, 1287, to the archbishopric, but owing to the death of Honorius IV., and the delay in appointing his successor, it was not until October, 1288, that Jørund was invested with the pallium at Nidaros.

The new archbishop had a very difficult part to play, and it can hardly be said he was equal to it, though the Saga says "he was firm in friendship, generous to his followers, and a dignified man." He began his episcopate in Nidaros by a liberal distribution of excommunications among the chiefs who had attacked the Church, including Jon Brynjulfssøn, whom we have before mentioned. The new archbishop and the bishops, were averse to continuing the strife with the State, in which Jon had suffered such a severe defeat, and seem to have desired, if possible, to come to terms with the king and his counsellors, as soon as they could. The Tønsberg Concordat was the high-water mark of the Church's power in Norway, and the attempt of Jon to carry it out in all its fulness, had provoked the reaction which led to his and the other bishops' banishment. Now the prelates were actuated with a desire to save as much as they could from the storm which had burst upon them.

Soon after Jørund's enthronement in Nidaros, a suitable opportunity occurred of coming to an understanding with the State. The king and his brother Haakon came on a pilgrimage to Nidaros (1289), and while there he and the archbishop seem to have come to terms. The following May, 1290, the king and Duke Haakon issued a letter in which they stated that they had come to an agreement with the archbishop and bishops, in which they had decided to revert to the old *Kristenret* which prevailed in the country before the Tønsberg Concordat, and that this should include tithes and fines, &c., about which so many complaints had been made by the people. Thus again the contending parties in Church and State went back to the ground they had before occupied. In the truce with Haakon Sverressøn in 1202 it was, "as in 1152"; so now it was, "as before the Tønsberg Concordat." The Church had, however, gained immensely in power from the time of the respite which followed the great struggle under Erik, and could afford to abandon its claims of supremacy over the State when it had obtained practical independence of royal control. The Tønsberg Concordat was not formally abrogated, but became a dead letter, and the peace now brought about lasted for a very long period. It was not until 1458 that the Tønsberg Concordat became again recognized, under Kristian I. of Denmark.

Peace having been thus secured, the archbishop turned his attention to the state of the Church in Norway, and called a provincial council in Nidaros in August, 1290. The bishops found that there were many matters in the life of the clergy and people which needed reform, and they issued a number of very useful canons. Among other things they ordered all parish priests to preach every Sunday and instruct the people about baptism and confirmation, and also to be diligent in teaching both young and old the Creed, Lord's Prayer, and *Ave Maria*, and to see that those who did not learn were punished. They were also to see that due reverence was paid to the Blessed Sacrament both in church and when it was borne to the sick and dying. The priests were not permitted to duplicate Mass on Sundays, except on the great festivals or where they had to serve two churches, &c.

In the monastic establishments it was ordained that sacred writings should be read at meal times, " so that the ears should not be open to slander and offence."

The remaining years of the reign of King Erik the Church and State never came into conflict. The archbishop, indeed, did his best to keep on good terms with the king, and agreed to be considered as one of the king's jarls, and did homage for his temporal possessions, which act was regarded with much disfavour by the Church generally.* The archbishop and the bishops were too much occupied in settling internal disputes to have time, even if they had the inclination, to enter upon any fresh conflict with the State.

In Norway, as in every other country of Europe, many disputes had broken out between the secular clergy and the mendicant orders, and as they went on almost exactly the same lines as elsewhere, we need not enter upon them at any length. In addition to these disputes, fierce quarrels broke out between the cathedral chapters and their bishops. In Nidaros a prolonged dispute was maintained between Archbishop Jørund and the chapter with regard to their respective rights, in which, after an appeal to the pope, the victory rested in the main with the chapter. A similar struggle went on at Stavanger with Bishop Arne, which lasted until the death of the latter in 1303.

The other disputes were between the cathedral chapters and the mendicant orders. The first was in Bergen, where the clergy and chapter were very hostile to the Dominicans. The latter decreed that none of the clergy should give them either "shelter, food, or alms." The bishop, Narve, who had himself been a Dominican, tried in vain to have this order recalled, but the hostility of the chapter and secular clergy was too strong for him.

In Oslo the dispute was between the chapter and the Franciscans. Duke Haakon had given the monks material for building a church, and they had set to work, when the chapter promptly gave orders to have it pulled down. The pope was appealed to, and ordered the bishop and representatives of the chapter to Rome, and they found it prudent under these circumstances to give way.

King Erik died in Bergen in July, 1299, in his thirty-first year. By his marriage with Margaret, the daughter

* This arrangement lasted until King Haakon's time, when it was done away with at Oslo in 1310.

of Alexander III. of Scotland, he had one daughter named Margaret. On her grandfather's death without leaving any son, she was accepted as the queen of Scotland, and it was arranged that she should marry Edward, the son of Edward I. of England. The "Maid of Norway," as young Margaret was called, sailed to take possession of her crown in 1290. She was then only eight years old. To the subsequent great misfortune of both Scotland and England, the young princess expired on her arrival at the Orkneys. King Erik married a second time, Isabella, the sister of Robert Bruce of Scotland, and by her he had one daughter, Ingeborg. On Erik's death his brother, Duke Haakon, succeeded him on the throne, and was crowned in Nidaros by Archbishop Jørund, in either the August or November following.

CHAPTER XV.

HAAKON V.

The last Male of Harald Haarfagre's line—New Law of Succession—
Archbishop Jørund's Council at Oslo—The King and Duke Erik—
The King procures the Appointment of a "Magister Capellarum
Regis"—His Policy in this—Death of Archbishop Jørund—Bishop
Arne of Bergen and his Quarrels—Murder of Duke Erik—Death of
Haakon.

HAAKON, who during his brother's lifetime had borne
the title of duke, succeeded Erik without any dispute. He
had for several years before his accession taken a prominent part in the government of the country, and practically
shared the royal power with the king. Haakon was a man
of much stronger character and force of will than Erik,
and he soon let it be felt, that he intended to rule with a
firm hand over both the barons and the Church.

He had seen, during his brother's reign, that the growing
power of the barons constituted a very serious danger to
the royal authority, and very soon after his accession he
detected some of them in treasonable correspondence, and
had Audun Hugleikssøn executed, and forced Bjarne
Lodinssøn to fly from the land.

The king was the last of the long race of Harald
Haarfagre in the male line, and not having any son he
was anxious to make a new arrangement with regard to
the law of succession. In 1302 he called an assembly
to meet in Oslo to arrange for this, and for the government of the country in the case of a minority. The
king had two daughters—one, Ingeborg, daughter of his
queen, Euphemia of Rügen, and another, Agnes, who was

illegitimate. Ingeborg was at this time only just a year old. The proposal respecting the inheritance was to permit the succession of the legitimate son of a legitimate daughter, next after the legitimate son's son, and before the legitimate brother. The king's object was in case his daughter Ingeborg lived, and became the mother of a son, that he should succeed. He also extended the legal period of a regency to the king's twentieth year instead of the twelfth. The regents were to be twelve in number, (and to include the chancellor); four of these were always to be attached to the king's person. The object of the reform was to include in the regency a certain number of officials, who would act as a check on the power of the barons. These changes, for some reason or other, the king omitted to have brought before the *Thing* for its formal acceptance.

Haakon now decided to find a suitable person to whom to betroth his infant daughter, and selected Duke Erik of Sweden, brother of the Swedish king Birger Magnussøn, a young man of great talents, and of a very ambitious turn of mind. He was the same year, 1302, betrothed to the baby princess Ingeborg. Duke Erik did his best to ingratiate himself with all the people in Norway, the barons and the clergy, and especially with the queen Euphemia, and set himself to form a party which he hoped might possibly be strong enough to place him on the throne. The king was mindful of all this, but for some years there was no open breach between him and the duke.

Archbishop Jørund and his chapter, had been on bad terms for a long time, and though an arrangement had been arrived at in 1299, the strife broke out again and raged more furiously than before. In 1302 the king went to Nidaros and held a *Thing*, and positively commanded the chapter to come to terms with the archbishop, which they did, but they were practically those of the last settlement, in which the archbishop got decidedly the worst of it.

The royal rebuke to the chapter was intended to save appearances, but the victory in reality rested with it.

Archbishop Jørund, however, did not spend all his energies in fighting with his chapter, but devoted himself as well to the care of his province. In 1306 he called a provincial council at Oslo, which was attended by all the Norwegian bishops, and also Erlend, of the Færoe Islands. Several very useful matters were arranged at this meeting. The rapid growth of the monastic establishments in Norway necessitated some attention to their condition. It was found that there was much ignorance amongst the brothers, and it was ordered that certain promising young men from the cloisters, were to be sent abroad to study, and maintained at the expense of these establishments.

A more serious abuse was dealt with in cases where it was found that nuns had received men as brothers into nunneries, and monks, women as sisters into monasteries. This was, in future, absolutely prohibited, and not to be tolerated "under any circumstances whatever." The bishops were directed to appoint suitable confessors.

The king now set himself to further curtail the power of the barons, or chiefs. From Oslo, in June, 1308, he issued an order by which the *sysselmænd* were brought directly under the king's control. The titles of jarl and *lendermand* were in future restricted to the king's sons and the jarl of the Orkneys. The present holders of these titles were to keep them for their lives. The king also created several new court officials, such as the standard-bearer, vice-chancellor, constable, &c. That Haakon was able to carry out such reforms was a manifest proof of his strength, and from this time onward, the growth of an aristocratic power in Norway, which might rival that of the king, seems to have been effectually stopped.

The relations between Haakon and Duke Erik had become more and more strained at this time, and the former saw plainly what were the duke's aims, and so he determined to break with him. The war which had dragged on for some years with Denmark was brought to an end in the September after the king's decree about the *lendermænd*, which we have just mentioned ; and an agreement was made by which the young princess Ingeborg was to be betrothed to Magnus, the son of the Swedish king, and nephew of Erik, king of Denmark. When Duke Erik of Sweden learned of this new arrangement, and saw that the king had decided to break with him, he, in the winter made a sudden attack on Oslo, and ravaged the country around. He failed, however, in an attempt on the fortress of Akershus, beside Oslo, and was obliged to retire to Sweden.

Just at this time King Haakon carried through a design which he had been meditating for some years, and which was intended to establish a powerful defence on his side against the authority of the bishops. We have seen how he had checked the growth of the power of the barons, and he wished also to enlist on his side an ecclesiastical force, which would defend him in any possible attacks from the archbishop and bishops.

The kings had before now felt, the want of a body of men who were learned and courtly enough to carry on negotiations, either with foreign powers or with their own people. At this time the clergy were practically the only men with any pretensions to learning in the kingdom. It had been usual from the earliest times for the kings to have attached to their persons, one or more priests (or bishops, as in the days of the two Olafs), who acted as what we would now call court chaplains. Some of these chaplains—*e.g.*, Martin, Sverre's chaplain—had become bishops, but the kings felt that if they were advanced to the position of diocesans and came under the direct influence of the Roman *curia*, they would soon very likely come into collision. Haakon's

idea, therefore, was to raise up in Norway a body of clergy
who were to be independent of episcopal control, and who
would be entirely devoted to the interests of the Crown.
There were at this time in his kingdom fourteen royal
chapels, to which the king, in spite of the various agree-
ments with the Church, seems to have retained the
patronage. The principal of these were, the royal chapel
in Bergen, known as the Apostles' Church, the Maria Kirke
in Oslo, St. Michael's Church in Tønsberg, and St. Olaf at
Agvaldsnæs,* not far from Haugesund. Some of the royal
churches were collegiate, and had a regular body of canons.
The king's idea was to unite these churches under one man,
with *quasi*-episcopal powers, and to form what, in modern
days, would correspond to an "exempt jurisdiction," or
"royal peculiar."

Haakon went to work very prudently. Instead of
negotiating with the archbishop, who was certain to oppose
such a scheme, he approached the pope directly. In
Clement V., the nominee of the French king, who brought
the papal seat to Avignon, he found the man for his purpose. After some delay he got the pope to issue a letter in
February, 1308, in which the pope stated that "on account
of the king's merits, which made him worthy of the favour
of the Apostolic see," he gave him leave to carry out his
plan. The provost of the Apostles' Church in Bergen was
to be the head of all the royal chapels, with the title of
"Magister Capellarum Regis," and to this officer was given
permission to wear a mitre and to carry a crozier, and to
"visit" the royal chapels under his care. The first man to
hold this office was Finn Halldorssøn, the provost of the
royal chapel in Bergen.

Thus Haakon triumphed over both the temporal aristocracy, and inflicted also a severe blow to the power of the

* This church can still be seen, with an ancient *bautasten*, or mono-
lith, beside it, known as *Jomfru Maria's Synaal* (the B. V. M.'s needle).

bishops. Indeed, at this time he was to all intents and purposes an absolute monarch.

Archbishop Jørund did not long survive this triumph of royal diplomacy. He died at Nidaros in April, 1309, and to the end of his days, in spite of the various " settlements" which had been made, kept up the fight with his chapter. He was not a man of the same lofty stamp as some of his predecessors, and his bad temper and quarrelsome disposition kept him always in conflict with others. He did much, however, to improve the internal condition of the Norwegian Church by the legislation carried through in the two important councils, over which he presided at Nidaros and Oslo. His successor was found in Eiliv Arnessøn, who is described as being "a great chief, of good manners."

During the concluding years of Jørund's episcopate Bishop Arne, of Bergen, was ruling his diocese with a strong hand. At a diocesan synod held in Bergen in 1307 he issued stringent orders to enforce celibacy among his clergy. Many of them, like the clergy in other parts of Europe, were living with what were called in Norway *friller* (focariæ), a state of things which was quite approved of by their people. It was only gradually, and after a long time, that celibacy was even partially enforced among the parochial clergy. They long resisted the demands of the bishops and the pope, on the ground that Cardinal Nicholas in 1152 had expressly granted them permission to live in matrimony. In his cathedral town he had a long controversy with the Hanseatic merchants, who wished to escape the payment of tithe, on the ground that they were only there for a time ; but the bishop held, that those who spent the winter in Bergen were undoubtedly liable, and after a prolonged dispute, the point was finally settled in the bishop's favour.

It was hardly to be expected that the Norwegian bishops

would view with equanimity the "Magister Capellarum Regis," whose office they would naturally consider to be an encroachment on their own authority. Bishop Arne especially was of a temper which would not look with favour on this new official, whose residence was in his diocese. We find that he very soon quarrelled with Finn Halldorssøn, and in 1310 a great dispute broke out between them with reference to fees and tithes, which the latter claimed. The bishop quickly threatened excommunication, and Finn referred the matter to the pope, who, not wishing to offend the king, temporized, and, while not altogether backing up Finn, he ordered that the bishop should perform all episcopal offices for the *Magister*, but he confirmed the right of the king's official to wear the episcopal garments, &c. There were other disputes with this Dean of the Chapels Royal, as we might call him, but the office ceased to be of importance as soon as the union with Denmark began.

The pugnacious bishop of Bergen had also a quarrel with his metropolitan. The new archbishop, Eiliv, who was elected in 1309, did not go at once to the pope for consecration. He received a summons with the other bishops to the council of Vienne in January, 1310. He was consecrated in 1311, probably at Avignon. It was after his return that the archbishop demanded what was known in Norway as the *pallie-hjælp*, or subsidy, which consisted of a portion of the tithes of the *hoved kirker*, to defray the expenses of the journey to Rome or Avignon. It seems doubtful if this tax was first levied in Eiliv's days, or whether it had existed before. There does not seem to have been any refusal to pay this, but Arne was very angry when the archbishop appointed Finn Halldorssøn to collect it, and at once threatened to excommunicate any one who paid it to Finn. Then both sides appealed to the pope, and the matter seems at last to have ended in the archbishop's favour. We must now turn back to the

events of King Haakon's reign, and it is necessary to be
clear about them, as they have much to do with the
subsequent history.

We have seen that King Haakon had quarrelled with
Duke Erik, and had made peace with Denmark and
Sweden, at Copenhagen, in 1309. The king of Denmark
made an expedition into the south of Sweden on behalf
of his brother-in-law Birger, who was at war with Erik
and Valdemar, but had to retreat. Then Erik and Haakon
again came to terms, and a new peace was made at Helsingborg in 1310, by which it was arranged that Erik was
now to marry a niece of the Danish king. The wily Erik,
however, had other ideas, but agreed outwardly, and went
to the pope to procure a dispensation, as the Danish
princess was within the forbidden degrees. He seems to
have arranged *not* to get this, and returned to Sweden,
and then, in September, 1312, he and his brother went to
Oslo, and Erik married Ingeborg, and Valdemar, the other
Ingeborg, daughter of the late King Erik of Norway and
niece of King Haakon. The Danish king was naturally
very angry, but a peace was again made in 1313 at
Helsingborg. Matters thus remained for a couple of
years, but the dukes were on very bad terms with their
brother, King Birger.

In 1316 Erik's wife Ingeborg bore a son, to the great joy
of King Haakon, who now had a grandson to whom the
crown should go on his death, and Duke Erik was con-
fident that, as the father of the future king, he could
accomplish his designs with regard to the royal power.
But a terrible tragedy was at hand. In December, 1317,
King Birger invited his two brothers to visit him at the
Castle of Nykjøping, and professed a desire to be fully
reconciled to them. The two dukes accepted the offer and
went to the castle. The next night they were seized and
thrown into a dungeon, and in a month after, both were

dead—probably starved to death, or in some other way murdered.

This terrible crime roused a storm of indignation against Birger, and he was forced to fly from Sweden. Haakon came to the country to support the claims of his grandson, and the party of the murdered dukes defeated Birger, who had collected some forces at Skaane, in 1318. Birger's son Magnus, who had been held as a captive, was executed in Stockholm in 1320 by the dukes' party, for fear he should escape and raise forces against them. King Birger, who had taken refuge in Denmark, died there in 1321.

The murder of the two dukes was a terrible blow to King Haakon, who seems to have been in poor health at the time, and he never recovered from it. Feeling that his life would not last much longer, he called a meeting of the chiefs in Tønsberg in April, 1319, and there he caused them to swear allegiance to his little grandson. The eight principal officials and chiefs of his kingdom undertook in the most solemn manner to carry out Haakon's arrangements made in 1302 with respect to the regency, and they further undertook to guard against foreigners being placed in positions of authority in the country. The king's foreboding as to his approaching death was verified. He died the next month, on May 8th, 1319, in the forty-ninth year of his age, and with him the race of Harald Haarfagre, in the male line, became extinct, after having furnished Norway with rulers for three hundred and eighty-six years.

Haakon V. was a man much loved by his people generally, and was in almost all respects a very noble king. He was, like some of his immediate predecessors, a man of considerable learning for his time. He understood and could converse in Latin, and caused to be translated, under his own supervision, portions of the Old Testament from the Vulgate into Norwegian, as well as a selection from the lives of the saints. These works were read to the king

and his courtiers on Sundays during dinner. In his reign
the Church in Norway had reached perhaps its most prosperous period during the whole of the middle ages. The
constant strife between the royal and ecclesiastical power,
which had been very injurious to the cause of religion, had
practically ceased ; and, under the wise and judicious rule
of Archbishop Eiliv, abuses were checked and attention
closely paid to the instruction of the people in the tenets
of the faith. The various councils which were held, kept
the bishops and clergy in touch one with another, and the
abuses which were so prevalent in the south of Europe,
from the worldliness of the higher clergy, were but little
known in Norway. After Haakon's death the prosperity
of the Church continued, but only for a short time, when
a calamity befell the nation and the Church, which is
perhaps the best explanation of the extraordinary paralysis
of national and ecclesiastical life which manifested itself in
later years. This was the visitation of the terrible *Sorte
Død*, the Black Death, the result of which produced effects
more far-reaching perhaps in Norway, than in any other
country of Europe.

CHAPTER XVI.

MAGNUS ERIKSSØN AND THE GREAT CALAMITY, THE *SORTE DØD*.

The Union of Norway and Sweden—Provincial Council at Bergen—
Duchess Ingeborg deprived of Power—A *Drotsete* (Lord Protector)
appointed—Fire at Nidaros—Archbishop Paul's Council at Oslo—
Discontent in Norway—Sodor and Man finally separated from the
Norwegian Church—The Black Death comes from England to
Bergen, 1349—Its Ravages—The Desolation of the Church—
Archbishop Olaf's Council at Nidaros—Death of Magnus.

THE death of Haakon V. left the little three-years-old
Magnus Erikssøn the sole heir of the throne of Norway, in
accordance with the law of succession established by his
grandfather eighteen years before. The council of regency
appointed by Haakon at once took charge of the affairs of
the kingdom. As the throne of Sweden was practically
vacant—King Birger having been driven out of the country,
and his son Magnus, though still alive, being held as a
close prisoner in Stockholm—young Magnus Erikssøn was
therefore, failing these, the heir to the Swedish as well as
the Norwegian crown, a state of things which Haakon V.,
with all his foresight, does not seem to have contemplated.

The party of the murdered dukes, Erik and Valdemar,
held a meeting in Upsala to consider the question of the
succession to the crown ; and the upshot of this was that a
deputation, headed by the bishop of Linkjøping, went to
Oslo to confer with the Norwegian chiefs, including Archbishop Eiliv and the bishop of Stavanger. It was then
agreed that on the return of the Swedish delegates they
should advise that Magnus Erikssøn be chosen as king of

Sweden. Accordingly another meeting was held at Upsala, and on July 8th, 1319, he was formally accepted as king of Sweden.

Thus for the first time Sweden and Norway were united under one king. The two kingdoms were, however, only bound together by " the golden link of the crown." In all other respects they were to remain, as before, quite distinct and separate, with their own laws and customs and their own revenues. The king was to reside for a portion of the year in each kingdom, and his Swedish advisers were to have no authority in Norway, and *vice versâ*. In many respects the arrangement made at this time, was very much the same, as that which prevails between Norway and Sweden in our own day.

Although young Magnus may be said to have succeeded to the throne on his grandfather's death, his formal acceptance as king of Norway did not take place until a gathering at Tønsberg in August, 1319. The young king's mother, Ingeborg (the widow of Duke Erik), had a good deal to do with the management of affairs. She was little more than a child when Magnus was born, and was left a widow when only seventeen. She unfortunately came very much under the influence of a Danish nobleman, Knut Porse, who had designs on the crown of Denmark, and her conduct caused very great dissatisfaction in Norway.

We must now revert to ecclesiastical affairs. In 1320 Archbishop Eiliv summoned a provincial council in Bergen, which was held at a time when the young king and his mother were in the city. All the Norwegian bishops attended, and the bishops of the Orkneys and the Færoe Isles. Many of the decrees of this council are interesting from the light which they throw on the state of life which prevailed in the Church in Norway at this time. Several of them were similar to those we find in other countries, but some, of course, were intended to deal with the peculiar circumstances connected with Church life in Norway. The regulation of the monastic establishments proceeded on the same lines as that of Archbishop Jørund's council in Oslo in 1306, but the rules with respect to the parochial clergy, and the exercise of discipline among the laity, are interesting.

We find further legislation directed against the state of concubinage, in which many of the parochial clergy lived, now that matrimony had been absolutely forbidden. It was ordered that if any priest had a *frille* within a month from receiving notice of the decree, he should be fined four marks for a priest of a *hoved kirke*, and two marks for a *kapellan*, or a deacon; continuance in this, doubled the fine in a few days, and ultimately led to a forfeiture of the benefice.

The priests were ordered to keep the baptismal font clean, and to procure oil for extreme unction from the bishop every year. Stringent rules were made respecting the duty of the parish priests to baptize infants and to shrive the dying. If a priest was guilty of negligence in these matters he was to be suspended, but it was ordered that those who required the services of the priest must send a horse for him to ride, or a boat if the journey had to be performed by water, and the priest was not to be required to row in the boat.

Great care was to be exercised in the carrying of the *viaticum* to the dying, and the priest was permitted to bring it in a little bag,* which was hung round the neck, when he had to traverse difficult mountain paths, or, as was often the case, places where no path existed. If the priest's vestments were worn out, they were to be burned in the church and the ashes placed under the altar.

In the mixed chalice it was ordered that there should be

* This was also permitted by Archbishop Jørund.—Council at Nidaros in 1290.

more water than wine. This was to be done by the priest himself, and not the server. The rule was possibly intended to economize the wine, which, as we have already seen, was difficult to procure in some places.

Rules were made to enforce morality among the laity, and marriage within the prohibited degrees was strictly forbidden. It would seem to have been customary for many of the people to live together after betrothal, before the regular marriage took place, but if children were born after the banns had been called, and before the marriage had been celebrated, they were to be taken as legitimate. The *viaticum* was not to be given to a *frille*, unless the man she lives with agrees to marry her, or she separates from him. No unmarried women were to be churched. Fresh regulations were made respecting the attendance of the clergy at diocesan synods. In a country so large, and so difficult to travel through in those days, it was hard for the priests to leave their parishes to attend the synods in the bishop's cathedral. It was arranged that the priests of the *hoved kirker* should nominate those who were to attend, and all parish priests were to be chosen in turn. Before the priest left his parish to attend the synod, he was to see that he left no infants unbaptized, or no one unconfessed or unhouseled. The priests who remained at home had to take charge of the parishes of those who went, and before the representative went to the synod, he was to announce who was to be left in charge. When on his way to the cathedral city, the priest in passing through a parish was liable to be called on to do duty, but could not demand any fee for the same. When he got home from the synod, he was to tell those who remained behind, what new decrees had been made.*

The dissatisfaction with the conduct of the king's mother,

---

* For fuller details of the decrees of this council, see *Norges Gamle Love*, Vol. III., page 246 ; and Keyser, Vol. II., page 198.

the Duchess Ingeborg, which had been felt from the first, grew stronger as the years passed, and the chiefs now saw that some steps must be taken to deprive her of all power in the affairs of the kingdom. In February, 1323, a meeting was called at Oslo, at which the archbishop and the bishops of Hamar, Oslo, and Skaalholt were present. It was decided to ask the archbishop to select a man in whose care the kingdom should be placed. He chose Erling Vidkunssøn, a great chief of Bjarkø, in Haalogaland. This choice was approved by a *Thing* at Oslo, and all the chief men promised to support him. Erling was known as the *Drotsete*— of which title, perhaps, the best translation would be lord protector, or lord high constable—and for nine years he ruled the country in the king's name with great wisdom and moderation. The object of his appointment was to get rid of the Duchess Ingeborg, and in this it was successful. She remained in Norway for a short time, but deprived of the power she formerly possessed, and in 1327 marrying Knut Porse, who had been made Duke of Sondre Halland, she went to live in Denmark. She was left a widow a second time in 1330, and after that remained principally in Denmark.

The Drotsete was not to rule Norway without some troubles, for about the time of his appointment, the Russians attacked Haalogaland and devastated a part of the country, including the Drotsete's own estate. The assailants were partly heathen and partly Greek Catholics, who were regarded as heretics by the popes. To repel this attack was therefore something of the nature of a crusade. The treasury of Norway was rather low at the time, after the extravagances of the Duchess Ingeborg, and the Drotsete felt anxious to obtain the necessary funds for the purpose. He therefore approached the Church in order to procure help. The wise and patriotic Archbishop Eiliv was willing to assist, but some of the other bishops were decidedly hostile to the proposal, especially Bishop Audfin of Bergen, with whom many controversies were carried on during his episcopate. There was much disputing about the matter, but nothing finally was decided at the time, as a peace with the Russians was made, and the money was not therefore required. The point in dispute was, however, too important to be allowed to drop, and at a provincial council which was held in Bergen in 1327 it again came under discussion. Here Bishop Audfin came forward as the champion of those who wished the Church to be exempted from all payment of *skat*, and claimed that Archbishop Jon Raude's *Kristenret*, which would have exempted them from payment, should be approved. This, however, was firmly resisted by the Drotsete, and aided by the kindly moderation of the archbishop, wiser councils prevailed. The "*Kristenret* of Haakon the Old and Archbishop Sigurd" was held to be the law under which the Church was to be ruled. This was formulated in a proclamation or letter signed by the king, the Drotsete, and the chancellor, and the matter was finally settled.

The office of chancellor, which seems to have been in abeyance for some years, was now revived, and it was intended to be a compensation to the Church, by having such a high official (who was one of the clergy) in a post which had so much to do directly with the government of the kingdom. The new chancellor was Paul Baardssøn, a man of great learning, who had studied at Paris and Orleans and was learned in canon law. He was first a member of the Bergen chapter, but was at this time in that of Nidaros, and afterwards, as we shall see, reached the highest post in the Church.

On Easter Monday, April 4th, 1328, a great disaster befell Nidaros. The beautiful cathedral of Christ Church, the monument of the work of Archbishop Eystein and his immediate successors, was almost destroyed by fire. All the internal woodwork was burned, and the walls suffered, but not irreparably. The bells also were much injured. The archbishop sent out an appeal to all his suffragans, and to the principal men in Norway, for help in rebuilding the cathedral, which was liberally responded to.

In 1332 the young king, having now reached his sixteenth year, assumed the nominal control of the government, and Erling Vidkunssøn, the Drotsete, resigned his post. He had discharged the rather difficult duties of his office with great skill, and his firm but prudent rule had secured peace to the land. After his retirement the chancellor, Paul Baardssøn, was the king's chief adviser. Paul was, however, not long to remain chancellor, for in November, 1332, Archbishop Eiliv died, having practically held the see for twenty-three years, though he was not consecrated until two years after his election. Eiliv was a man who was universally respected in Norway, and under his wise government the Church attained very great prosperity in every respect. Though a strong Churchman he was not an intemperate advocate of her claims, and by his skilful pilotage he avoided many of the dangers which had so frequently caused strife between the Church and the State. He was too good a patriot not to recognize the injury which the fierce controversies of previous generations had done to Norway, as well, indeed, as to the Church over which he was called to rule. Paul Baardssøn was chosen as Eiliv's successor, and resigned his office as chancellor.

In the year 1335 the young king married Blanche, or Blanca, as she was called in Norway, the daughter of the duke of Namur, a woman of great cleverness, who soon acquired a complete ascendency over her weak husband. The year following Magnus was crowned in Stockholm as king of Sweden. It is not easy to arrive at an exact estimate of the character of Magnus, for the Swedish writers paint him in very dark colours, and ascribe all kinds of

vice and immorality to him, and the name which was
given to him of *Smek*, or the trifler, indicated that he had
but small regard for the responsibilities of his office.   But
on the other hand, the Norwegian writers speak of him in
a very different way, and some called him "The Good," and,
we are told, after his death regarded him as almost a saint.*
The truth probably lies between the two accounts, and it
was the hostility between the two countries which, when
one denounced the king as an evil-living trifler, caused the
other to paint him as a good and saintly man.   He was
certainly not a strong king, and utterly unfitted to hold
two kingdoms under his sceptre.

Magnus's weak rule, and his continued absence in
Sweden, led, as was only to be expected, to much discontent in Norway, which had been so long accustomed to its
own king.   To try and arrange matters the king called a
meeting at Baahus in August, 1339, but nothing definite
was arrived at.   It was, however, settled that during the
absence of Magnus in Sweden the archbishop and Bishop
Haakon, of Bergen, were to look after the government of
Norway, and with this, things were quiet for a time.

The year 1343 was remarkable for the consecration of
no less than six bishops in the province of Nidaros to fill up
sees vacant by death or resignation.   These were, Bergen
and Stavanger, the two Icelandic bishoprics of Skaalholt and
Hole, and Garde in Greenland.

Notwithstanding the arrangements mentioned above, the
discontent with Magnus burst forth again, and a strong
party desired the separation of the kingdoms of Norway
and Sweden.   At a meeting at Vardberg, in Sweden, in
1343, it was arranged that the king's two sons should
succeed him at his death, the elder Erik, taking Sweden,
and the younger Haakon, Norway.   Both of them were at
this time only children, but the arrangement seemed to

* See Daae's *Norges Helgener*, page 188.

promise (when it came into being) an end of the very unsatisfactory state of things which then prevailed.

In 1346 Archbishop Paul died, having held the see for a little more than twelve years. There was no very important event to mark his episcopate. During the latter part of it, he issued a long pastoral letter to the clergy and people, in which he gave many directions respecting the observance of the Church's rules in connection with holy baptism, confirmation, confession, &c., which showed how carefully all these sacraments were at this time administered in the Norwegian Church.

Paul's successor was Arne Einarssøn, who was one of the Nidaros chapter, and a nephew of Archbishop Eiliv.

We have already noticed that though the political connection between Norway and the Western Isles of Scotland and the Isle of Man had practically ceased, yet for ecclesiastical purposes the bishopric of Sodor and Man still remained a part of the province of Nidaros. About this time, however, the ecclesiastical connection was also to come to an end, though nominally it continued for a considerably longer period.

The last bishop of Sodor and Man who seems to have gone to Norway was Marcus, who was present at the coronation of King Erik in 1280. The bishops seem to have had a not unnatural objection to facing the dangers and discomforts, of the long voyage across the North Sea to Nidaros to receive consecration, and to have preferred the shorter journey to England, or the more interesting one to Avignon. In 1348, on the death of Bishop Thomas, William Russell, abbot of the Cistercian monastery of Rusheen, was chosen as his successor. Instead of going to Norway, he proceeded to Avignon, where he was consecrated by the cardinal bishop of Ostia. The reason for this was explained to the archbishop of Nidaros, by Pope Clement VI., in a letter which he wrote the following year (April, 1349). In this he mentions that his action in having William Russell consecrated was "by no means to be ascribed to any intention of the pope to detach the Sudreyan see from the *Provincia Nidrosiensis*, or to give any prejudice to his metropolitan rights, but only to the circumstance that this episcopate, as all others, or in general all ecclesiastical benefices, had been reserved by the pope for his own provision."* Thus, although nominally respecting the rights of the metropolitan of Nidaros over Sodor and Man, the pope's action practically put an end to them, and from this time onwards, no bishop of that see was consecrated at Nidaros. Still, for nearly a hundred years longer, Sodor and Man was officially regarded as a part of the Nidaros province.

Magnus in 1348 attacked the Russians as a sort of crusade, and gained some successes; but on his retirement they overran Finland, and again attacked Haalogaland and Sweden, and this still more increased the hostility of the Swedes to the king.

Archbishop Arne, following the example of his predecessor Paul, sent out another pastoral letter very much on the same lines as that of the latter, and with the same careful attention to details in the religious life of the people. There is no doubt that at this time the Church in Norway was in many ways an example to the other national Churches of Europe. Its remoteness had preserved it from many of the abuses and corruptions which at this time were manifesting themselves in other lands, and the constant succession of provincial councils which we have noted, were an evidence that the primates desired to maintain a high standard of life, both in the monastic establishments and among the secular clergy, even if the rules laid down were not strictly adhered to. But a great disaster was

* See "Chronica Regum Manniæ et Insularum," edited by P. A. Munch, page 147; and Appendices 17 and 18.

now to fall upon the land and to inflict a blow from which the Church never fully recovered, and which crippled its usefulness down to the day, when the avarice of the Danish kings and their courtiers, swept away most of its fabrics, confiscated its revenues, and broke the long line of the historic episcopate.

In 1349 an English merchant ship sailed into the harbour of Bergen and brought to Norway the awful plague which had devastated so many European lands, and in an incredibly short time the Black Death (the dreaded *Sorte Død* of Norway) swept the land from one end to the other.*

Terrible as were the results of this visitation in England and other countries, they seem to have been even worse in Norway, and down even to the present day signs of its desolating progress may be traced. Many districts which are now but sparsely inhabited, were once (for Norway) thickly populated. Valleys which in the olden days contained comfortable farms and patches of cultivated land, are now merely used for *sæters*, or dairy farms, to which for a few months the cattle and sheep are driven in the summer to feed on the rich pasture.

The Norwegian annals are full of stories of this great disaster, and the imagination of the people depicted the plague as a terrible old witch, who went through the land bearing with her a rake and a broom ; where she raked some survived, where she swept with the broom none were left behind. It is estimated that more than a third of the population of the land died, and when the pestilence ceased there was no heart left in the people. In one valley, the great Jostedal (according to the legend which seems not to be improbable), every soul perished except one little girl, who, almost wild with terror, managed to support her life through the winter, and was discovered

---

* Dr. A. L. Faye's *Den Sorte Død*, contains much interesting information respecting the Black Death.

the next summer by the people of Lom, who crossed the mountains to see what had become of their neighbours. Her descendants again peopled the valley.*

Even the very existence of churches was in some places forgotten, as all the inhabitants of the parish had been swept away.† No district of Norway seems to have

* A family tracing its descent directly from this girl, who was known as *Jostedals Rypa* (*rypa*, the ptarmigan), on account of her having been found like a wild bird, still live near Amble in Sogn.

† A very remarkable instance of this is the case of the parish church of Hedal, not far from the northern end of the Spirillen lake, in Valders. The story of the recovery of this church in later years is a strange and interesting one: "Some centuries ago a man in pursuit of *Ryper* traversed one of these formerly inhabited, but now deserted, places. As he shot an arrow at a bird on one of the trees he heard a peculiar sound, as if the arrow had struck against something. Full of curiosity, he approached the place, where, to his astonishment, he came upon an old church. Mindful of the ancient idea that if it was a work of witchcraft it would immediately disappear if brought into proximity to steel, he seized his tinder-box and threw it over the church. On the spot where it fell, a farmhouse was afterwards built, which to the present day bears the name of Ildjernstad (the tinder-box place). After taking this precautionary measure he proceeded to investigate the church. The key stood in the church door, which was half open. In the middle of the floor stood a large bell, and at the foot of the altar a great bear had taken up its winter quarters. It was slain by the brave hunter, and its skin was hung up in the church as a memorial of this strange occurrence, where the remains of a large bear-skin are still to be seen. In the church he is said to have found, among other things, some pictures, a little brass shrine, four large bells and one small one. It was against one of these that the hunter's arrow had struck and produced the sound which attracted his attention." ("A. Faye, Norske Folkesagn," quoted by Dietrichson, "Norske Stavkirker," page 354.)

The little brass shrine, once used as a reliquary, is still preserved in the church, and is remarkable for its representation of the martyrdom of St. Thomas à Becket, of Canterbury. This interesting relic of the middle ages (see picture next page) is believed, on the best authority, to have been made about fifty years after the martyrdom, and is therefore one of the very earliest, if not the earliest, representations of the murder of St. Thomas of Canterbury. It is worthy of note how the cult of "the holy blissful martyr" of Canterbury prevailed in Norway

RELIQUARY IN HEDALS CHURCH

(probable date, 1220), depicting in the lower panel the Martyrdom of St. Thomas of Canterbury. The photograph is from a replica in the Bergen Museum.

[To face p. 246.

escaped the pestilence; it stalked north, south, east, and
west, and the memory of its desolating presence has never
been effaced from the minds of the people. Other nations
of Europe suffered from the same terrible plague, but they
have forgotten it. The memory of it still survives among
the bønder of Norway.

There was, however, one bright spot in the universal
gloom which the plague spread over the land, and that was
the heroic devotion of the bishops and clergy. None of
them seem to have flinched from the post of duty and
danger. Through it all, they stood firm and ministered to
the sick and dying, but the price paid was a terrible one.
The archbishop and every bishop in Norway died of the
plague, with the sole exception of Salomon of Oslo. In
Bergen in one day eighty persons were buried at a single
church, and among these were fourteen priests and six
deacons. The chapter of Nidaros was almost entirely
swept away, and the same thing happened in Bergen and
other cathedrals. In Agder seven parishes were swept of
their inhabitants. The bishop of Stavanger sent many
priests and deacons to minister to the sick and suffering,
and in a very short time all of these brave men fell victims
to the plague. These terrible disasters filled the minds of
the people with horror and remorse for their sins, and it
was thought they were but a prelude to the Day of Judgment, which was everywhere expected in Norway in 1357.

The plague began, in the natural course, to abate, and a
special prayer which the pope is said to have written for
the suffering people, as well as a special mass which was
said, helped to comfort and reassure them.*

during the middle ages. The famous church of St. Thomas of Canterbury,
near Nystuen, on the Fille Fjeld, was only finally swept away in 1808.

* In 1359, and again in 1371, terrible epidemics raged in Norway,
which carried off many people, including, in 1371, Archbishop Olaf,
who died at Oslo.

It is easy to understand what a terrible blow this desolating pestilence proved to the Church in Norway. All its best and wisest men were carried away, and the ranks of the clergy were most terribly thinned, and no suitable men left to take the vacant posts. The Nidaros chapter had only one member left, and the pope nominated Olaf, abbot of Nidarholm, to the vacant see. In this instance the pope made use, for the second time at Nidaros, of the power which the papacy claimed of appointing to vacant sees *per provisionem*, and overriding the rights of the chapters. There were, of course, cases in which this might manifestly be for the benefit of the Church, as, for example, where, from disputes or other causes, there was an unreasonable delay in filling up vacancies. In the case of Archbishop Olaf it was a very wise step, but the papacy did not confine the exercise of its power to such instances, but proceeded in many cases to deliberately overrule the decisions of the chapters and appoint its own nominees to vacant sees. Another instance of this happened on the death of Bishop Salomon of Oslo (the only survivor of the Black Death among the bishops), who died in 1351. After his death the chapter chose Gyrd, one of their number, and he was consecrated by Archbishop Olaf ; but the pope declined to recognize him, and appointed Sigfrid, or Sigurd, bishop of Stavanger, who was in Rome at the time. The canonically-chosen bishop gave up his post, but, Clement VI. dying soon after, his successor, Innocent VI., appointed Gyrd to the see of Stavanger.

The new archbishop at once set to work to try and reorganize the shattered Church. To fill up the many vacancies, it was absolutely necessary to lower the canonical age for ordination, and many lads of eighteen years of age were put in charge of parishes. These young men had, of course, neither the learning nor experience needed for the posts which they held, and many abuses soon manifested

themselves.   Their lives and conversation were very much
below the standard of upright living which had characterized their predecessors, and for a time at any rate there
was a great declension in the state of the spiritual
life of the Church.   The archbishop called together a
council at Nidaros in August, 1351.   At this many of
the older regulations were renewed and new ones added to
cope with the state of things then existing.   It was
especially enjoined on the clergy the necessity of leading
clean and pure lives and of avoiding being mixed up in
quarrels among their people.   The old regulations respecting
the *friller* were again re-enacted, and great abhorrence was
expressed that some of the clergy had regularly and openly
taken *friller*, and had had public betrothals to them.
Although, on paper, the laws always existed, yet we know
that down to the Reformation, from the time of the *Sorte
Død*, these regulations were never enforced, but that the
clergy continued to contract these irregular unions, and
that it was practically acquiesced in by their superiors, who
in many cases, if we are to believe Theodore of Niem, themselves had their *friller* as well as the parochial clergy !

A wise provision of the council was that the older clergy,
who had survived the plague, should instruct the new and
untried ones in all matters pertaining to the right and
proper performance of the Church's offices.

The new prelates strove, as far as they could, to remedy
the state of things which they found around them as the
result of the Black Death, but it was a long time indeed
before matters were finally reduced to order, and the revival
of religious life was again checked, by the desolations which
accompanied the break with Rome, under the Danish kings,
in the early part of the sixteenth century.

If ecclesiastical affairs in Norway at this time were in an
unsatisfactory state, things were no better as regards
temporal matters.   The feeble King Magnus's unpopularity,

caused largely by his continued absences from the country, increased year by year. It will be remembered that he had arranged that his second son, Haakon, was to have the kingdom of Norway, but Haakon was still a child. In 1350 Magnus was in Bergen, and seems to have agreed to nominate as "drotsete" Orm Eysteinssøn, who practically ruled the country for five years, until 1355, when young Haakon was declared of age and took over, nominally, the government of the kingdom. Magnus now remained king only of Sweden. His other son, Erik, who had been brought up in that country, was not on good terms with his father, chiefly on account of Magnus's favourite, Benedict Algotssøn, whom he imagined, his father wished to make his heir. An arrangement was made, however, in 1357 by which Erik and Magnus divided Sweden, but the peace did not last long. Erik suspected, with apparently good reason, that his father was intriguing with the Danish king Valdemar against him. In 1359 young Haakon of Norway was betrothed to Margaret, Valdemar's daughter (afterwards the famous queen), and the marriage took place in 1363.

In 1359 Erik of Sweden died suddenly at the age of twenty-two years, supposed to have been poisoned,* and his wife and two children died soon afterwards. Magnus thereupon resumed the government of Sweden, and Valdemar attacked and conquered the district of Skaane. The Swedish chiefs were very furious with Magnus on account of what they believed to be his secret compact with the Danish king, and in 1363 they offered the crown to Albrekt of Mecklenburg, son of Euphemia, Magnus's sister. Albrekt accepted the offer and went to Stockholm. But Haakon came to his father's assistance, and there was much

---

* According to another account, he was carried off with his young wife and infant twin children, by the visitation of *barnekopper* (small-pox), which visited the north in 1359—60.

hard fighting.   At Enkjøbing a battle (March, 1365) was
fought, in which Magnus was taken prisoner and Haakon
wounded. The war continued with varying successes, until
at last, in 1371, an agreement was made by which Magnus
was set at liberty.   Magnus was to have the revenues of
some Swedish provinces and to bear the title of king during
his life ; Haakon renounced on his part, his claim to Sweden,
and left the government to Albrekt.   Magnus did not long
survive this peace; he was drowned while crossing the open
Bømmel Fjord, to the north of Stavanger, in December,
1374, and thus ended his long and inglorious reign of fifty-
five years.

CHAPTER XVII.

THE CHURCH UNDER MARGARET AND ERIK.

Queen Margaret gains Denmark for her son Olaf—The Pope appoints
Nicholas Ruser Archbishop—Erik of Pomerania chosen King—The
Union of Kalmar—Bishop Eystein Aslakssøn of Oslo—His Mission
to London—History of St. Birgitta—The Order of the Saviour—
The State of the Norwegian Church as recorded by Theodore of
Niem.

DURING the concluding years of the fourteenth century
the history of the Church in Norway does not present any
special features of interest. It had not recovered from the
shock of the disasters of 1349—50, and in 1371 another
outbreak of plague still further paralyzed its powers. The
energetic Archbishop Olaf, who had done his best to revive
life in his diocese and province, fell a victim to the plague
in 1371. He was succeeded by a man named Thrond,
about whom practically nothing is known. It will give
some idea to what a low ebb the Church had been reduced
by the Black Death when we are told that in the diocese of
Nidaros, Archbishop Thrond found only forty priests (old
and feeble), where formerly there were three hundred! In
the Bergen diocese there was only one priest to every three
or four churches, and when the enormous extent of most
parishes in Norway is borne in mind, the wonder only is that
there was any religion left in the country. There is no
doubt that a very great falling-off in the religious life of
the people, was the result of the lack of a properly instructed
priesthood. Even in the towns this was noticeable, and
the energetic Bishop Jakob of Bergen, in a pastoral which
he issued in 1390 to that city, paints in very dark colours

the state of morals then prevailing, and set himself
vigorously to remedy these evils.

King Haakon, who after his father Magnus's death, was
the sole king in Norway, had a son, Olaf, born to him in
1371, and in 1375 Valdemar Atterdag of Denmark died
without leaving any male issue.   Queen Margaret at once
claimed the Danish crown for her infant son, although she
was not the eldest daughter of Valdemar.   The question of
the election of a new Danish king came before the diet at
Odense, but the adherents of Ingeborg, duchess of Mecklenburg, Margaret's elder sister, attended in force, and the
decision was postponed.   Meanwhile Margaret did much to
ingratiate herself with the most influential men in Denmark,
especially among the clergy, and the result was that at
another gathering, held at Slagelsee in 1376, her son Olaf
was chosen as king, and his mother was entrusted with the
government on his behalf.   King Haakon did not live long
after this triumph of his energetic queen, but died at Oslo
in 1380.   The year following Margaret and Olaf came to
Norway, where the latter was accepted as king at Nidaros,
and a "drotsete" appointed to govern the country during
the absence of the young monarch and his mother.   Queen
Margaret was now making her power felt in both Denmark
and Norway, and her ambitious design of uniting the three
Scandinavian kingdoms under one sovereign, became more
apparent.   But it was not only in the State, but in the
Church as well, that she desired to place in office, those who
would carry out her will.   A very curious incident occurred
at this time in the Norwegian Church which showed that the
queen's influence was no less powerful with the Roman
curia than in Denmark or Norway.

In 1381 Archbishop Thrond died, and the Nidaros
chapter elected Haakon Ivarssøn as his successor.   He
started for Rome in order to be consecrated in 1382, but
had only got as far as Germany, when he learned to his

astonishment that the pope had already selected and consecrated an archbishop for Nidaros in defiance of the
chapter's election of himself. This was one Nicholas Ruser,
or Rusare, a man of a noble Danish or German family, who
had been in favour with Valdemar, the late king, and also
with Queen Margaret. It seems very probable that this
man was not originally in holy orders at all. It was true
he had been a canon of Roskilde, but this did not necessarily
imply that he was in orders, as such posts were sometimes
given to laymen as a reward for services rendered to the
Crown.* It is clear, however, that Archbishop Nicholas
arrived in Denmark fully invested with papal authority in
1382, and was welcomed by the queen. In confirmation of
the opinion, which many in his day held, that he was merely
a layman, it may be noted that he never exercised any
episcopal powers. He never consecrated any bishops, or
performed any other duties of his office, except to preside
at a council which was held at Tønsberg in 1383, but this
was not an exclusively ecclesiastical gathering. One thing,
however, he did do. He went to Nidaros and helped himself to many of the treasures of the see, and with these he
retired to Denmark, where, fortunately for the Church, he
died in 1386.

King Olaf died in 1387, at the early age of seventeen,
and there was now no direct heir to the kingdom of
Norway. Queen Margaret, however, was determined not
to lose her grasp of the royal authority. She was accepted
as regent of Denmark the same year, and in 1388 of
Norway as well, but the Norwegians would not accept a
woman as their Sovereign. Margaret had, however, a
candidate for the vacant throne in the person of Erik of
Pomerania, then a child only six years old. Erik was

---

* Bp. Bang, in his *Udsigt over den Norske Kirkes Historie*, makes
this point clear, as against Keyser's assumption that the possession of
a canonry implied being in holy orders.

Margaret's grandnephew, his mother being Marie, the daughter of Margaret's sister Ingeborg, who married Henry of Mecklenburg. This prince was nephew of Magnus Erikssøn, and great-grandson of Haakon V.* Though Erik was so remotely connected with the royal house of Norway, he was accepted as king through the influence of Queen Margaret, who was thus enabled to maintain her rule over the kingdom and to carry on the government in young Erik's name.

Margaret had now the complete control of two of the Scandinavian kingdoms, and she determined to add Sweden to the number, and to unite them all under one sceptre. She soon found an opportunity, as King Albrekt had grown very unpopular with his people, chiefly on account of his partiality for his German friends. With her usual diplomacy, Margaret skilfully availed herself of this, to stir up the Swedish magnates against their king, and she so far succeeded that in May 1388, a number of the chiefs formally declared themselves on her side. This at once led to an open rupture, and both parties took up arms, and the result was that the next year, 1389, King Albrekt was utterly defeated, and taken prisoner, at Falkøping and carried to Denmark.

There was still some resistance on behalf of Albrekt by the Germans, who held Stockholm, and were supported by the Hanseatic towns of Rostock and Wismar, and they encouraged privateers, known as the *Vitalie-brødre*,† to harry the Norwegian coast, in the course of which they burnt the city of Bergen. The struggle continued for

* See genealogical table.

† The *Vitalie-brødre* (brethren) were a kind of joint-stock company formed for bringing provisions to the Germans in Sweden; from their supplying them with victuals they received their name; and from being harmless provision merchants, they ended by becoming dangerous pirates.

some years longer, and at last the imprisoned king Albrekt, having failed to pay the ransom demanded of him, was obliged to surrender Stockholm, and, being set free, retired with his son to Germany.

Queen Margaret had now gained all the three kingdoms. In 1396 she had secured the kingdom of Denmark for Erik, and later in the same year he was chosen king of Sweden. Thus for the first time Norway, Sweden, and Denmark were united under one king. On Trinity Sunday, June 17th, 1397, young Erik was solemnly invested with the crown of the three kingdoms at Kalmar.

At this time the famous union of Kalmar was formed, and a constitution was promulgated under which it was to be maintained. The principal points of this important agreement were as follows :—

(1) The three kingdoms of Norway, Sweden, and Denmark were in future always to remain united under one king.

(2) The king should be chosen by all three kingdoms. If the deceased king left sons, one of them was to be selected, but if there was no issue, the representatives of the kingdoms were to select the best man they could find.

(3) The three kingdoms were to be united in all foreign matters, but under their own laws, &c., with respect to domestic affairs.

(4) If any one country was attacked, the others were to help it, but at the charges of the former.

This triple alliance of the kingdoms of Scandinavia seemed to promise well for the future peace of the North ; and had there been a strong man upon the throne, or a succession of wise and prudent kings, it would doubtless have led to very important consequences. Erik was, however, a mere cypher, and when the strong-minded Margaret passed away, the jealousies and quarrels between different nations, and the ambition of the Danish kings, soon broke up the union, leaving only Denmark and Norway united, the latter country soon to become a mere province of Denmark, and practically bereft of national life, until the beginning of the nineteenth century saw its revival once more.

From this necessary digression, into the political history of the countries under Margaret's rule, we must return to ecclesiastical affairs in Norway at the end of the fourteenth century.

Nicholas Ruser's successor in the primacy was Vinalde Henrikssøn. He was probably a Swede by birth, but had lived all his life in Norway, and had been " Magister capellarum regis " and keeper of the royal seal. He was consecrated in 1387, and got back to Norway the same year. He was a good man, but his activity was manifested chiefly in political matters, in which he took a very leading part as a supporter of Queen Margaret. He died in 1402. A more prominent ecclesiastic of this period was Bishop Eystein Aslakssøn of Oslo (1386—1407), who has left a remarkable inventory of the property of the Church in his diocese, which was known as "The Red Book," so called from the colour of its binding. He issued also a pastoral letter with respect to the state of the Church in the Telemark, which was at that time, and for centuries after, a remote and very turbulent district, where the authority of both Church and State was but lightly regarded, and where tithes were but seldom or ever paid. It throws a remarkable light on the life of the people at that period, and shows the difficulties with which the clergy had to contend, amongst their very fierce and quarrelsome parishioners.

One interesting fact concerning this bishop is worthy of notice. When the Norwegian bishops left their sees it was, as a rule, to visit one of the Scandinavian kingdoms, or to go to Rome, on matters directly connected with the affairs of the Church in Norway. Bishop Eystein Aslakssøn

was, however, an exception to this rule, and paid a visit
to England in 1405. After the death of her son Olaf, Queen
Margaret, on her grand-nephew Erik having been accepted
as king, decided to procure an English consort for him, and
negotiations were opened with the English court in order to
obtain the hand of the Princess Philippa, the daughter of
Henry IV., for Erik. Six envoys were selected for the
purpose, and Bishop Eystein was placed at the head of the
mission. They met at Jønkøping in November, 1404, but
were prevented by bad weather from setting out until the
spring of the following year, when they safely reached
London, where the bishop was lodged "with one John
Scrivener, of Fleet Street."* The efforts of the mission
were crowned with success, and the marriage of Erik and
the English princess was celebrated by proxy on November
26th, 1405. The Norwegian bishop proved himself very
acceptable to the English court, and had the honour of
being invited to preach in Latin before Henry IV., which
he did, and his eloquence was much admired.

During his stay in England he visited St. Albans, where
he charmed the monks with his knowledge of their patron
saint, to whom the famous cloister at Selje was dedicated.

The latter part of the fourteenth century saw the foundation of a new religious order, the only one to which the
North gave birth—the famous order of the Holy Saviour,
which was due to that most remarkable woman St. Birgitta.†

Britta, or Birgitta, was born in the year 1303 or 1304.
Her father was Birger Pederson, the "lagman" of Finstad, in
Sweden, and her mother Ingeborg Bengtsdatter, of Ulfaasa.
Both parents belonged to well-known families, and her
mother was connected with the Swedish royal line.
From her earliest childhood she seems to have manifested a

---

* See Wylie's "History of England under Henry IV.," *passim*.

† One of the most recent accounts of the life of St. Birgitta is
"Den Hellige Birgitta," by A. Brinkmann, Copenhagen, 1893.

From a Photograph by]   **SELJE.**   *[Rev. D. G. Cowan.*

Ruins of the Benedictine Cloister of St. Alban, founded in the 11th Century.

[To face p. 258.

very devout and mystical frame of mind, and even at eight years of age is said to have had visions.

At thirteen she was married to Ulf Gudmarson, who was himself only five years older than his very youthful bride. The marriage turned out to be in every way a happy one, as Ulf was of a very similar disposition to his wife. Their family consisted of four sons and four daughters, one of whom was afterwards the famous St. Katharine of Sweden. About the year 1340 Birgitta and her husband went on a pilgrimage to the far-famed shrine of St. James of Compostella. On the way back he fell very ill in Flanders, and on his recovery vowed (with Birgitta's approval) to renounce the world, and enter upon a religious life. This he did and joined the monastery of Alvastra, but he did not long survive, and died in 1344.

It would seem that it was at this time, that the natural mysticism of Birgitta's mind became much more marked, and she began to have those wonderful visions and revelations which afterwards led to the establishment of the order which bears her name.

On account of her high rank she was attached for a time to the suite of Blanche of Namur, the wife of King Magnus Erikssøn, who seems to have treated his saintly relative with but very scant courtesy. During this time she was disturbed by the continued wars between France and England, and is reported to have said: " If the king of England will not observe the Divine plan he will prosper in none of his transactions, and will end his life in pain and leave his kingdom and his children in tribulation and anguish. His family will set themselves against each other and cause a confusion all will wonder at."* Was the miserable death of Richard II. and the struggles between the houses of York and Lancaster, the fulfilment of this prophecy?

After her widowhood, and finding the residence in the

* Butler, " Acta Sanctorum."

court very distasteful, she retired to her own home, and in 1346 she finally left Sweden for the south. Her natural instinct led her to Rome, where, like many another before and after her, she hoped to find "the streets paved with imperishable gold—the blood of the holy martyrs—and where through the merits of the saints and the absolution of the pope, the speediest way to heaven was to be found." Visits to various shrines filled up some time, and then, like her sainted contemporary, Catharine of Siena, she did her best to make the Avignon pope, Urban V., return to Rome, which he did at length in April, 1367, in spite of the opposition of the French cardinals. But a short time sufficed for Urban, and he decided to return to his native land in 1370. Birgitta, however, declared that the Blessed Virgin had revealed it to her, that if he went back he should die, and strangely enough her words proved true. Urban V. died within two months of his return to Avignon, and the fame of Birgitta grew more and more.* In 1372, accompanied by two of her sons and her daughter Katharine, she went on a pilgrimage to Jerusalem and the holy places of Palestine, and returned to Rome the next year, where she died on July 23rd, 1373.

Birgitta was much reverenced for her sanctity throughout Europe. The remarkable "Revelationes St. Birgittæ" have been collected, and contain an extraordinary series of "for the most part mystic rhapsodies, visions of the Saviour and the Virgin, full of strange pious allegory."† St. Birgitta in many ways, closely resembled her more widely known contemporary Catharine of Siena, especially in the way in which

* The election of Urban's successor, Gregory XI., at first filled Birgitta with much joy, as she hoped that he would finally end the papal residence at Avignon. Gregory, however, temporized, and said that there were difficulties in so doing while the war between France and England continued. He received her admonitions with pious inactivity and professed great gratitude for them.

† Milman, "History of Latin Christianity," Vol. VIII. page 27.

she believed the revelations were directly given to her by our Lord Himself, and that it was by His direct command that she founded the order, and from Him received the details as to its constitution.

In 1391, at the request of King Erik, the pope, Boniface IX., canonized her on October 7th, which was afterwards observed as her day in the calendar. The order of the Holy Saviour quickly spread over the North. The plans for it she had drawn up before she left Sweden for Italy, and submitted them to Pope Urban V. who approved of her idea and sanctioned the establishment of the order in August, 1370.

Birgitta selected Vadstena, on lake Vettern, as the home of the order, and began the building of the cloister, and from this spot it spread, the Abbess of Vadstena being the head of the whole community.

A remarkable feature of this new order was the fact that both monks and nuns lived in the one establishment, but, of course, in their own separate parts of it.

Each cloister of the order consisted of sixty nuns (*sorores*), thirteen priest-monks (*fratres presbyteri*), four deacons (*fratres diaconi*), and eight lay brothers (*fratres laici*).

The thirteen priests were to represent the thirteen Apostles—*i.e.*, including St. Paul—the four deacons, the four fathers of the Church. The sixty nuns, four deacons, and eight lay brothers were intended to represent our Lord and his first disciples. The abbess was to rule all, and to represent the Blessed Virgin. The nuns were the real core and centre of the cloister, and the monks were merely added to perform the Church services and to manage its secular affairs. Every church contained thirteen altars. One priest was chosen as *confessor generalis*, who acted as secretary and adviser of the abbess.*

The body of Birgitta was brought from Rome to

* Lange's *Norske Klostres Historie*, pages 53 *et seq.*

Vadstena, where it now rests, along with that of her daughter, St. Katharine of Sweden.

In spite of the revival of Church life in the North, of which the new Order of the Saviour was an evidence, there is unfortunately but little doubt that the ordinary religious life of the people was at a very low ebb at the end of the fourteenth century. The terrible visitations of the Black Death and the other plagues which followed, brought about the usual results which such disasters have produced in different lands. There were those who, like many in days when pestilence raged, plunged only deeper into dissipation, and sought to drown the thoughts of death and judgment, in carousing and debauchery. On the other hand, there were others who turned to the opposite extreme, and whose religion became a sort of fanatical mysticism, and lost that practical form which manifests itself in a "godly, righteous, and sober life."

Norway, bereft by the plague, of priests whose "lips should keep knowledge," and having only young and ignorant men, who ministered in the priest's office, soon fell away from the high standard which had been maintained in former generations.

We have preserved to us an account of the condition of the Church in Norway at the close of the fourteenth century from the pen of the well-known Theodore of Niem, who was bishop of Verden, afterwards archbishop of Cambray, and who died there in 1417.*

In his account of the state of the Church in the North of Europe he says, speaking of Norway :— †

"The clergy here are, as a rule, poor in dress and

* Theodore, or Dietrich, was probably born early in the 14th century. He was employed in the papal *curia*, where he was "abbreviator and scriptor" under Urban VI. His "Nemus Unionis" is a large work dealing with schism, printed at Basle, 1566. The most recent Life of Theodore is that by Georg Erler, " Dietrich von Nieheim."

† "Nemus Unionis," Chapter xxxv.

adornments, and perform the Divine service with few ceremonies and no solemnity. Neither are they to any great
degree imbued with liberal arts or other sciences. But from
habit or custom in Norway, both clergy and laymen drink
equally hard, and if any one cannot drink himself drunk
in beer beyond all measure, he considers himself to be very
unhappy. They challenge one another to drinking bouts,
and no one who had not seen it, can imagine how much
both sexes can drink at a time, and they continue at this
until they fall to the ground in a state of intoxication.
Whoever is best able to empty his cups is considered to
have beaten the others in bodily strength and vigour.

"In these places (Ireland and Norway) it is permitted
to bishops and clergy publicly to keep concubines, and
when the bishop twice a year visits his diocese he brings
his beloved one with him to the houses of the priests. The
concubine herself would not allow her episcopal lover to
go on these visitations without her, partly because he fares
sumptuously with the priests, and into the bargain receives
gifts from those who are visited, and partly also because she
wishes to look after her lover, lest he should fall in love with
another who should be better looking, and so do an injury
to her.

" If by chance any of the priests who are being visited have
no concubines, they are looked upon as traitors to the inherited custom, and have to give the visiting bishop double
hospitality. And so it is the custom that in these countries
the priest's concubine, or wife, should have precedence and
rank in Church and at table, in walking and in sitting,
and standing before other women, even the wives of
knights."

It is not easy to say exactly, how much truth there is in
this very unfavourable account of the bishops and priests
of Norway ; but it is more than probable that it was very
grossly exaggerated, and that Theodore wrote about matters

of which he appears to have had no personal knowledge, as he never seems to have visited Norway. It is very doubtful if the bishops, surrounded as they were by many of the regular clergy, who would only have been too ready to report their faults to Rome, would have thus dared so openly to set canon law at defiance. We have plenty of evidence as to the way in which they attempted to prevent the priests contracting these unions, which, though forbidden by the Church's law, were yet quite in accordance with the law of the land, and as such recognized by the priests. Theodore was scarcely in a position to criticize too severely the morality of the Norwegian bishops, and his virtuous indignation merely expended itself in words, which were not exactly in accordance with his actions. In an inventory of the various possessions bestowed on him by the Roman *curia*, Cecchus casually mentions (without wishing to cast any reproach on Theodore's morality) a house as that which his concubine inhabited!* But the description of the drunkenness of both priest and people is a sad and probably true one, and rendered all the more sad when contrasted with the picture drawn some centuries before by a much greater writer, Adam of Bremen.

* " Dietrich von Nieheim," p. 406.

CHAPTER XVIII.

ERIK—TO THE DEATH OF KRISTOFER OF BAVARIA.

Condition of the Church—Erik's Ecclesiastical Policy—Action of the Scandinavian Prelates in the Great Schism—Aslak Bolt, Archbishop—His Work for the Church—Council at Oslo—Denmark and Sweden reject Erik—Norway follows and Elects Kristofer—Short Reign and Death of Kristofer (1448).

Though the state of the Norwegian Church at the close of the fourteenth century was far from being a satisfactory one, still it certainly did not altogether deserve the severe strictures of the future archbishop of Cambray. It is possible, indeed, that, in some respects, it might even have contrasted favourably with the condition of some of the other national Churches at that particular period, but it had undoubtedly fallen away from the very high standard of life and morals, for which it had been remarkable in the earlier days. There were, however, evidences of a revival of Church life, such as the newly-established Order of the Holy Saviour, which soon found a home for itself in Norway as well as in Sweden, and the rules of this new order made the preaching of the Gospel, in the language "understood of the people," one of its most prominent features. Had the times been more favourable, the revival might have progressed and the Church of Norway regained the ground it had lost by reason of the Black Death. The political conditions, however, reacted unfavourably on it, because the Government of Margaret and Erik made use of all the important ecclesiastical posts to serve its own purposes, and so checked and stunted the growth and development of the Church's life. The highest offices were bestowed as rewards for political services.

We find, therefore, that a very considerable number of Danes and Swedes were preferred to the vacant sees and canonries in Norway, to the exclusion of the native Norwegian clergy. This was not necessarily in itself a bad thing, as the infusion of new blood might have helped in a great measure to revive the life of the Church, at a time when it was at such a low ebb. But the men who were appointed were not, as a rule, of a type likely to advance the prosperity of the Church.

Nicholas Ruser, for example, was hardly the kind of archbishop to whom we might look for any development of religious life in his province, and his sole aim during his brief tenure of the seat of Eystein, seems to have been his own personal aggrandisement, and, having accomplished that, he spent the rest of his life in Denmark. These foreign prelates never seem even to have attempted to win the regard of their clergy and people. Many of them were cordially hated in their dioceses, and their oppressions and exactions helped to fan the fire of discontent which was smouldering in Norway.*

Archbishop Vinalde Henrikssøn died in 1402, and his successor was Askell, or Eskill, who was a native Norwegian. His episcopate, which lasted until 1428, was entirely uneventful. He was not consecrated until 1404.

The Norwegian bishops were, of course, summoned to the Council of Pisa (1409), but none of them went to it. At the beginning of the great schism in the papacy (1378) the Norwegian Church supported Urban VI. and his side. When at the Council of Pisa the confusion in the Church was made still worse by the appointment of a

---

* The policy of Margaret and Erik was very like that of the English Government towards the Irish Church in the eighteenth and early years of the nineteenth century.

third pope, the allegiance of the North seems to have been divided. At first Queen Margaret and Erik, with the clergy generally, in Sweden and Denmark, and presumably Norway (though we have no certain information), maintained the cause of Gregory XII. Some of the Swedish bishops and chapters gave their support to Alexander V., and eventually the queen and King Erik, and the bishops and clergy of the three kingdoms, took the same course.

In 1412 the great Queen Margaret passed away, having for almost forty years practically guided the destinies of Norway and Denmark, and for a somewhat shorter period of Sweden as well. She had been to Flensborg, in Jylland, and had gone on board her ship to return home, when she was suddenly seized with illness, and expired on October 28th at the age of sixty.

Margaret is undoubtedly the most remarkable woman we meet with in the history of Norway. The daughter of Valdemar "Atterdag," * with whose accession a new era of life and prosperity began to dawn upon Denmark, after a long period of national disaster and internal strife, she inherited many of the characteristics of her father; her ambition was boundless, and she never hesitated as to the means which she used to compass her ends. She knew more of statecraft than any of the monarchs with whom she came in contact, and there can be no doubt that at Kalmar she laid the foundation of a scheme, which only wanted capable men to direct it, and might have materially altered the history of the North of Europe.

Whilst we cannot fail to admire her great genius, it is impossible to shut our eyes to her overweening ambition and love of power both in Church and State. It was her

---

* He probably received the name of "Atterdag" (the new day) from this fact. Other explanations of the name are given, such as his usual adage, "To-morrow we shall have a day again"; or his frequent use of the German expression of surprise, "der Tage!"

father's opinion that Nature had made a mistake in her case—she should have been a man, and not a woman ; and, indeed, she it was who played the man, whilst her feeble husband and most of the other chiefs in her day, were but as puppets in her hands. The greatness of her personal power can be seen by the way in which, as soon as she died, the fabric she had built up with such skill began to crumble to the ground.

The queen's body was not taken from her native land. She was buried in the great cathedral of Roskilde, the Westminster of Denmark. There, just behind the high altar, a white marble effigy marks the spot where, " after life's fitful fever," the great queen who had welded the three Scandinavian nations into one kingdom, sleeps her last sleep.*

But now there came a temporary revival of the Church life in Norway under the rule of a new and energetic archbishop. In 1428 Archbishop Askell died, and the chapter chose as his successor Bishop Aslak Harniktssøn Bolt, of Bergen, to which see he had been consecrated in 1408. It was not, however, until January 1430, that the pope agreed to permit his translation from Bergen to Nidaros. The new metropolitan was a man of a different stamp from his immediate predecessors. He was a strong man in every way, and though possessed of a rather violent temper, was admirably suited to the needs of the Church in his time. He was learned in the Scriptures and the canon law, and during his episcopate did much to raise the standard of religion in Norway. He was the first archbishop who acted as papal legate.

As soon as his translation to Nidaros was accomplished, he set himself vigorously to work to improve the condition

---

* Though we cannot fail to recognize the political genius of the queen, we may perhaps demur to the inscription on her tomb, " To the memory of that Princess whom posterity cannot honour beyond her merits."

of the finances of the Church, and especially of his cathedral. A diligent visitation of his diocese, which was undertaken immediately after he went to Nidaros, revealed the fact that the old-established contributions authorized by the *Kristenret* had not been paid regularly. These had been granted for the support of the cathedral, and had customarily been paid either in money or in kind. They were known as the " Olaf's corn " and the " Michel's corn " ; the latter received its name from being paid at Michaelmas. The devastating fire at the cathedral, caused by lightning, in July, 1431, made the demand for these contributions specially opportune. Another instance of the archbishop's zeal is shown by the compilation about the year 1440 of an inventory of all the property of the Church in his diocese, which he caused to be made in the same way as the bishop of Oslo (Eystein Aslakssøn) had done fifty years before. The archbishop's inventory was known as Aslak Bolt's " Jordebog " (book of temporalities), and still survives.*

It was in the first half of this century, that the Birgitta order began to spread in Norway, and the archbishop, when Bishop of Bergen, had introduced it into the country in conjunction with Stein, the abbot of the Benedictine cloister of Munkeliv, in Bergen. This monastery had purposely, it seemed, been allowed to become almost empty, and afforded an opportunity for converting it into a habitation for the new order (1426). This was approved by the head cloister of the order at Vadstena, in Sweden, in 1434, and it thus

---

* The " Jordebog " was published in Christiania in 1852. It was edited by the late Professor P. A. Munch. In the introduction to the volume Professor Munch mentions the way in which this inventory survived. It was taken from Trondhjem, along with other archives, by the last archbishop, Olaf Engelbrektssøn, when he fled to Holland in 1537. From thence it was carried to Heidelberg, and finally to Munich, where it remained until 1830, when a vast variety of documents relating to the three Scandinavian kingdoms, were restored to their respective countries.

became the first establishment belonging to the new community in Norway.

Archbishop Aslak determined to revive the practice of holding provincial councils, which had been abandoned since the time of Archbishop Olaf; but his first attempt in this direction was not very successful. In 1435 he summoned a council to meet in Bergen, but to his great chagrin none of his suffragans put in an appearance. The bishop of Bergen alone among the Norwegian prelates, had any legitimate excuse for being absent, as he was in Sweden on business for the king. The bishops of Hamar and Oslo, who were Danes and very unpopular, seem to have been the most obnoxious in this passive resistance to the archbishop's authority. Aslak, however, refrained from any open quarrel with them, but suspended the abbot of Halsnø for his disobedience, and, in spite of the absence of the other bishops, proceeded with some legislative measures. Among others, laws were passed for the purpose of preventing the begging monks collecting contributions without a licence from the bishop of the diocese. Though he had been to a very considerable extent thwarted in his plans for reform, the archbishop did not give up the intention of holding councils, and summoned another to meet at Oslo in December, 1436.

Before this met, however, the discontent which had long existed in Norway, ended at last in open rebellion. King Erik had for many years ceased to visit that part of his dominions, and had not, it would seem, been there since 1405. The administration of the law and collection of taxes, was entrusted by the king chiefly to Danes, who ground down the people, and whose exactions produced very bitter feelings. The increased taxation on account of the Slesvig war was also extremely unpopular. The centre of the discontent was in the diocese of Oslo, whose bishop, Jens, or Jon as he is called by some, was very much hated. Appeals were made to King Erik for justice, but they met with no response, and in the summer of 1436 the people rose in rebellion under Amund Sigurdssøn at Tønsberg. The king's men met the rebel leader, and a truce was arranged for a short time, but on the expiration of it Amund proceeded to Oslo, where he seized the bishop's palace, but was in his turn besieged there by the royal adherents. Finally a peace was made in December of 1436, and Amund was promised an amnesty for himself and his followers.

Immediately after this the provincial council called by the archbishop met on December 20th, and this time several of the bishops were present, but *not* the bishop of Oslo. The legislation of this council proceeded on the usual lines, and enforced various regulations which had been made at other like assemblies, regarding morals and discipline. The most important work, however, was an effort made by the archbishop to improve the learning of the native clergy, and so to take away the excuse of appointing foreigners to posts in Norway on the ground of their better education. To do this he appropriated a part of the tithe which the *Kristenret* gave to the poor—an illegal proceeding doubtless, but one which the exigencies of the time seemed to demand. We may here mention that some sixteen years before this, the University of Rostock had been established, and from that time onwards the clergy of the three northern kingdoms who were educated abroad, chiefly studied there instead of in England or France, as had been the custom in the earlier days. This was not without its effect on the subsequent history. It largely helped to sever the close connection between the Churches of England and Norway, which had existed from the time of the first introduction of Christianity into the latter country. Henceforward Norway came under the influence of German thought and theology. If the old historic connection with England had been maintained, the results which followed the breach with Rome in the next century might have been different, and the Church in Norway have followed in the same course as that of England, and not have lost, with the historic episcopate, its place in the Catholic Church.

The council at Oslo, before separating, called together a number of representatives from the discontented part of the country, and addressed once more, a strong appeal to the king to assert his authority, and to put away the abuses which were everywhere complained of. They seem to have been actuated by a spirit of great loyalty to their unworthy monarch, when the two other sister nations had rejected him, and were only anxious he should come and rule over them, with some of the old spirit which had marked his ancestors. But this appeal was practically useless. King Erik had had enough of his three troublesome kingdoms, and Denmark and Sweden had no wish to have him any longer.   In 1437 he left Denmark and went to Gotland, thus practically abdicating, but taking no formal step.   The Danes now offered the crown to Kristofer of Bavaria, Erik's nephew, the son of his sister Katharina, who had married John of Bavaria, and declared Erik deposed.   The Swedes also deposed the king, and nominated Karl Knutssøn as governor of their country.

Norway, however, still held to her lawful but worthless monarch, and actually attacked the Swedes on his behalf, but without any important result.

Then the chiefs made one more appeal to Erik, and sent men to ask that he would appoint a " drotsete," which he did, and nominated Sigurd Jonssøn (1439).

After this, when both Sweden and Denmark had accepted Kristofer as king (he was crowned at Upsala in September, 1441), they wished Norway to join with them.   Meanwhile the Norwegians had held a meeting at Oslo, under the presidency of Archbishop Aslak, and decided to send once more to Erik, representing the state of the country, and intimating that if he could not do something they must abandon his cause. The ambassadors appointed never reached the king, as they were stopped in Denmark. One more appeal seems to have been made to Erik, but, like the others, it led to nothing. After this a meeting with the Swedes was held at Kalmar, but the question of the king was not decided.

In 1442 the Norwegians finally abandoned Erik, and at a meeting held at Lødøse the archbishop and the Norwegian representatives agreed to accept Kristofer as their king, and he came to Norway in July of the same year, and was crowned at Oslo.

Erik had reigned nominally for fifty-two years over Norway, though, as we have seen, he practically spent but little if any time in the country ; and in the early part of his life all the real power lay in the hands of Queen Margaret. After his deposition he continued to live for some years in his strong castle at Gotland, where he exhibited perhaps the only trace of his historic ancestry, by following the lucrative occupation of a sea rover. In 1449 he retired to his domains in Pomerania, where, after another ten years, he died in 1459 at the age of 76.

Kristofer's reign over Norway was of short duration, but under it the country settled down, after its disturbed state in the closing years of Erik's reign. The " drotsete " surrendered his office when the new king was crowned, and no events of importance, ecclesiastical or civil, have to be recorded. Kristofer died suddenly at Helsingborg in 1448, having been king of Norway for a little over five years. Though personally very popular from his genial nature, he was not the man to overcome the difficulties with which he was confronted. In Denmark he was entirely helpless to withstand the arrogance of the nobility, and in other parts of his dominions, the Hanseatic league was too strong for him. Had he lived longer and proved a capable governor, many of the subsequent troubles of Norway might have been averted, and instead of a period of practical extinction of national life, which lasted for over three hundred and fifty years, Norway might have held a position of importance among the nations of Northern Europe.

But this was not to be. We have now to enter upon the dark period of the history of Norway in both Church and State, one marked by but few episodes to relieve the gloom which everywhere prevailed. When we think of it, we are filled with surprise that there was no one upon whom the spirit of the kings in the heroic days descended, who would go forth as a leader of men to free the Fatherland, and restore to it once more, that national life which in the earlier days had been so strong and vigorous.

CHAPTER XIX.

NORWAY UNDER DANISH KINGS.

THE death of Kristofer of Bavaria, and the events which followed, showed how feeble were the links which held the three nations together in the Kalmar union. The regular course on the death of the sovereign of the united kingdoms, would have been for the duly accredited representatives of each nationality to have met and chosen a successor, as the last monarch had left no heir. Instead of this, Sweden and Denmark set to work on their own account. It must be remembered that they were *elective* monarchies, while the crown in Norway, according to law, was hereditary. Kristofer died in January, 1448, and in the following June the Swedish Assembly, or *Rigsdag*, met in Stockholm, and forthwith chose Karl Knutssøn as king, and he was at once crowned at Upsala.

The Danes, on their part, made overtures to Adolf of Slesvig to occupy the vacant throne; but he induced them to accept in his place, his nephew Kristian, or

T 2

Christiern, Count of Oldenborg, and he was chosen as king in the month of September.

Norway was now without anyone as a claimant for the throne, and in default of heirs, the law provided that the bishops and chief men should meet at Nidaros and select a suitable person as king. This, however, was not done, and the archbishop was in Nidaros while the chief men of the kingdom were at Oslo, and so matters were left for the time, with Sigurd Jonssøn in authority. Meanwhile both Sweden and Denmark had provided themselves with kings, and each country was anxious for Norway to join in the arrangement which they had made. There were now two parties in the Norwegian Council, one, under Archbishop Aslak, in favour of the Swedish king, Karl, and the other, led by Jens, bishop of Oslo, supporting the claims of Kristian of Denmark. There was, however, one man who claimed descent from the old royal family of Norway— namely, Sigurd Jonssøn, the "drotsete," who was a descendant of Agnes, the illegitimate daughter of Haakon V., and who might have been chosen as king of Norway, only he declined the honour. The majority of the council were in favour of the maintenance of the Kalmar union, and no step was taken at the end of 1448.

In February, 1449, the Norwegian Council again met, and after some discussion, it was decided to send Bishop Jens and Hartvig Krummedike as their representatives to Denmark. According to some accounts they went with express instructions *not* to tender the crown to Kristian, but according to others they were under no restrictions. The two ambassadors were Danes, and there seems no doubt that they offered the crown of Norway to the Danish king. The next month they returned to Oslo, bringing some Danish chief men with them and a writing from Kristian. Finally a majority of the council agreed to accept Kristian as king of Norway, and a meeting was arranged to be held at Marstrand in July, where Kristian was present. The meeting was duly held, and the newly-chosen monarch issued a manifesto to Norway. It was also settled that Kristian should proceed to Nidaros the next year to receive his crown. Meanwhile the government of the country was left in the hands of the archbishop and Sigurd Jonssøn.

So far all seemed to be regular, and the choice of King Kristian a free election on behalf of the Norwegian Council; but the Norwegian chiefs asserted later, that all that they had done, both at Oslo and Marstrand, was under compulsion, and that Bishop Jens and his brother ambassador, came back supported by a body of 2,000 Danes, and the archbishop and the Norwegian-Swedish party were obliged to agree to the proposals of Bishop Jens.

Meanwhile the supporters of Karl of Sweden had not been idle. In May of the same year, he had been chosen as king at a *Thing* held at Nidaros, and in October he came from Sweden to the Oplands, and was also accepted by a *Thing* at Hamar, at which the bishop was present. Then he went north to Nidaros, and Archbishop Aslak, who had by this time returned home (on the ground that he had acted under compulsion at both Oslo and Marstrand), received him, and crowned him in the cathedral on November 20th. A few days after Karl retired again to Sweden. There were now two kings formally accepted by the people in different parts of Norway, and the preponderance of the popular vote was undoubtedly given to Karl. The bishops were divided, the archbishop, and Bishop Jens of Oslo, heading the rival parties, and it seemed as if a civil war was inevitable. In the winter Karl made an attack on Oslo, the headquarters of the Danish party, but afterwards retreated to Sweden.

When the spring came, negotiations were opened between Kristian and Karl, and a conference held between their representatives at Halmstad. Here, it would seem, Karl's cause was betrayed; the greater prelates were hostile to him, and anxious for union with Denmark, and the result was that his claim to the crown of Norway was surrendered.

In July, 1450, Kristian sailed for Nidaros with a strong fleet, and met with no opposition; the archbishop had died at the end of 1449, and there was no one to lead the national party. On St. Olaf's day he was crowned in the cathedral, possibly by Marcellus, bishop of Skaalholt, of whom we shall hear more presently, but it is not quite certain. Before he left Nidaros, Kristian issued a proclamation to the people, defending his title to the crown in opposition to Karl of Sweden.

From Nidaros the new king went south to Bergen, where he held a meeting of the council. At this it was decided that Norway and Denmark were hereafter to be for ever united under one king, but that each kingdom was to be entirely independent. This completed the union of Norway and Denmark, which led to such disastrous consequences to the former kingdom, and which survived for the long period of 364 years. We have seen the active part which the prelates of Norway took in this matter. It is difficult, perhaps, to say that the archbishop's conduct was very straightforward throughout, though if it be true, as was asserted by the Norwegian party, that on the return of Bishop Jens he had with him a Danish army, then it is likely that Archbishop Aslak was compelled, against his will, to assent to Kristian's nomination. He justified his subsequent action on that ground, and there is no doubt that he honestly believed that the Swedish king's rule would be likely to be more advantageous to his country than that of Kristian. Bishop Jens of Oslo seems, like Nicholas, his notorious predecessor in that see, to have been a crafty and treacherous man, and to have betrayed the interests of Norway to the Danes. He was himself a

Dane, and was very much hated by the people in his extensive diocese, so much so, that an effort was made at one time to have him translated to Viborg, and the bishop of that see (who was a Norwegian) placed in Oslo; but the arrangement fell through, and Jens remained in possession of his see until his death.

We shall now see the result to the Church in Norway of the rule of the Danish kings, and the manner in which they deliberately set themselves, with the papal sanction, to destroy the right of free election, for which the Church had so long and zealously striven. The efforts of the king and the popes, were directed to placing in all the highest offices of the Church, men who had no interest in the country, and were, as a rule, ignorant of its language and customs, and who were appointed as a reward for services rendered to the papacy or the Danish court.

The accession of Kristian I. was marked by the commencement of a long conflict, which left the Church in Norway without a primate for a period of nearly ten years, and in which the struggle between the popes and the king, against the canonically-elected archbishop, did infinite harm to the cause of religion in Norway.

Archbishop Aslak Bolt died, as we have seen, at the end of 1449, and before the arrival of Kristian I. in Norway. On his death the chapter of Nidaros elected, as his successor, one of their own body, Olaf Throndssøn. This took place, it would seem, before July, 1450, in which month Kristian arrived at Nidaros. There was nothing to be alleged against the newly-chosen archbishop, but King Kristian had a fixed policy in his mind, which was to fill the sees of Norway, especially the primacy, with those upon whom he could depend to carry out his wishes. Kristian at once protested against the election of Olaf Throndssøn, on the ground that his approval had not been first obtained.

The king's object in this, was to secure the post for a
man on whom he reckoned to support his policy. This
was Marcellus, a Franciscan monk, whom he had succeeded
in inducing the pope in 1448 or 1449 to appoint as bishop
of Skaalholt, in Iceland. Marcellus, however, merely drew
the income of his distant diocese, but never went there.
The previous life of the bishop of Skaalholt seems to have
been open to grave suspicion, and it was supposed that he
had been in prison for frauds of one kind or another. It
would, however, appear that these charges, if not groundless, were "not proven," for the pope appointed commissioners later on to investigate them, and they practically
acquitted him.

In Marcellus King Kristian thought he had the man he
wanted as archbishop. At first, however, the chapter of
Nidaros were unwilling to give way, but a compromise
was arranged by which it was agreed to refer the dispute
between the king and the chapter to arbitration. The
arbitrators (among whom, curiously, was Marcellus himself) decided in the king's favour, and upheld his
contention that his consent was necessary for the election,
and recommended to the chapter Marcellus, "the king's
chancellor and bishop of Skaalholt and papal legate."
Now followed, perhaps, the most scandalous episode in the
history of the Church in Norway. Kristian and Marcellus
entered into a formal contract before a notary, the terms
of which still exist,* by which, as a reward for carrying
out the king's plans, he was to become archbishop of
Nidaros. Marcellus was to go to Rome, and there persuade
the pope to recognize the right of the king to present
to the bishoprics in Norway and Denmark, and also
to the appointment of clergy, and further that the
pope should sanction the union of the three kingdoms
under Kristian. If Marcellus did not accomplish this

* "Diplomatarium Norvegicum," Vol. II., 789.

before the Christmas twelvemonth following, the bargain
was to be at an end, and the king might appoint someone
else to Nidaros. When this shameful compact had been
made, Marcellus was, by some of the chapter, chosen as
archbishop in place of Olaf, whose election had been
declared invalid, and Marcellus went off with his monarch
to Denmark.

The king and Marcellus, however, reckoned without
their host. The pope (Nicholas V.) had himself another
candidate.* It is not quite clear if Marcellus went at
once to Rome in accordance with the compact, but in any
case he was not able to fulfil his part in time, though the
king did not abandon him as his candidate on this account.
The pope declined to recognize him, and in February,
1452, he nominated to the see of Nidaros, Henrik Kalteisen,
a German by birth, and one who had proved himself most
useful to the Holy See at the Council of Basel. Kalteisen
was a learned man of upright life, and had been Inquisitor-
general in Germany. He was then well advanced in years,
and quite ignorant of the language and everything else
connected with Norway.

The position of affairs was now a curious one. Three
men had been nominated to the vacant see. There was,
first, what we might call the national candidate, Olaf
Throndssøn, who represented the Norwegian Church, and
had been duly chosen by the Nidaros chapter after the
old and lawful manner ; secondly, there was the royal
nominee, Marcellus, who represented the claim of Kristian
to control the election; and, thirdly, Henrik Kalteisen,

---

* The reader will note how this case presents an exact parallel to the
state of affairs in England, in the famous dispute which ended in
Stephen Langton's elevation to the throne of Augustine. There was
King John's nominee, John de Gray ; the elect of the chapter of
Canterbury, Reginald ; and the papal nominee, Stephen. Unfortunately
for Norway, however, Henrik Kalteisen did not turn out a Stephen
Langton.

whom the pope wished to force on both the national Church and the king.

Armed with papal authority, Kalteisen betook himself at once to Kristian in Denmark. The king for the moment found it wisest to give way, and, abandoning his candidate, sent Kalteisen to Norway. Early the next year, 1453, the new archbishop was in Bergen, and in May he reached Nidaros. On his arrival, Henrik found that his new post was very far from being a pleasant one. The chapter, with more courage than we might have expected under the circumstances, protested against having as archbishop an old and feeble man, who would be unable to withstand the fatigues which the administration and visitation of his vast diocese must entail, and who, moreover, could not speak the language of his people. It was only natural that a man who had been accustomed to the comforts and mode of living of the south of Europe would, in his old days, shrink from the duties which lay before him. Henrik, who was a conscientious man, believed it to be his wisest course to resign the archbishopric.

At a meeting of the council, which was held in Bergen in October, at which the king was present, he expressed his willingness to resign. This course met with the unanimous approval of the council, and a letter to the pope was drawn up, begging him to accept Henrik's resignation and to appoint either Olaf or Marcellus, as his successor. This, however, the pope refused to do, and matters were again at a deadlock.

The next year Marcellus appears to have gone to Rome to urge his claims, but apparently without success, and on his way home he was attacked, plundered, and imprisoned at Köln, apparently by the townsfolk, but, as has been supposed, at the instigation of the Roman authorities. Marcellus appears soon to have obtained his release, as the next year we hear of him with the king in Denmark,

THE MARIA KIRKE, BERGEN.

Founded before 1183, later on the Church of the Hanseatic Merchants, hence called Tyske
(German) Kirken. The German language was used in the Services as late as 1868.

[To face p. 282.

whilst Henrik had left Norway and returned to the papal court.

While matters were in this state with respect to the primacy, a terrible tragedy occurred in Bergen in September, 1455—one happily unique in the history of the Norwegian Church.

The bishop of Bergen was now Thorleif Olafssøn. Before his preferment to that see he had been chaplain to King Erik, and afterwards bishop of Viborg. The governor of the city of Bergen was Olaf Nilssøn, who was extremely unpopular with the German merchants of the Hanseatic league, on account of the way in which he defended the rights of his countrymen against these traders, who sought to control all the business of the town. His unpopularity became so great that the king removed him from his post, whereupon Olaf, getting together a body of men, captured the Swedish stronghold of Elfsborg, and offered it to the king on condition of receiving back again his post at Bergen. This was agreed to, and Olaf Nilssøn returned to that city. Bishop Thorleif was friendly to the governor, and endeavoured to adjust the differences between him and the German residents.

The return of their old enemy with his power confirmed by the king, roused the German traders to madness. In vain the bishop did his best to make peace, but the merchants refused to listen to any conditions. Matters became so threatening that Olaf Nilssøn was obliged to seek refuge in the great cloister of Munkeliv, which crowned the ridge which divides the harbour (the opposite side of which was occupied by the German merchants) from what is now called the Pudde Fjord. To this place of refuge the bishop himself went, along with two priests.

On the 1st of September the outbreak took place. Swarming out from their quarter, the Germans and their followers, to the number of 2,000, marched round the end of the

harbour and attacked the great cloister. It would appear
that Olaf Nilssøn and the bishop were not prepared to
resist the assault. When the attack was made the bishop
was in the chapel. The doors were burst open, and a mob
invaded the sacred precincts. The bishop went to the
altar, and, taking the Host with him, calmly walked
forward to meet his foes; but, notwithstanding the fact
that he was their bishop, and that he carried in his right
hand the sacred Host, he was at once cut to pieces, as
well as his few brave adherents. Olaf Nilssøn had taken
refuge in the tower of the monastery, but this was promptly
set on fire. The smoke soon obliged him to surrender,
and on doing so he was at once put to death. The flames
spread to the rest of the building, and soon the great
Munkeliv cloister was but a heap of smouldering ruins.

This terrible outrage Kristian at first hesitated to
punish; but the pope acted with greater decision. All
concerned in the rising were at once excommunicated and
heavily fined, and the duty of rebuilding the cloister was
laid upon the German residents in Bergen.

Kristian, however, turned this matter to his own advantage. In his defence to the pope, he pointed out that this
disturbance and murder of one of the highest officers of
the Church, was an evidence of how much the country
suffered from the want of its proper ecclesiastical head,
and he again pressed forward the claims of Marcellus;
but neither side would give way. Soon another point in
dispute seemed about to arise between the king and the
pope. To fill the vacancy in the see of Bergen caused
by the murder of Bishop Thorleif, the king nominated
Joachim Grubbe, a Danish noble, but as he was under
canonical age it was necessary that he should obtain a
papal dispensation. This the pope promptly refused, and
nominated an Italian, Paolo Justiniani. Fortunately, however, in the interests of peace, Grubbe died at this time,

and the king, seeing that the papal nominee might be very useful to him, passed over the pope's arbitrary action in appointing Paolo to the vacant see.

It was in 1457 that, Karl Knutssøn having been expelled from Sweden, Kristian was elected king, and again united the three kingdoms under one monarch. He now decided to send Paolo Justiniani to Rome to try once more to gain the papal approval of Marcellus' appointment to Nidaros. This mission, however, was a failure, and in 1458 the pope (Calixtus III.) died and Pius II. succeeded him.

But now at last Kristian abandoned the cause of Marcellus, and consented to recognize Olaf Throndssøn. Henrik Kalteisen having persisted in his resignation, the pope agreed to accept Olaf, and he was consecrated in 1459, more than nine years from the date of his election by the Nidaros chapter. Marcellus had to be content with his Skaalholt bishopric, which he never visited, and in 1462 he was drowned off the Swedish coast.

We must now revert to the year 1458, when an important meeting was held at Skara, in the month of January.

King Kristian called together the principal ecclesiastics and chief men of Norway, in order to induce them to accept his son Hans, then a child of only two years old, as his successor to the crown of Norway. This, it seems, he had no difficulty in doing, the monarchy in Norway not being elective, as in the two other countries, and when Kristian was recognized, it followed by the Norwegian law that his eldest son should succeed him.

At this gathering Olaf Throndssøn was present, and though the king had practically withdrawn his opposition to him, he was yet only archbishop-elect. Along with him were the bishops of Oslo, Hamar and Stavanger, and some other prominent clergy. In the month of February they induced Kristian to accept the Tønsberg Concordat, which had been abandoned since the time of Erik, one hundred and sixty-eight years before. This was, at first sight, a great triumph on the part of the Church over the royal power, and we may wonder how it was that Kristian, who was determined to make the Church as much as possible subservient to him, would for a moment have consented to such a proposal. A little consideration, however, will make us see how this came about. In the first place, the king was very anxious to obtain the support of the Church in Norway for his young son Hans, and to obtain this, was prepared to make very great apparent concessions.

In spite of the state into which the Church had fallen, it was still the greatest power in the land, and, as most of the old Norwegian great men and chiefs, had been replaced by Danes, the ecclesiastics represented the popular feeling in Norway more than any other class. Again, it must be borne in mind that the very great concessions of the Tønsberg Concordat were at this time of comparatively little importance; the whole state of things had changed. The power of the papacy was widely different from what it had been, and although a power was given to the Church beyond anything which it had before, except for the few years in which the concordat lasted, yet, as has well been pointed out, it was only an authority on paper, and the very worst instances of oppression and disregard of the rights of the Norwegian Church took place, we shall find, under his successor. The semblance of power was given, but none of the reality. It is only fair to Kristian to say that he seems, on the whole, for the rest of his reign to have refrained from interference in the internal affairs of the Church in Norway.

We must here mention a political event which affected the Church, as it tended to further reduce the limits of the province of Nidaros. We have already seen how the diocese of Sodor and Man had become detached from it, and now another portion of the British Isles was about to follow in the same way. Kristian, unable to find the dowry (60,000 gylden) of his daughter Margaret, who married James III. of Scotland, promised in lieu of it (1469) to abandon the tribute which the Scottish kings had paid for the Hebrides since the time of Magnus Laga-bøter. This, however, was not enough, so he was obliged to pledge first the Orkneys, and then the Shetlands, and thus the ancient authority of the kings of Norway over these portions of the British Isles finally disappeared, as the money to redeem them was never afterwards forth-coming. The transference of authority was of course nominally only civil, and the Orkneys with their bishop still remained in the Nidaros province; but practically from this time onwards they were detached from their ancient ecclesiastical allegiance.*

Archbishop Olaf died in 1474, and his successor was Gaute Ivarssøn. Olaf had been for fifteen years recog-nized as archbishop, but was, twenty-four years before his death, elected by the chapter.

In 1474 Kristian went on a pilgrimage to Rome, and while there obtained the consent of the pope to the founding of a university at Copenhagen, but it was not finally established until 1479. The new university diverted the attendance of the Norwegian and Danish clergy from Rostock to Copenhagen, and was a great benefit to the cause of higher education in Norway and Denmark. Kristian I. died at Copenhagen in May, 1481, and was buried in Roskilde.

The death of Kristian I. was followed by a short inter-regnum. His son Hans had been, as we have seen, accepted by the Norwegian bishops and chief men as his

* A few years later, however, we find the Orkneys forming a part of the province of St. Andrews, and that bishopric is mentioned in the bull of Pope Sixtus IV. (raising the see of St. Andrews to metropolitan rank) as one of the suffragan sees in the new province.

father's successor at the meeting in Skara in 1458, but in spite of this, after Kristian's death the Norwegian government was carried on by the council, with the archbishop at its head, and it was not until January, 1483, at a meeting in Halmstad, that Hans was formally taken as king in Norway and Denmark. On February 1st the new king issued an important manifesto, which was known as the " Halmstad Recess," and which was intended to reassure his Norwegian subjects and to remove the grievances which were complained of. In this document Hans promised, among other things, to support the Church and uphold all its privileges. He would not interfere with the rights of election, or force foreigners into office in Norway, and the clergy were to be exempted from the civil courts in all ecclesiastical matters. The murderers of Bishop Thorleif were to be punished.

These promises were made by the king apparently for the purpose of securing the support of the Norwegians, but he afterwards violated them in almost every particular, and the Church in Norway, during his reign, was subjected to many indignities. At first, however, things seemed to go well. Hans came to Norway, and in July, 1483, he was crowned at Trondhjem * by Archbishop Gaute. After an absence of about three years, during which there was a considerable amount of discontent, the king returned to Norway, and after a meeting with the bishops and chief men at Bergen better relations were again established. In 1489 Hans secured the recognition of his son Kristian, then eight years of age, as his successor to the Norwegian throne.

There were at this time in Norway two distinct parties. Many of the people and clergy were hostile to the Danish rule, and wished for an opportunity of freeing their country

* The old name of Nidaros was abandoned for the modern Trondhjem a little before this time.

from it; but, on the other hand, there was a less numerous, but more powerful, body of the Danish noblemen who had received property in Norway from the king, and a certain number of officials. Many of the Danes had intermarried with Norwegians, and as time went on their numbers increased considerably, and eventually this led to the complete subserviency of Norway to the Danish kings, and brought the country into the position of merely a province in the kingdom of Denmark. These two rival parties had, as their leaders, Alf Knutssøn and Hartvig Krummedike. The former was, on his mother's side, a scion of a very old Norwegian family, closely connected with the ancient royal line; whilst the latter was a well-known Dane, whom we have met with before, in connection with the negotiations which ended in the election of Kristian I. to the throne of Norway.

Although Norway had accepted Hans in 1483, it was not until 1497 that Sweden came under his rule. Both countries were quite ready, when the opportunity offered, to try and get rid of their Danish monarch. This was presented to them in the year 1500. Kristian I. had received from the Kaiser Frederick III. the country of the Ditmarsk, in Holstein—a region lying between the Elbe and the Eider. The inhabitants of this district were a hardy race, who carried on a ceaseless warfare against the encroachments of the North Sea, and whose coast was defended by dykes, as in Holland. The land was in parts rich and fertile, but there was much fen country, and the narrow roads had usually a deep dyke on each side. The Ditmarskers were a brave and independent folk, and they did not approve of being handed over to a neighbour who, as such, was likely to exercise much greater authority over them than the kaiser. Kristian I., however, did practically nothing with regard to the country, and it fell to the lot of Hans to try to make his power felt.

At the beginning of 1500 the king and his brother, Duke Frederick, assembled an army with the intention of crushing out the independence of these hardy peasants. The forces of the king consisted largely of mercenaries, and his total strength is estimated at from twelve to fifteen thousand men. Without meeting any opposition he took possession of the town of Meldorf, and then in an evil hour decided to complete his conquest of the country, by going north to Heide. The distance was very short (between eight and ten miles), but the difficulties of the way were very great. The road lay between dykes, and was a narrow one, and rendered heavy by a thaw which had just set in. On February 17th the army started on the ill-fated march. The peasants were determined to make a stand for their liberty, and assembled under Wolf Isebrand. With difficulty the king's army made its way along the heavy road until they reached Hemmingsted, where, to their utter surprise, they found the enemy awaiting them, who at once opened fire upon the Danish forces. The cavalry were in the van, and were thrown into confusion, and the horses sank in the mire. The water in the dykes rose, as the people had opened the sluices, and the Ditmarskers at once attacked their foes. Twice they were repulsed, but the royal forces could not leave the narrow road and follow their agile assailants. To retreat or advance was impossible, and a third attack broke all attempt at resistance; the helpless soldiers were hewn down like sheep, and those in the rear alone were able to escape. King Hans and his brother managed to make their way out of the scene of slaughter with a mere fragment of their powerful force, and the victors (fortunately for them) did not attempt to follow up their success.

After this terrible defeat of King Hans the spirit of rebellion, which had long been smouldering in Norway and Sweden, soon broke into a flame. The chiefs of both parties were dead, but their sons, Knut Alfssøn and Henrik Krummedike, took their fathers' places. In 1501 Knut Alfssøn gathered men in Sweden, and attacked and captured Akershus at Oslo, and Tønsberg, and there seemed to be a prospect of breaking the Danish yoke. Henrik Krummedike, however, came to defend the cause of the king, and gained some advantage over Knut. The latter was now anxious to make terms, and was induced, in August, 1502, to go on board Henrik's ship under the promise of a safe conduct. When he got there he was at once treacherously murdered and his body thrown overboard. All his property was confiscated to the Crown. Thus, deprived of their leader, the Norwegian national party had no alternative but to submit. The Swedes, however, still continued the struggle.

The spirit of rebellion was not quite extinguished in central Norway, and only awaited an opportunity to manifest itself.

In 1507 King Hans sent his son, Duke Kristian, to Norway as governor. He was a young man of ability, but cruel and treacherous, and he soon had an opportunity of displaying these qualities. In 1508 the people of Hedemark rose in rebellion under Herluf Hufvudfat, but Duke Kristian quickly crushed it, and took the leaders prisoners and had them put to death at Akershus. According to some authorities it is said that before their death, they accused Karl, bishop of Hamar, who had only been three years bishop at the time of the rising, of having instigated the rebellion. Whether the bishop was guilty of the charge or not, Kristian determined to punish him. By deceit he induced Karl to come to him,* and at

---

* How little the bishop expected such treatment is shown by the fact that before he left his palace, he told his people he would return in eight days bringing back the duke as his guest. It was this which probably induced the bishop's servants to open the palace gates at once.

once threw him into prison, and started with an armed force for Hamar. Pretending that he and the bishop were pursued by the Swedes, the doors of the *bispegaard*, or palace, were thrown open to him. The place was then sacked by the duke and his followers, and the adjoining cathedral plundered. That this unparalleled outrage, which, by its attack on the bishop, entailed immediate excommunication on the duke, did not at once raise a storm throughout the land was a proof of the weakness of the Church and the power of the king. The duke left the bishop in prison without bringing him to trial. Archbishop Gaute does not seem to have done much on his suffragan's behalf. He wrote, indeed, to the king, and Kristian was called upon to defend himself to the pope, which he did with many false statements. The pope appointed two bishops, a German and a Dane, to investigate the case, passing over the archbishop. Nothing definite seems to have come of this, and the unfortunate bishop still remained a prisoner. His despair of ever obtaining justice, led him to attempt to escape, and in doing so he broke his leg, which seems to have hastened his death, for when, after four years' imprisonment, he was released in 1512, he died almost immediately after at Oslo.

Two years before this Archbishop Gaute Ivarssøn died, having filled the see of Nidaros for thirty-four years, a longer period than any of his predecessors. He seems to have been in ill-health and extreme old age at the time of Bishop Karl's imprisonment, or he would probably have taken some more energetic steps to obtain justice for him. The events which followed the death of Gaute showed the way in which King Hans observed the conditions of the Halmstad Recess. The chapter immediately elected John Krabbe as Gaute's successor, and he at once started for Rome to receive, as he expected, consecration.

King Hans and Duke Kristian between them had anti-
cipated the death of the old archbishop, and were determined,
in spite of the solemn promise to the contrary, to place a
Dane at the head of the Norwegian Church. They selected
as their candidate Erik Valkendorf, a canon of Roskilde
and chancellor and secretary to Duke Kristian, and they
seem to have arranged matters with the pope (Julius II.),
who was willing to have the royal nominee. Krabbe,
therefore, found he was not to be Gaute's successor, and
the pope, in August, 1510, overruling the choice of the
Nidaros chapter, nominated, *per provisionem*, Erik Valkendorf as archbishop, and he was forthwith consecrated.

We have seen that these events occurred during
the time the unfortunate bishop of Hamar was still in
prison. We have no certain knowledge if the new archbishop interfered on his behalf, but it was decided that
on his release, Karl was to be sent to Erik in Trondhjem,
but death, at Oslo, ended his troubles before this could be
carried out.

The arrest, and imprisonment of a bishop without trial
was, however, not a matter which could altogether be
passed over without notice, even by a pope friendly to
the duke and his father. By Kristian's act he was in law
ipso facto excommunicated, and it was necessary that he
should receive absolution. The papal nuncio Grave was
ordered to remove the Church's ban at the end of 1512,
and on Pope Leo X.'s accession (1513) he issued a bull to
the archbishop and the bishop of Roskilde directing them
to convey the papal absolution, if the duke would clear
himself by oath of having caused the bishop's death.
This Kristian did to their satisfaction.

King Hans, who had practically given over Norway to
his son, died, after a fall from his horse on his way to
Aalborg, in February, 1513, after a reign of thirty years.
We have seen the way in which he treated the Church in

Norway, notwithstanding the promises which he made at the commencement of his reign. It would perhaps be unfair to judge him too hardly in the matter of the barbarous treatment of Bishop Karl, but there can be no excuse for the deliberate policy which he sanctioned of filling all the highest offices in the Church with Danes instead of Norwegians, when he had distinctly pledged his royal word not to do so. More and more feeble grew the Church under its foreign rulers, darker and darker its prospects, and the end was not far off.

CHAPTER XX.

KRISTIAN II. AND FREDERICK I.—THE BEGINNING OF THE END.

Kristian's promises to the Church—Archbishop Erik's zeal—Dyveke and her Mother—Kristian's marriage—Erik leaves Norway—His death in Rome—Lutheranism in Denmark—War with Sweden—The "Bloodbath of Stockholm"—Kristian deposed, 1523—Olaf Engelbrektssøn, the last Archbishop, elected—His Character—Position of Affairs in Norway—Henrikssøn of Østeraat—Vincent Lunge—Norwegian Council accepts Frederick I.—His Manifesto from Ribe—Attacks on Church Property—Norway uninfluenced by the Reformation—The Bishops of Norway—Affairs of Denmark—*Herredags* at Odense, 1526-1527—First Lutheran preacher in Bergen—Destruction of Churches in Bergen—Lunge and Eske Bilde—Bishop Olaf Thorkildssøn Consents to the Destruction of his Cathedral—Archbishop Olaf powerless—The Norwegian Church turns to Kristian II.—He Abjures Lutheranism—Comes to Norway—Frederick Relieves Oslo—Surrender of Kristian under promise of Safe Conduct—His long Imprisonment and Death—The Rebellion Crushed—Death of Frederick.

As we are now rapidly approaching the time when the great blow fell upon Norway, which severed its connection with the Catholic Church of Western Europe, it is very necessary that we should note carefully the historical events which led up to this. We have seen the way in which the Danish kings Kristian I. and Hans had treated Norway, both ecclesiastically and civilly, and how their policy was to bring it into entire subserviency to Denmark. The few feeble attempts which the Norwegian people made to regain something of their old independence, show us how almost entirely, the spirit of the country had died out—or perhaps it would be fairer to say, how destitute the

land was then of a single capable leader, who would unite
the people, and lead them to victory and independence
once more.

The story of the disestablishment of the ancient Norwegian Church, and the erection in its place of the
Lutheran community, is one which presents few, if any,
redeeming features. Everywhere we note the rapacity of
the king and his courtiers, who destroyed in a wholesale
manner churches and monasteries, and almost for the time
swept all religion from the land; and on the other side we
find, with few exceptions, that the bishops and clergy
made but little resistance, and seem to have lost every
chance which offered to them, of taking decisive action at
a critical moment, when the whole situation might have
been changed.

Kristian II. (like his father before him) had been
accepted as king when he was only eight years old, during
Hans's lifetime, and at that monarch's death there was no
opposition to his claim in either Denmark or Norway.

Hans died in February, and in the July following
Kristian issued the customary manifesto, which contained
almost exactly the same promises to the Church and State
as that of the Halmstad Recess. It did not, apparently,
seem at all incongruous, that the man who had imprisoned,
and kept without trial for four years, a bishop of the
Norwegian Church, should promise to respect all its rights
and privileges, and that none of the high offices should be
filled with others than native Norwegians, when he had
been the means a short time before, of displacing the
canonically elected archbishop, in order to install a Danish
ecclesiastic in the primacy.

The year following he was crowned king of Norway at
Oslo, in the month of July.

The new archbishop, Erik Valkendorf, was a man who
had a very high sense of the duties of his office, and set

himself to look after the Church and province committed to his care. He had been chancellor and secretary to the king, during the time he had ruled Norway in his father's name, and Kristian, in forcing him on the Nidaros chapter by the exercise of the papal power, expected to find in him a willing agent for all his schemes with respect to the Norwegian Church. But Kristian found, as other kings before him had found, that a subservient chancellor and secretary, could become a very different kind of man when placed at the head of a national Church, whose interests might often come into collision with the head of the State.

At first, however, all went smoothly. Archbishop Erik devoted himself to the care of his diocese and province. Among other plans, he was very anxious to revive the connection with the distant diocese of Garde, in Greenland, which had almost ceased to exist. The Norse colony there had suffered a great deal from the attacks of the Eskimo, and the trade, which had at one time been fairly brisk between Iceland and Greenland, and through the former country with Norway, had practically come to an end. Bishops for the see of Garde had been consecrated, it is true, and were recognized as suffragans of the archbishop of Nidaros, but few, if any of them, ever went to their distant diocese. They acted as vicars for bishops, like Marcellus, who was bishop of Skaalholt, but never went to Iceland, and religion in Greenland had come to a very low ebb indeed.

We gain a very extraordinary picture of the state of the diocese of Garde from a bull issued by Pope Alexander VI. in 1492, in which he says:

" We understand the church of Garde is situated at the end of the world, in the country of Greenland, in which the people there living, for lack of bread, wine, and oil, are accustomed to make use of dried fish and milk, and on

account of the very rare voyages to the said land, caused
by the intense freezing of the waters, so that no ship is
believed to have made the voyage thither for eighty years;
and if any such voyage were to be made it is believed it
could only be done in the month of August, when the ice
is thawed. And for these same reasons the church there,
is said to have had for these eighty years, no bishop or
priest over it personally residing there. On account of
which absence of Catholic clergy it has resulted that
many who were once Catholics, and had received baptism,
have left the faith—shame be it said! Also that the
inhabitants of that land have nothing left in memory
of the Christian religion, but a *corporal* which is exhibited once a year, upon which, a hundred years ago,
the Body of Christ was consecrated by the last priest
remaining there." *

Archbishop Erik laid down plans for re-opening the
communication with this distant part of his province, and
made careful enquiries from all available sources as to the
voyage thither, &c., and there seemed a reasonable prospect
of something being done for Greenland. King Kristian,
however, declined to fall in with the archbishop's plans,
and the attempt failed. In 1519 or 1520 the last bishop
of Garde, Vincentius Kampe, was consecrated for a diocese
which, from his predecessor's neglect, might well be described as *in partibus infidelium*.

Kristian II. was unmarried when he ascended the
throne, and in 1515 he formed an alliance which tended
to considerably enhance his position among the princes
of Europe; but before we come to it it is necessary
to advert to an incident in his earlier life which had,

---

* " The Norse Colonization in America, by the light of the Vatican
Finds," by Marie A. Shipley. Lucerne, H. Kneller, 1899. Many
interesting details about Greenland will be found in Dr. Luka Jelic's
L' Evangélisation de l'Amérique avant Christophe Colomb.

indirectly, a most important influence on his subsequent history.

During Kristian's stay in Norway (in 1507), before he became king, he was present at a gathering at Bergen, where he met a very beautiful Dutch girl named Dyveke. The duke, as he then was, became enamoured of the fair foreigner, and took her with him to Oslo, along with her mother, Sigbrit, a very bad but clever and ambitious old woman, who speedily acquired a great influence over Kristian, which she used to the uttermost, and which eventually turned out to be most disastrous to him.

In 1515 Kristian arranged for his marriage with Isabella, daughter of Philip of Burgundy and sister of Charles of Burgundy, afterwards the Emperor Charles V. The following year the king sent an embassy, of which Archbishop Erik was the head, to fetch his bride from the Netherlands. Isabella arrived in Copenhagen in August, and was married and crowned there. It appears that Charles, the new queen's brother, had heard rumours of the king's connection with Dyveke, and wrote to Kristian on the subject. He also spoke plainly to the archbishop, before his sister's wedding, as to the importance of ending the affair, but, being then only a very young man, his remonstrances were unheeded. The archbishop both wrote and spoke to the king on the subject, and by this, not merely incurred the displeasure of Kristian, but drew down upon himself the anger of Sigbrit, Dyveke's mother, who vowed vengeance on him, and who, as we shall see, did not forget her vow. Kristian appears to have treated his young wife with great indifference, which she seems to have felt very keenly. The Emperor Maximilian, hearing of this, sent a special ambassador, Sigismund Herberstein, to remonstrate with Kristian, and try and induce him to break off all communication with Dyveke and her mother; but even this did not make any change in the state of

affairs. Indeed, it seems as if it only confirmed him in his
infatuation for them both.

Matters continued in the same way for some time longer,
and Dyveke and her mother lived close to the royal palace
in Copenhagen. In 1517, probably in June, Dyveke died
suddenly, not without suspicion of having been poisoned
in revenge for her interference in some court intrigues.
The death of his mistress, however, did not free Kristian
from the malign influence of her mother, the clever and
unscrupulous Sigbrit; indeed, it only seems to have riveted
the chains which bound him to this remarkable woman.
She was his chief adviser in matters both of Church and
State, and contrived to fill all the offices which fell vacant
in Norway, with those upon whom she could rely on being
faithful to her, and who would harass and thwart the
archbishop as much as possible. One of these was Hans
Mule, who, though a priest, was nominated as the adminis-
trator of Akershus, a purely civil office. In this post
Hans deliberately set himself to oust Bishop Andreas Mus,
of Oslo, from his see, and the unfortunate man was perse-
cuted in every possible way by Mule and his adherents.
The archbishop did his best to protect him, and wrote to
the king in 1519 to complain of Mule's actions. In 1520
there seems to have been an open rupture between Erik
and Mule, but Kristian was at this time engaged on his
expedition to Sweden.

The archbishop now determined himself to go to Denmark
and put his case before the king. In May, 1521, he made
arrangements in Trondhjem for a prolonged absence, and set
sail; but by stress of weather he was driven out of his course,
and found himself at the end of June, in Amsterdam, instead
of Copenhagen. Curiously enough King Kristian came to
the same place at that very time, as he was engaged in
some negotiations with his brother-in-law, Charles V. He
tried to have the archbishop arrested, but the authorities

refused, and, after an interview with the king, Erik went to
Utrecht, where he remained until November, when he
started for Rome, which, however, he did not reach until
February, 1522. Meanwhile he had written a long defence
of himself to the council in Denmark, in which he charged
Sigbrit with influencing the king against him in every
way. He came to Rome just at the time of the death of
Leo X. His successor was Adrian VI., with whom the
archbishop was personally acquainted, and from whom he
might well have expected to obtain justice. Unfortunately,
however, Adrian was delayed in Spain for some months
after his election, and did not arrive at Rome until the end
of August, whilst the unfortunate archbishop, worn out with
anxiety and the fatigues of his journey, died in November,
1522. Erik Valkendorf, although a Dane, had proved
himself a true friend to the Norwegian Church.* He had
set himself firmly on the side of morality and justice, and,
like many another before him, found the reward to be exile
from his country. The king's treatment of one who had served
him faithfully, only helps to show us what a treacherous
and worthless man he was. When the old archbishop, sick
at heart, found himself on his death-bed in Rome, without
having had his cause vindicated, he might well have used
(but with far greater truth) the bitter words of Pope
Gregory VII., " I have loved righteousness and hated
iniquity, therefore I die in exile."

During the time the archbishop was seeking to have his
case considered, the continued persecution against Andreas
Mus, the bishop of Oslo, had produced the desired result of
forcing him, in 1521, to resign his see, nominally of his
own free will. He, however, made a good bargain, and

* In Archbishop Erik's time, printing was first used for the Church
service books in Norway. He had the missal printed in Copenhagen and the " Breviarium Nidrosiense " printed in Paris, both in
1519.

was allowed to retain a considerable amount of the income. The chapter now proceeded to elect Hans Mule, but he was not then consecrated, and continued to hold his office under the Crown.

We must now retrace our steps a little and follow the course of events in Denmark.

The Swedes had been more successful than the Norwegians (after the defeat of Hans in 1500) in throwing off the Danish yoke, and maintained their independence under Sten Sture, and his son of the same name. Kristian, however, was watching his opportunity to recover what had been lost.

In 1517 the preaching of Luther had, as we know, aroused the attention of Europe, and Denmark, from its situation, was naturally soon affected by it. The sale of papal indulgences went on in Denmark and Norway, as well as in other countries, and in 1517 the papal legate, John Arcemboldus, came to Denmark* to sell them, and also to act as a mediator between Kristian and Sten Sture. On his arrival he made an arrangement with the king, by paying him the sum of 1,100 gulden, for the privilege of selling indulgences in his dominions, which he did largely in Denmark and Norway through his various agents. After spending a profitable and pleasant time in the former country he, in 1518, proceeded to Sweden, having gained Kristian's confidence and led him to suppose that he was entirely on his side. When, however, he came there, Sten Sture found it easy to bring him over completely to his views. Information of Arcemboldus's betrayal of his cause reached Kristian in 1519, and the king was furious and tried to seize him, but he managed to escape to Lübeck with a great deal of the money he had taken. Kristian,

* Full particulars as to the mission of Arcemboldus in Denmark and Sweden will be found in Paludan-Müller's " De første Konger af den Oldenborgske Slægt."

however, was able to secure some of it in Norway * and other places.

Enraged at the duplicity of the papal envoy, Kristian now decided to be revenged, by patronizing Luther. In 1520 he applied to the Elector of Saxony, who sent him a priest named Martin Reinhard, who arrived that year in Copenhagen. A Carmelite monk, Paul Eliæsssøn, seems to have been the person who suggested this course to the king, and when Reinhard came, he translated his discourses, as the former could not speak Danish. The efforts of Reinhard seem to have had no effect, and Eliæssøn, finding Luther went too far for him, gave up his emissary. It was about this time, and from no religious motives, that Kristian suppressed the nunnery of Gimsø, at Skien, in Norway.

In 1520 Kristian resolved to attack Sten Sture and, if possible, bring back Sweden to the Danish crown. In this he was successful. The king's army crossed into Sweden, and Sten Sture, defeated and mortally wounded at the battle fought on the ice at Bogesund, died very soon after. Now Sweden lay at the mercy of Kristian, though it was some months before he completed the conquest of the country.

On November 4th, 1520, Kristian was crowned at Stockholm, and there he assembled many of the principal nobility of Sweden, who, unsuspicious of any treachery, responded to the king's invitation. The coronation feast, however, was marked by a most horrible atrocity. The enemies of Sten Sture, headed by the Archbishop Gustav Trolle, determined to be revenged on their former antagonists. On the night of November 7th a number of the guests were suddenly arrested, and the next day taken to the

* The amount of money which Arcemboldus managed to get together by his sale of indulgences must have been considerable, as we learn that in Bergen alone, the king's man, Jørgen Hanssøn, contrived to seize a sum of no less than between 3,000 and 4,000 marks.

market place and there put to death one after another. No less than eighty persons are said to have been thus murdered, including the Bishops Matthias of Strengnæs and Vincent of Skara and many of the chief men in Sweden. This barbarous slaughter is known in history as the "Bloodbath of Stockholm," and the storm of indignation which it aroused was ultimately the cause of the downfall of Kristian.

The strength of the king's forces, for the present, held the Swedes in check; but the next year they rose in rebellion under the leadership of the famous Gustav Vasa, they drove out the Danes, and finally chose him as their king.

Kristian, during the progress of the struggle, demanded fresh supplies from Denmark. But now the end of his rule over that country was at hand. The nobles of Denmark were leagued against him, and offered the crown to his uncle, Duke Frederick of Slesvig. It is only fair to Kristian, to say that in spite of his many crimes, he was very popular with the bønder and the burgers of Denmark, whom he had always protected from the rapacity of the nobles. But in this crisis of his fate no one seems to have made any movement in his favour, and Kristian himself appears to have made no effort, though he had a certain number of troops at his disposal, to retrieve his fortunes. He decided to seek safety in flight, and in April, 1523, he left Copenhagen for the Netherlands, taking with him his wife and family, and, unfortunately, his evil genius Sigbrit, whose ascendency over him had not in the least diminished, and was popularly ascribed to witchcraft.

The tidings of the death of Archbishop Erik Valkendorf in Rome, do not seem to have reached the chapter at Trondhjem until the 30th of May, nearly six months after his decease; but as soon as it became known to them they decided to lose no time in exercising their rights, and a couple of days after, chose their dean, Olaf Engelbrektssøn, as Erik's successor.   The last archbishop of Nidaros was a Norwegian of an old noble family from the neighbourhood of Stavanger.   He had studied at Rostock, and was a man of some learning, and of a very considerable amount of worldly wisdom, which was manifested by his desire to keep himself right with whatever party was uppermost in the State at the time.   He was called upon to rule the Church at the most critical period of all its history, and unfortunately he was not the man for such a post at such a time.   Had he been a strong archbishop, and one who knew how to act promptly in an emergency, the history of the Church in Norway might have been different, as will be seen later on.   Immediately on his election he started for Rome, but instead of going *via* Copenhagen, where Frederick was now in power, he went to the Netherlands, and at Mechlines met the exiled Kristian II., who was still (legally) sovereign of Norway, and swore allegiance to him.   After this he proceeded on his way to Rome, where he was consecrated at the end of 1523.   On his way back to Norway he travelled by Germany and Denmark, and visited King Frederick I. at Flensborg in response to his invitation.   There seems no doubt that, to make himself quite safe with whichever king might reign, the new archbishop did homage there to Frederick, a trait in his character which does not exhibit him in a very pleasing light.   He reached Trondhjem in May.

Norway was placed in a rather peculiar position by the flight of Kristian II., who, though he had abandoned his throne, was still *de jure* king of Norway, until repudiated by the council, the Norwegians being under no binding obligation to accept Frederick (whom the Danes had proclaimed) as his successor.   Another difficulty was that the head of the council, and the chief director of affairs, in the case of a vacancy of the throne, was the archbishop, and at the time when Kristian fled the see was vacant. The two chief men in Norway were now Nils Henrikssøn of Østeraat (a spot at the entrance of the Trondhjem Fjord), who was a man of great wealth and power, especially in the north, and Olaf Galde, who possessed an equal influence in the Oplands and the south. Henrikssøn's wife was Fru Ingerd Ottesdatter, a woman who played an important part in subsequent events. By her Henrikssøn had no sons, but five daughters, all of whom were married to Danish noblemen, who occupied, as we shall see, most important positions in Norway. When Kristian fled, the council met and decided, during the vacancy in the see of Nidaros, to divide the government of the country between Henrikssøn and Galde, the former taking the north and west, and the latter, the south and east. There was, however, another powerful man in the country who represented the Danish interests, and whom we have met with before—namely, Henrik Krummedike, the treacherous murderer of Knut Alfssøn, the head of the Norwegian party, in 1502. He had been a strong supporter of Kristian II., but seeing his cause was hopeless, he at once made overtures to Frederick, and became the champion of his cause in Norway.

We now come to another man who exercised no small or unimportant influence on the history of this critical period—namely, Vincent Lunge. He was a Dane of noble family, and a man of great learning; he had been professor of law in the University of Copenhagen, and in 1521 was its rector. The studious atmosphere of a university life, however, did not meet with his wishes, and he abandoned it for the more exciting and dangerous paths of political life. In 1523 he came to Bergen to support the interests of Frederick, having first been to the north, where he married Margaret, one of the daughters of Nils

Henrikssøn. In November of this year Henrikssøn (to whom it was intended to give over the command of the Bergenhus, the fortress and royal castle at Bergen), was dying, and on his death the bishops of Bergen and Stavanger decided that Vincent Lunge was the best man to whom to commit the care of the fortress, as after his marriage, he seemed to have identified himself with the Norwegian interests. Thus Lunge became one of the principal men in Norway, and a member of the council.

Such was the state of affairs when the new archbishop, Olaf Engelbrektssøn, returned from Rome in May, 1524. No time was now lost in making arrangements for a successor to Kristian II. upon the throne. The council was called, and met in Bergen in August, with the archbishop at its head. Their first act was to renounce their allegiance to Kristian, and, the throne becoming vacant, they had to choose another king. Frederick was apparently the only candidate, but the council was not by any means prepared to elect him unconditionally. Vincent Lunge, who was naturally a supporter of his, was, however, quite as decided as the others in his determination to preserve, as far as possible, the entire independence of Norway as to internal affairs, while accepting the Danish monarch as king. In pursuance of this policy the council decided to draw up a manifesto, which was to be submitted to Frederick, and if he agreed to its terms, they were willing to tender him their allegiance. At the same time a letter was written denouncing Henrik Krummedike as an enemy of Norway.

The manifesto of the council was at once dispatched to Frederick, in charge of Vincent Lunge, who met the king at Ribe, in Denmark. At that place, in November, 1524, Frederick I. accepted the proposed terms and affixed his seal to them.

This manifesto followed mainly the lines of similar

x 2

documents which had been issued by the previous Danish kings to Norway, and bound the king to the observance of terms which his predecessors had accepted but never kept. But in this new manifesto fresh conditions were inserted, in view of the advance of Lutheranism, which it is very necessary for us to note.

After the usual promise to protect the Norwegian Church and to give freedom of election, &c., Frederick solemnly vowed that he would never permit heretics, Lutherans or others, to preach contrary to the faith of the holy Church ; and wherever such heretics were found in Norway, he would punish them with loss of life and goods. In addition to this he promised that appeals should not be permitted to Rome, before the Norwegian prelates had considered the matter. It will be seen by the above that the bishops in Norway were alive to the danger which threatened them, and they desired to bind the king down very strictly, by a promise to check the spread of the doctrines of Luther, especially when they knew that the Danish kings, chiefly from political motives, had been inclined to favour the German reformation movement.

The purely civil points in the manifesto were promises to rule according to the law of St. Olaf and the national customs, &c. He was not to claim the throne by hereditary right, as it was now made an elective monarchy. The Orkneys and Shetlands were to be redeemed and restored to Norway, from which country they had been alienated without the consent of the Council.

Frederick accepted these conditions to obtain the crown of Norway, but accepted them without (as his subsequent actions showed) the least intention of being faithful to his promise.

The king at this time was of the mature age of 53, and there was, therefore, less excuse for his deliberate breach of faith with the Norwegian Church. The only excuse for him was, that he was more or less in the hands of the Danish nobles and others, who hoped to profit, as they did largely, by the spoliation of the Church. The Danish party were determined, as soon as possible, to crush out the independence of Norway and to reduce it to the condition of a province of Denmark. On this account Vincent Lunge, who was now on the side of Norwegian independence under the Danish Crown, became very unpopular, and the court decided to get rid of him, if possible, and to place Danish nobles in command in all the Norwegian strongholds. The first step in this direction was to remove Olaf Galde (in 1527) from the charge of Akershus and to set a Dane in his place. Needless to say, this was entirely contrary to the terms of the manifesto issued from Ribe.

The next year (1528) the king determined that the command of the fortress at Bergen, should be transferred from Vincent Lunge to Eske Bilde, another Danish noble, who had married a daughter of the notorious Henrik Krummedike. This change of command was carried out early the next year.

Vincent Lunge was, however, allowed to hold many possessions in the north, and was further given the Nonnesæter cloister at Bergen, which was seized by the king from the Antonius order. This cloister lay on the neck of land between the two small lakes to the south of Bergen, and Lunge quickly transferred it into a well-defended house for himself, and called it Lunge's *Gaard*.* These two lakes now preserve his name, and are known as Lungegaardsvandene.

We now come to the time when the Norwegian Church had to enter upon the conflict in which she was crushed, and when all the ancient possessions wherewith the piety

* Some remains of the cloister may still be seen, including the doorway of the chapel.

of her sons and daughters had endowed her from the earliest days, were to be swept away into the pockets of the king of Denmark and his needy courtiers. Never was there a more wanton spoliation than that which befell the Church of Norway, and never had religion less to do with it. The attack on, and the plunder of, the Norwegian Church was practically something entirely apart and distinct from religion. In other countries of Europe—in Germany, Holland, Denmark, &c.—the teaching of Luther had profoundly impressed the minds of the people, and they accepted the principles of the Reformation, on thoroughly conscientious grounds. The abuses and corruptions of the time had called aloud for reform, and when the various councils which had been held were found powerless to effect this, and the occupants of the Roman See were men less and less likely to combat them, it was only natural that in the Teutonic races, the old spirit of independence should assert itself, and make an effort to cast off a yoke which had proved too galling.

But it cannot be said with truth that there was in Norway any real desire for change. We have noticed before, that the Church in Norway had escaped many of the corruptions which prevailed in other lands, on account of its remote geographical position. It is quite true, of course, that it did not escape altogether, and that, especially after the desolations caused by the Black Death, there was much to lament over; but to assert that the disestablishment and disendowment of the Church in Norway had any real popular support, would be entirely and altogether contrary to fact. The popular movements which we meet with in England during the middle ages, against the abuses of the Church, and the evil lives of many of the monks, had no counterparts in Norway, possibly from the very reason just stated. But the fact remains that in Norway there was no reformation movement whatever. No Wyclif was

found among her parish priests ; no Lollards ever caused
disquietude to the bishops; no Piers Plowman ever dreamed
dreams or saw visions on the Norwegian hills.   Priests
and people alike lived contentedly within the fold of the
holy Church.   Its spoliation therefore was completely
a political movement, and the work of a king who had
solemnly pledged his royal word, a few years before, to
do everything in his power to support the Church and to
prevent the spread of the teaching of Luther.

It was a very unfortunate thing for the Norwegian
Church in this critical time, that the five sees were filled
with men of very different calibre from many of their
predecessors.   Had they been men of power, it would
hardly have been possible, that the wholesale destruction
which went on from 1528, could have taken place.   It
would be unfair to assert that it was because they were
more or less nominees of the Danish Government, for
Erik Valkendorf was a Dane, and he proved himself a
strong and capable archbishop and a defender of the
Norwegian Church's privileges ; and now the occupant of
the see of Nidaros was a member of an old Norwegian
family.

It may be well here to call to mind the names of those
who were the bishops at this time.   Of the primate we
have already spoken.

The bishop of Bergen was Olaf Thorkildssøn, who was
consecrated in 1523.   He seems to have been the most
feeble of all the prelates, and was unfortunately in the
place where a very strong man was specially needed.   He
was, it is believed, personally a good man, but when the
storm came, his only idea was to get away from it, and
leave his unfortunate diocese and cathedral city to shift
for themselves.

Stavanger was filled by Hoskold Hoskoldssøn, who was
consecrated in 1513.   He was a graduate of Rostock.   Like

his brother of Bergen, he was timid and feeble, and was entirely at the mercy of the Danish nobles, who dominated the land.   The occupant of the see of Oslo was a man of very different type from the bishops of either Bergen or Stavanger—the unscrupulous and time-serving Hans Reff, who was consecrated in 1525.   He had succeeded Hans Mule, who, as we have seen, forced Andreas Mus to resign his see in 1521, but Mule was not consecrated until 1524 by Archbishop Olaf in Bergen.   He, however, was drowned very soon after his consecration.   Hans Reff was a Dane, and had studied in Paris, and before his election he had been a canon of Nidaros.   He was a very shrewd man of business, and was not willing to allow his opinions to interfere with his worldly prospects.

The remaining diocese, that of Hamar, had as its bishop Magnus Lauritssøn, who was a man diligent and conscientious in the discharge of his duties, but otherwise not of any great power.

Such were the rulers of the Norwegian Church when the struggle commenced in 1528, and in a few years after, with one ignoble exception, we find them all scattered, and the historic episcopate of Norway a thing of the past.

We must turn again for a moment to the history of Denmark, in order to see the progress which the reformation movement was making in that land.   Frederick I., though posing as a defender of the faith in Norway, had always been inclined to the opinions of Luther, while his son, Duke Kristian, was openly a Lutheran.   The prospect of the progress of the reformation movement, began to alarm the bishops and clergy in Denmark, and the question came before the national assemblies.   In 1526 the king held a Diet, or, as it was called in Denmark, a *Herredag*, at Odense, and at it he proposed that, instead of going to Rome for confirmation, the bishops should only apply to the archbishop of Lund, and the money thus saved should go to national defence. There was no special objection to this, on the part of the *Herredag*, especially as it was but a return to ancient and lawful custom in the Danish Church; but then it was to be remembered that the see of Lund was vacant, and it meant that the king was to be the person to confirm the election of the bishops.

The bishops, in return for this concession, asked the king not to grant letters of protection to any persons enabling them to preach, as it was their right to give such licence. Frederick was, however, very skilful in evading any direct answer to these demands; indeed, he denied that he had ever given such letters, and when again pressed on the subject, he managed to avoid a reply, and kept the bishops at bay until he left Odense.

The next year another *Herredag* was held at the same place in August, and now the king's designs became more and more manifest. Still, he had to be cautious, because it was necessary that he should have the nobles on his side, and do nothing by which he should lose their support while the exiled King Kristian II. lived, whose popularity with the bønder and towns-folk was a standing danger to Frederick. But notwithstanding this, it was clear that he intended to grant, at any rate toleration, to the Lutherans throughout his dominions, and this, in spite of the prelates, he was able to do, and to carry the *Herredag* with him in his reforms. What was decided practically established religious liberty and toleration for Lutherans, and gave permission to the priests and monks to marry, if they thought fit.

It was only natural that these very revolutionary changes should excite the greatest hostility on the side of those who still held by the Roman allegiance, for they at once opened the door for the spread in every direction of the tenets of the Lutherans, and the king's son, Duke Kristian, was a strong supporter of Lutheranism. In

Denmark, at any rate, the reformed doctrines were widespread among the people, and the continual controversies between the nobles and bishops, prevented any effective opposition to them, on the part of the adherents of the old faith.

As was only to be expected, it was not long before these changes in Denmark began to make themselves felt in Norway as well. Hitherto no teacher or preacher of Lutheranism had come to the country, but when the king began to grant letters of protection, they soon put in an appearance.

In 1528, the year after the *Herredag* at Odense, the first preacher arrived in Bergen. His name was Antonius; but beyond this we know little, and he seems to have devoted himself chiefly to the German residents in the city, and afterwards he was the priest of St. Halvard's Church. It would appear that the preaching of Antonius was attended with success, for we find that he required help, and in the next year, 1529, two more Lutheran teachers arrived in Bergen, with a letter from the king to Eske Bilde, announcing that he had granted his permission to them. The names of the new preachers were Herman Fresze and Jens Viborg. It would seem that in the same year teachers appeared also in Stavanger.

King Frederick in 1529 sent his son Duke Kristian to Norway, on a mission which had more of a political than ecclesiastical character. He was anxious that Kristian should be accepted as the heir to the throne of Norway, but at the time of his own election, in 1524, the Norwegian Council had made it clear that they did not recognize any hereditary right to the throne. The duke held a meeting in Oslo, at which the archbishop and all the Norwegian bishops (except Hans Reff) were conspicuous by their absence. The mission of Duke Kristian was a failure as far as the recognition of his rights was concerned, and instead of spending some considerable time in the country, and visiting Bergen, he left Oslo in September for Denmark.

We must now turn our attention to the extraordinary attack which was made upon the Church in the city of Bergen and see the amazing and shameful way in which the bishop seems to have betrayed his trust. We have already seen that the Nonnesæter cloister had been secularized in 1528, and handed over to Vincent Lunge as his private residence. About the same time it would appear that the Dominican cloister, which stood near to the royal residence and the castle (Bergenhus), had been burned down. It is not quite clear how this came about, but it is believed that Vincent Lunge and the prior Jens Mortenssøn divided the spoils of the monastery between them and then set the place on fire.* The prior received compensation for the loss by a grant of some farms. Another act of spoliation at this time was the stripping of the Apostles' Church (the chapel royal) of all its valuables, and these Vincent Lunge handed over to the king on his visit to Denmark in 1530.

It would seem that Lunge took this journey in order to try and regain the royal favour, but in this he does not appear to have been very successful. On his return to Bergen he tried, by a daring stroke, to regain possession of the Bergenhus or fortress. Eske Bilde was, as we have seen, placed in command there in 1529 by the king in place of Lunge, and was naturally his most formidable rival. Lunge, when he came back to Bergen, at once applied to Bilde to surrender the fortress to him, on the ground that he had received the command of it from the king during his stay in Copenhagen. Eske Bilde promptly declined to do any such thing without written authority, and applied

---

* Lange, in his *De Norske Klostres Historie*, seems to make no doubt about this; he also adds that the prior Jens Mortenssøn appears to have taken service in Vincent Lunge's household afterwards.

to the king, 'who repudiated Lunge's statement and confirmed Eske Bilde in his post.

Now began the wholesale destruction of ecclesiastical buildings in the city of Bergen, which marked the rule of the Danish governors, and swept away many noble edifices which had adorned the town. This was especially the work of Eske Bilde, and it gained for him the unenviable title of *Kirkebryder*—the puller-down of churches.

Clustering around the Bergenhus, with the noble hall built by Sverre's grandson, Haakon Haakonssøn, there stood at that time a number of churches.* The first in importance was the cathedral, the greater Christ Church, so closely associated with the national history (second only in this respect to the Domkirke in Trondhjem), and the burial-place of kings and bishops. Then there was the little Christ Church, a short way from the cathedral, and of earlier date, having been built about the time the town was founded by Olaf Kyrre; in it rested the remains of St. Sunniva, which had been brought from Selje in the twelfth century. In the precincts of the royal palace stood the Apostles' Church, which was the most beautiful building in Norway. It was the third church which had borne the name. The first was of wood, and was destroyed by fire; the second, of stone, was consecrated by Cardinal William of Sabina in 1247. Then in 1302 Archbishop Jon returned from Paris, bringing with him a "Holy Thorn," which he had received from Philip III. of France, and for this relic a third church, somewhat in the style of *Sainte Chapelle* in Paris was erected, and adorned with statues of the twelve Apostles. This church, like its predecessors, was the royal chapel in Bergen. The archbishop's palace and the residences of the canons completed

* For a description of Bergen in the Middle Ages, see Dr. Yngvar Nielsen's valuable work, entitled, *Bergen fra de ældste Tider indtil Nutiden*. Christiania, 1877.

the ecclesiastical buildings, the Dominican cloister having been just burned down. Such were the buildings which now lay at the mercy of Eske Bilde.

Here was a chance which a Cromwell might have envied for earning the title of *Kirkebryder*. But even Eske Bilde could hardly embark on this without some excuse, and a convenient one was found. It was discovered that these various churches interfered with the defensive works of the fortress, and that the exigencies of the public service demanded their removal. King Frederick, therefore, in 1530 ordered Eske Bilde to begin, and promptly the Apostles' Church became a thing of the past, and its treasures were carried to Denmark. The next to be attacked was the cathedral, but here even Eske hesitated. As a skilful soldier he saw that the great monastery of Munkeliv, on the opposite side of the harbour, would be a much better position for a fortress, than the one which he occupied, which was commanded on all sides by hills; he was willing to leave the cathedral alone and build a new fort on the site of Munkeliv. His scheme, however, was not carried out, and the doom of the cathedral was pronounced. We might well wonder what the bishop of Bergen was doing at this time, and why he had not taken some very decided steps to have the Church's property protected, and to stop the destruction of churches and other ecclesiastical buildings, in which he would have had ample support in the ancient law of the land. But he did absolutely nothing, and was actually a consenting party to their destruction. In February, 1531, the bishop and the archdeacon made a bargain with Eske Bilde and others to permit the cathedral to be pulled down,* along with the bishop's residence, on the ground that it was needed for the defence of the town, and in lieu of the cathedral, &c.,

---

* They abandoned it " of their free will, well-considered counsel and consent . . . to be broken down and carried away."

the bishop was to have Munkeliv for his cathedral and residence. This scandalous bargain having been made, the bishop actually issued an invitation to the people of the town and its neighbourhood, to come and help in the pulling down of his ancient cathedral church, and in May of this year, the place was levelled to the ground. These attacks on the Church in Bergen naturally emboldened the adherents of the Lutheran party, and, far from becoming popular with them for his acquiescence in the designs of the Danish nobles, the bishop was openly insulted in the streets. The Lutherans now seized upon the Kors Kirke (Church of the Holy Cross) and established the reformed service there. Not long after this, the German merchants put an end to the service in the Maria Kirke, and placed there a German pastor instead of the Norwegian priest, and in St. Halvard's Church the same course was adopted. These measures provoked reprisals, and an attempt was made to burn down the house of one of the German preachers.

The feeble Bishop, Olaf Thorkildssøn had now taken up his residence in the Munkeliv cloister, from whence the Birgitta order had been expelled, and here he remained for a while without any attempt to save the Church in his diocese. It might naturally have been expected that when the attack was first made in the beginning of 1530, on the churches around the fortress, he would have appealed at once to the primate for aid, not merely as his metropolitan, but as the head of the council in Norway. But incredible as it may seem, it was not until the devastation was completed, that he informed Archbishop Olaf of what had taken place. What he might have done to assist his suffragan in the defence of the Church's property under other circumstances, it is hard to say; but just at this time the archbishop had his hands full in his own diocese, for there, as well as in Bergen, attacks

were being made on the property and privileges of the
Church. The archbishop's principal antagonists were
Nils Lykke and his mother-in-law, the well-known Fru
Ingerd (widow of Nils Henrikssøn), whose eldest daughter
had, as we know, married Vincent Lunge. Lykke had
secured possession of the monastery of Tautra, and Fru
Ingerd had got herself elected abbess of Reins cloister,
both entirely illegal acts, which afterwards received the
royal sanction. Fru Ingerd and her party were nominally
inclined to the Lutherans, but it seems probable that they
adopted that course, merely out of hostility to the archbishop, and not from any conscientious motives.

With this threatening state of affairs, and the evident
intention of the king to consent to the secularization of the
Church's property and to give free scope to the spread of
Lutheranism, the archbishop and others began to turn their
thoughts to the exiled king, Kristian II., in the hope that
he might prove a deliverer. The previous record of that
monarch was not indeed an encouraging one. During his
reign the attack on the monastic establishments had begun :
his manifesto on his accession he had disregarded in quite
as flagrant a manner as Frederick had done ; and his conduct during his government of Norway in his father's lifetime, was not such as to inspire any confidence in him.
Still there seemed no one else to whom the archbishop and
his party could turn for help in this emergency; and besides,
it was to him, that the archbishop had first sworn allegiance
after his election to the primacy, and on his journey to
Rome to be consecrated in 1523.

Kristian II., after his flight from Copenhagen in 1523,
had, as we have seen, taken up his residence in the Netherlands with his wife and family, and also the notorious
Sigbrit. There he was received with scant courtesy, on
account of his having encouraged Lutheranism, and also for
his having, after his marriage with Isabella, refused to

abandon Dyveke, and his still being under the influence of her mother. Queen Isabella died in 1526, and left one son, Hans. While Kristian's mother-in-law, the Duchess of Savoy, lived, her influence prevented Charles V. from doing anything to help him, but after her death in 1530 his prospects improved. A few months before, Kristian had had an interview with his imperial brother-in-law at Augsburg, and found him ready to give him some help, but not unconditionally. Before Charles V. would do anything, it was absolutely necessary that Kristian should purge himself from any suspicion of being tainted with Lutheran heresy. Where his own interests were concerned, Kristian was quite ready to abjure any form of faith which the emperor might desire. Charles then entrusted to Cardinal Campeggio, the task of reconciling his unworthy brother-in-law to the Church, and before the cardinal, Kristian solemnly declared his abhorrence of all the doctrines of Martin Luther, and submitted with good grace to the severe penance which Campeggio imposed upon him, for his previous backsliding from the Catholic faith.

Having thus made his peace with the Church and regained a measure of the favour of his powerful relative, Kristian awaited a favourable opportunity of making an effort to recover his lost dominions. King Frederick had always feared lest he should be attacked by Kristian, knowing how popular he had been with the people in Denmark, but without imperial support Kristian had not the means of equipping any force powerful enough to attack Denmark or Norway. He had, however, his agents, who were watching the course of events, and when he learned of the attacks which had been made on the Church in Norway and elsewhere, he began to think that the prelates would— in spite of his previous record—be ready to welcome him as a deliverer.

It is difficult to say if the archbishop had been in any

treasonable correspondence with the exiled king; on the whole it is probable he had not, but his conduct in 1531, before the arrival of Kristian, was, to a certain extent at any rate, open to suspicion. In May, 1531, King Frederick issued summonses for a *Herredag* to be held at Copenhagen in the June following, and to this the archbishop and bishops of Norway were duly cited. Eske Bilde, who, in spite of his love for destroying churches, seems to have been a more honest man than his rivals Vincent Lunge and Nils Lykke, was very anxious that the archbishop should be present at this meeting, and that he should come to better terms with the king. The archbishop, however, did not seem inclined to go, and in May he found a suitable excuse in a great fire which broke out in Trondhjem, and which destroyed some of the churches and almost again ruined the cathedral. This calamity sufficed to keep Archbishop Olaf at home; but the bishops of Bergen, Stavanger, and Oslo started for Copenhagen, and thither also went Vincent Lunge, Eske Bilde, Nils Lykke, and all the chief Danish nobles from Norway.

This was the opportunity for which Kristian was waiting. His trusty men went through the country preparing the people for the revolt, and received much encouragement from the Church. They passed through the Oplands and on to Trondhjem and collected supplies, which were sent to Kristian in the Netherlands. By means of this money, and the help of the emperor, Kristian got together an army of 7,000 men, and a fleet of twenty-five ships, and at the end of October, 1531, he set sail for Norway. The voyage from Holland proved a most tempestuous one; some of his ships were lost, and much of his treasure and artillery. He did not reach the Norwegian coast until November 5th, and the next day he issued an appeal to the people of Norway, in which he said he came to them as a deliverer and asked that representatives of the country should meet him at

Oslo, to which place he made his way, having written to the archbishop to meet him there. On his arrival at Oslo he found the fortress of Akershus in the hands of Gyldenstjerne, the Danish commander, who declined to give up the place until he had communicated with Frederick, but promised if he did not hear within a reasonable time, he would surrender. Kristian was foolish enough to agree to this, but it is also probable that, having lost all his guns, he found an attack would not be successful.

The crafty bishop of Oslo, Hans Reff, now found himself obliged to accept Kristian's authority, and he authorized the clergy in his diocese to give up all the silver belonging to their churches, except what it was absolutely necessary to retain. This was largely done, and the churches were much impoverished.

The archbishop did not respond to Kristian's invitation to join him at Oslo, but contented himself with proclaiming him and sending his manifesto round his diocese. In January, Kristian wrote from Oslo to the archbishop, directing him if possible to seize Vincent Lunge and Fru Ingerd, but in this he was not successful, as they escaped to Bergen.

Early in the month of January, 1532, Kristian, finding he could do nothing against the fortress of Akershus, went on an expedition against the Swedes, who had invaded the country near Baahus. This expedition was successful, and the Swedes were driven back. In the meantime, however, the brave defender of Akershus had not been idle. Finding that Kristian was absent, he, on January 21st, made a sortie from the fortress, and, crossing the ice, attacked the monastery on Hovedøen, and seizing the abbot, who was asleep in his bed, little dreaming of danger, burned the cloister, and carried off all the treasure to Akershus. When Kristian heard of this, he quickly returned to Oslo, and made another attack on the fortress,

which was repulsed, and Gyldenstjerne now considered he was strong enough to hold out until help came in the spring.

It seems strange that Kristian should have wasted his time in the investment of Akershus, instead of consolidating his power in Norway, which was now nominally under his authority, but he seems to have always failed to act with energy, even when he had a sufficient force behind him.

Meanwhile Frederick was busy preparing to crush his nephew. As soon as he heard of the invasion of Norway he saw it must be a struggle to the death with Kristian, and he set to work at once to gather his forces. The Lübeckers, at the end of November, 1531, sent him some ships and a promise of more help later on. Kristian had been wise in choosing the winter for the time of his attack on Oslo, as the ice in the fjord rendered it impossible for a Danish fleet to reach the town, and it was not until the spring that the expedition to relieve it could start. The months went by and Kristian remained inactive before Akershus. At last, on May 7th, Frederick's fleet, of twenty-five ships and 6000 to 7000 men, reached Oslo and relieved Akershus. Kristian then entrenched himself at Oslo, but the Danish forces set fire to his ships, and on the 12th he began negotiations for surrender.

While this was going on, Eske Bilde sent Otto Stigsen, Thord Roed, and others from Bergen to attack the archbishop in Trondhjem. He retired to his castle at Stenviksholm, but the Danes set fire to the archbishop's palace and some of his farmhouses.

Frederick had not come in command of the army and fleet sent to relieve Oslo, but gave the expedition into the hands of four men, to whom also he entrusted full authority to treat with the enemy. These were Knut Gyldenstjerne (the Bishop of Fyen), Nils Lykke, Von Heiderstorp, and the brave defender of Akershus, Mogen Gyldenstjerne,

Y 2

brother of the bishop. Along with these men he sent his secretary, with his royal seal, and gave them full authority to act in his name.

The negotiations were prolonged between Kristian and the Danes, but finally it was agreed that Kristian was to be given a safe conduct to Copenhagen, in order that he might have an interview with his uncle Frederick. There can be no doubt that the four commissioners distinctly pledged themselves to this, and that if no definite agreement was made between the kings, Kristian should be brought in safety to Germany. But between the opening of negotiations for the surrender at Oslo and the month of July, it is said that Frederick sent two of his men with strict orders to Gyldenstjerne and the others, to make no terms with Kristian except absolute and unconditional surrender, and that when they reached Oslo the conditions, though agreed upon, had not been signed. Gyldenstjerne and the others declined to obey, as they had unlimited authority given to them, but on the other hand, they did not tell their victim of the king's fresh orders.

On July 8th the betrayed man embarked for Copenhagen, which he reached on the 24th. When he got there he soon saw the deceit which had been practised upon him. Frederick refused to see him, and he was not allowed to land. Still ignorant of his fate, he was taken nominally to Flensborg, where he expected to find the king; but when the ship proceeded to the castle of Sønderborg, he saw he was betrayed, and burst into tears.

At the beginning of his imprisonment another heavy blow fell upon him; his only son, Hans, died at Augsburg in August, 1532, and now all hope of deliverance was gone. At Sønderborg he remained for seventeen years, at first treated fairly, but afterwards with great severity. At the end of that period he was removed to Kallundborg, where he was left until in 1559 death at last set him free at the age of seventy-eight years.

The violation of the promised safe conduct was undoubtedly an act of the greatest treachery, and for which we cannot acquit King Frederick. He had first given the four commissioners full authority and his royal seal, to sanction all that they did in Norway, and his messages sent when the negotiations were concluded (though not signed) could hardly be well set against this. The blame must, of course, be shared by those who refused to tell Kristian in time, of the message they had received, so as to give him an opportunity of leaving Norway for the Netherlands, or some other safe place. It remains, however, a lasting stain on the character of Frederick, and that he felt his conduct needed explanation is shown by his letter addressed to the princes of Germany, in which he tried to defend himself.[*]

In spite of the treachery shown towards him, and his long and weary incarceration, it is hard to feel much sympathy for Kristian II. During those twenty-seven years of imprisonment, he had ample time to reflect upon the terrible crimes which had darkened his life. In the silent watches of the night, the memory of his own harsh imprisonment of the hapless bishop of Hamar, must often have come before his mind, together with the recollection of the way in which he had broken the promises made at the time of his accession to the throne. Visions of the awful "Blood-bath of Stockholm" may well have filled him with horror. Those terrible words to a guilty conscience, "With what measure ye meet, it shall be measured to you again," may well have rung in his ears. The long years of his weary imprisonment may (let us hope) have led the discrowned king in his old age to reflect upon the irreparable

* C. Paludan-Müller, "De første Konger af den Oldenborgske Slægt." p. 560.

harm that he had done to the countries over which he had been called to rule, and have taught him that the highest glory of a king was to do justice and right, and that to keep faith with his people, was a more noble ornament than the triple crown which had once been his.

With the surrender at Oslo all resistance to the authority of Frederick in Norway came to an end. Nils Lykke was sent from the king, with full power to deal with those who had been concerned in the rising. Frederick does not seem to have had any desire to deal severely with the rebels, or to drive the bishops and clergy to extremities. Nils Lykke came first to Bergen, and then with Vincent Lunge went to Trondhjem, where they negotiated with the archbishop, who still remained in his castle at Stenviksholm.

Matters were at last finally arranged, and the archbishop, on again taking an oath of fidelity to Frederick, escaped with a fine of 15,000 Danish marks.

Meanwhile Hans Reff, the Bishop of Oslo, had gone to Copenhagen, where he made his peace with Frederick, and after being, like the primate, mulcted in a fine, was taken back into the king's favour. The bishop of Hamar also escaped with a fine, and the bishops of Bergen and Stavanger, who had taken no part in the rising, were not punished in any way.

The monastery of Hovedøen (which, as we saw, had been burned by Mogen Gyldenstjerne in January, 1532) was secularized, while a similar fate overtook the priory of Værne as a punishment for the help which these establishments had given to Kristian II.

Finally, at a meeting of the council held at Trondhjem in November, 1532, all renewed their allegiance to Frederick, and peace was re-established in the land. Frederick did not long survive his triumph over Kristian. He died at Gottorp on Maundy Thursday, April 10th, 1533, after a short reign of a little more than eight years over Norway, during which time he had never been crowned. His reign over Denmark was only two years longer.

The manner in which he endeavoured to promote the spread of Lutheranism in his dominions, very highly incensed the bishops and clergy against him, and not without cause, when we remember that he had given a distinct pledge to both Norway and Denmark, at the time of his accession, in the Ribe Manifesto, to discountenance in every way the spread of Lutheran teaching. Of his very harsh treatment of the unworthy but betrayed Kristian II., we have already spoken.

CHAPTER XXI.

THE INTERREGNUM, TO THE SIEGE OF COPENHAGEN.

THE death of Frederick I. in 1533 was followed by a
period of four years during which civil war raged in
Denmark, and the crown of Norway was vacant. The
government of the country was carried on by the council,
under the presidency of the archbishop. Had he been a
man of real power, he might at this time have succeeded
in shaking off the Danish yoke, and regaining for his
country the independence which had practically been lost;
but at the most critical moments he failed to act decisively,
and it ended in the complete subjugation of Norway, and
the sweeping away of the ancient Church establishment.

It will be necessary to sketch the course of events in
Denmark and Norway during the interregnum. Frederick
I. had been twice married, and by his first wife he left a
son, Duke Kristian, who at the time of his father's death
was thirty years of age. He was an open and avowed
Lutheran. By his second marriage Frederick left several
children, the eldest of whom, Duke Hans, was at this time
thirteen years old.

When Frederick died, parties in Denmark were divided

between these two sons. Many of the nobles were in favour of Duke Kristian, but the bishops and the country people, as a rule, were supporters of Hans, who had been brought up in the Catholic faith.

A special meeting of the Danish Council was at once called by the chancellor, and it was decided to postpone the election of a king until a joint meeting with the Norwegian Council could be arranged, and this, after a very considerable delay, was fixed for June 24th, 1534, at Copenhagen.

When the news of Frederick's death first reached Norway, the archbishop summoned the council to meet the following August, in spite of the suggestion of Eske Bilde that it should be deferred, until a short time before the joint meeting, intended to be held the next year. Nothing was decided at the council, which met under the presidency of the archbishop, and matters remained unchanged.

As the time for going to Copenhagen drew near, the archbishop began to hesitate, and finally only got as far as Bergen, when he should have been at Copenhagen. Meanwhile Eske Bilde and Vincent Lunge had started on their journey, the former by sea and the latter by land. As matters turned out, it was as well for the archbishop that he had remained at home.

The *Herredag* at Copenhagen never met, for matters had taken quite a new turn in Denmark. In place of two parties, those of Duke Kristian and Duke Hans, there arose a third, and for a time it seemed as if it was to be the victorious one, both in Denmark and Norway.

Kristian II., the prisoner in Sønderborg, had, in spite of his many crimes, still a following in Denmark, and his party secured the powerful help of the city of Lübeck, which for commercial reasons was ready to render the needful aid to place Kristian once more upon the throne.

They assembled an army under the command of Count

Kristofer of Oldenborg, and with the aid of the Lübeckers' fleet, soon produced an entirely new state of affairs in Denmark. The count landed in Sjælland on June 22nd, 1534, Copenhagen declared for Kristian II., and the castle soon afterwards surrendered. Eske Bilde, all unconscious of this revolution, arrived at this moment in Copenhagen from Bergen, and was at once arrested, and remained a prisoner for nearly eighteen months. In a very short time Count Kristofer had all the principal islands and the province of Skaane in his power, and Duke Kristian's supporters were only to be found in Jylland. They were now forced to agree among themselves, and, abandoning Duke Hans, united in choosing Kristian as king. Vincent Lunge (who, having travelled by land, escaped the fate of Eske Bilde) joined Duke Kristian's party. The contending parties in Denmark now looked to Norway, and felt that the side which it supported would gain the upper hand. Now that Eske Bilde and Vincent Lunge were absent, Norway practically meant Archbishop Olaf, and the balance of power now lay in his hands. But he failed to rise to the occasion, and when he might have acted it was too late. Count Kristofer had now achieved his greatest success. Gustavus Vasa joined with Duke Kristian and the tide began to turn against Kristofer. In January, 1535, a defeat at Helsingborg lost him the Danish province in Sweden, and, Kristian having made a successful attack on Lübeck a short time before, the Lübeckers superseded Count Kristofer and appointed Albert of Mecklenburg in his place. Soon, however, the cause of Duke Kristian was everywhere successful in Denmark, and the struggle known as the *Grevens Feide* (the Count's war) came to an end.

We have now to consider the position of affairs in Norway. During the quarrel the country had remained neutral, and Kristian having won, his supporters were anxious that he should be at once acknowledged by the Norwegian Council. In February, 1535, Duke Kristian wrote to the council, but no decisive step was taken. The archbishop called a *Rigsmøde* for May, 1535, but this was first postponed, and finally never met. The supporters of Kristian in the south of Norway now wished to force the archbishop's hand, and in the month of May they issued a letter or manifesto, signed by Vincent Lunge, the bishops of Oslo and Hamar, and the chancellor, Morten Krabbe, accepting Kristian as king, provided he would respect all the old laws and customs of Norway. This they dispatched to the archbishop, hoping to secure his approval and that of the northern members of the council. But the archbishop was not yet ready to give way, and a new candidate appeared upon the scene.

This was Frederick the Count Palatine, who was just about to marry the daughter of the imprisoned Kristian II. As Kristian's son had died (in August, 1532) the Emperor Charles V. adopted Frederick as a candidate to represent his unfortunate brother-in-law. The emperor wrote to the archbishop from Spain in April, 1535, and the Count Palatine also from Heidelberg a few months later; but Frederick lost much time in making a move, and then his marriage, which took place in September, delayed him still longer. To these communications Archbishop Olaf adopted a temporizing attitude. He knew that the count and the emperor would be favourable to the cause of the Church, but they were a long way off, and Kristian of Denmark was very near at hand. Meanwhile Frederick went on with his preparations.

Now the party of Kristian felt that they must take more decisive steps before the emperor and his *protégé* should make a move. Vincent Lunge and his friends at Oslo had, as we have seen, formally accepted him as king, and were waiting for the northern chiefs and the archbishop to agree.

Kristian now sent to Norway Klaus Bilde and Eske Bilde (who had been just released from prison) with instructions to do their best to advance his cause. Early in December they reached Oslo, and decided at once, in spite of the opposition of Vincent Lunge, who wished to ignore the archbishop, to proceed to Trondhjem. Along with them went Lunge and Hans Reff, the bishop, and, after being joined *en route* by the bishop of Hamar, the party came to Trondhjem at Christmas, 1535.

Before we advert to the remarkable events connected with this meeting, it is well to mention that another leading man in Norway was already in Trondhjem, but not of his own free will. This was Nils Lykke, Vincent Lunge's brother-in-law. His wife Elina having died in 1532, he was very anxious to marry his deceased wife's sister, Lucie, which was, of course, contrary to the law both of Church and State. He appealed to the archbishop in order to get the necessary dispensation; but Olaf temporized, and although inclined to look leniently on the offence, yet he could not openly approve what was so entirely contrary to the Church's law. The conduct of Nils Lykke very much enraged his brother-in-law, Vincent Lunge, and he was very angry with the archbishop for his failing to take action against Lykke. Meanwhile the latter wrote to his friends and to Duke Kristian for their support, but received no encouragement. He had been living with Lucie as his wife, and she bore him a son early in 1535, who, however, only lived a couple of months.

Now the archbishop began to discover—if he had not known it before—that Lykke was more or less tainted with Lutheranism, and would favour the Danish as opposed to the Norwegian national party; and so, to bring Vincent into a more friendly state of mind towards him, he caused Nils Lykke to be arrested in July, 1535, and imprisoned him in his castle at Stenviksholm. Next month he was

accused before the council of heresy and other misdemea-
nours, and sentence was given against him. The penalty
of death to which he was liable was, however, not then
exacted, and he remained a prisoner in the archbishop's
castle. Under these circumstances naturally Nils Lykke
was to take no part in the coming council. Another
vacancy was caused by the death in May, 1535, of Olaf
Thorkildssøn, the weak bishop of Bergen, who, after
witnessing the destruction of his cathedral and the practical
establishment of Lutheran teaching in Bergen in 1531, took
refuge in Voss, and remained there until death ended his
troubles. No new election was made immediately, but
afterwards Geble Pederssøn, the archdeacon, was elected,
but was never consecrated, and conformed to the wishes of
the king, as we shall see later on.

Such was the state of affairs when the Danish king's
representatives and the other leading men, met at Trondhjem
in the last days of December, 1535. At this time there
seems to have been gathered together in the city a very
large number of the principal bønder of Trøndelagen, and
although the famous Øre *Thing* of the ancient days was
now never called to approve of the choice of a king, it would
seem that some of the old spirit lingered among the bønder.
But it was the council, with all its officials and Danish
noblemen, who now chose the king of Norway instead of
the freemen at the *Thing*. When the council met, Vincent
Lunge, and the others who had already in Oslo decided for
Kristian of Denmark, urged his election by the assembly,
and further demanded the payment of *skat* to him. This
claim was resisted on two very legitimate grounds—first,
that the king had not formally been chosen; and, secondly,
that no payment of *skat* could be claimed until the king
had by the usual manifesto sworn to govern according to
the laws of Norway and to preserve inviolate the rights
of both Church and State.

It would now appear that the bønder in Trondhjem appealed to the archbishop for his guidance, and he seems to have called a meeting of them at the palace, and there he explained matters to them with regard to the proposed election and the payment of *skat*. It is hard to know the exact truth of what followed, but it would seem that the people clamoured for the arrest of the bishops of Oslo and Hamar and Klaus Bilde, and the death of Vincent Lunge and the chief Danish supporters of Kristian. Rushing from the meeting they went to the house of Vincent Lunge, who was at once killed,* and Klaus Bilde and Bishop Hans Reff of Oslo narrowly escaped with their lives. They were, however, arrested by the archbishop, and, along with Eske Bilde, placed in safe keeping at Tautra. It is very hard to know how far the archbishop was responsible for the murder of Vincent Lunge. The later Danish writers do not hesitate for a moment to accuse him of it, and to assert that he was drunk when he gave an order for his death, but had endeavoured to recall it when too late. The most reasonable supposition seems to be, that there was a genuine outbreak of the people, and that it is very likely they were inflamed by the speech of the archbishop, and, although he did not intend them to do so, they at once attacked and killed the chief man of the unpopular Danish nobles, who was especially hated in the north. Very probably the archbishop intended to imprison and hold as hostages, all the chief Danish men then in Trondhjem, for he had, but a very short time previously, received the letters from the emperor and the Count Palatine, announcing the proposed expedition to Norway, and the new candidate's prospects would be vastly improved by the captivity of all the leading Danish nobles in the country. It was a

---

* It is probable that Kristofer Throndssøn Rustung, the archbishop's principal follower, was the leader in the attack on Vincent Lunge which ended in his murder.

great chance for the Count Palatine, but he was not able to avail himself of it.

Archbishop Olaf was not a great or very scrupulous man, but we cannot believe that he would have permitted the murder of his chief opponent if he could have prevented it. Another crime still more mysterious was laid to his charge by later Danish writers, and with even less ground, and that was the death of Nils Lykke, who was said to have been smothered soon after Vincent Lunge's death in the castle of Stenviksholm. The circumstances connected with his death are very obscure, and there seems no evidence that the archbishop was responsible for it. As Lykke had practically been condemned to death, there does not appear to have been much sympathy for him, either amongst Danes or Norwegians.

The archbishop had now to all intents and purposes burned his boats, and there was nothing left for him but to do his best on behalf of the Count Palatine, and hope for his speedy arrival in Norway. In pursuance of this policy the archbishop sent out two expeditions, one to the south over the Dovre and through the Oplands to Oslo, and the other to Bergen.

The object of the first, which was accompanied by the bishop of Hamar, was to attack and, if possible, seize the fortress of Akershus, and on the way to spread the news that the Count Palatine was coming with a powerful force supplied by the emperor. The governor of Akershus (Gyldenstjerne) sent off in haste for help to Kristian in Denmark. Meanwhile he was able to hold out, and the archbishop's forces had to retreat in March, 1536.

The expedition to Bergen, which was under the command of Kristofer Throndssøn, fared still worse. Thord Roed, who still held the Bergenhus (which Eske Bilde had placed in his hands), was warned of the attack and induced the people of the town to accept Kristian III. In order to strengthen his position he destroyed the great monastery of Munkeliv,* on Nordnæs, the peninsula which formed one side of the harbour, lest it should be used (as it might probably have been) as a fortress, and when Throndssøn came he found he could do nothing. He then opened negotiations with Roed, but he was seized, whilst under promise of safe conduct, in the house of Geble Pederssøn, the bishop-elect, and sent off to the fortress at Baahus.

Thus both of the archbishop's attempts ended in failure, and there was no appearance of Frederick the Count Palatine. Kristian had strengthened his position very much by making peace with the Lübeckers, and protecting himself on the south, while he pressed forward the siege of Copenhagen, which alone held out against him. The archbishop now saw that his best course was to try and make terms with Kristian. He accordingly released his prisoners, and proceeded to negotiate with them in order to obtain favourable terms. To this they were willing to accede, and Klaus Bilde promised to let bygones be bygones, if the archbishop would agree to the choice of Kristian III.

Klaus Bilde now went to King Kristian and conveyed the news about the archbishop's willingness to surrender. Kristian was still vainly endeavouring to subdue Copenhagen, and he felt that time was pressing, for the Count Palatine's expedition would soon be ready to start, and with Copenhagen unsubdued, he could not safely go north. He therefore was apparently very glad to find that the archbishop would accept him, and

---

* After the Birgitta order had been driven out, the cloister was granted to Geble Pederssøn, who resided there. Thord Roed asked leave to station some men in the church tower, and managed to convey into it some barrels of tar, which were set on fire, and the great buildings were destroyed.—See Lange's *Norske Klostres Historie*, pp. 313—315. No traces now remain of this famous foundation, which stood on what is now an open space called *Klostret*.

agreed to a meeting being held in Bergen on July 29th, at which the archbishop promised to be present, and Kristian ordered that a safe conduct should be issued to him. This gathering, however, never took place, and when the time came that it should have been held, Kristian III. was in a position in which he could afford to despise the archbishop, and proceed with his plans for making an end of the ancient constitution both of Denmark and Norway, as regards the Church.

On June 1st the bishop of Stavanger (Hoskold Hoskoldssøn), Eske Bilde, Geble Pederssøn (the bishop-elect of Bergen), and others issued a letter in which they asserted their readiness to accept Kristian III. as king of Norway, and thus almost all the country, except the north and part of the Oplands, proclaimed its willingness to receive the Danish monarch as its king.

CHAPTER XXII.

THE CHURCH'S DOWNFALL—LOSS OF NATIONAL INDEPENDENCE.

The Emperor unable to help Frederick Count Palatine—Copenhagen taken by Kristian III.—Episcopacy suppressed in Denmark, and the Property of the Bishops seized—The Recess—Norway made a Province of Denmark—Archbishop Olaf sends in despair to Holland for help—His ignoble flight from Trondhjem, April 1st, 1537—The Bishop of Hamar taken a Prisoner to Denmark—The Bishop of Stavanger imprisoned—The Bishop of Oslo secures the King's favour and is made a Superintendent—Conclusion.

WE now come to the day which saw the destruction of the ancient Church of Norway and the national independence of the land. Church and State, which had been so closely connected there, more so perhaps than in most countries of Europe, were now to lie helpless at the foot of the conqueror. The Church founded by the two Olafs, and which had flourished so vigorously for so long a time, was to be swept away, and the country in its civil aspect made but a mere province of Denmark.

Events moved with great rapidity after June, 1536, and it is little less than amazing the way in which, by the will of one man, such an ecclesiastical and political revolution could have taken place.

As the events of these months are so important, it is necessary we should consider them in detail.

We have seen how in the early months of the year 1536 Archbishop Olaf, after the failure of his attacks on both Akershus and Bergen, was convinced that no aid was to be expected from the Count Palatine and the Emperor Charles V., and so decided to make the best terms he could

with Kristian III. But matters were not at the moment
in such a desperate condition with respect to the count.
Indeed, but for an unforeseen event, he might have arrived
in Norway with a very formidable force, and have completely changed the whole aspect of affairs. Unfortunately
for the count, however, the outbreak of a war between
Francis I. of France and the emperor, and a sudden attack
of the Duke of Guelderland, disconcerted the emperor's
plans for assisting his nephew, and the forces which had
been collected for the invasion of Norway were required
elsewhere. A fleet of twenty - five ships had been
assembled in the Netherlands, but was useless, as there
were no men ready to embark.

Kristian III. now saw that if, in this emergency, he
could recover Copenhagen his position would be secure.
He accordingly redoubled his efforts to capture the
town. The inhabitants, left without help from the
emperor, were at last forced to yield. On July 29th
(the feast of the patron saint of Norway) the town
capitulated, and Kristian had thus the whole of Denmark
under his rule.

In Norway the archbishop was in despair; his only
chance of succour seemed to have failed him, and as a
last hope he dispatched his trusty Kristofer Throndssøn*
to the Netherlands, to see if there was any prospect of

* Throndssøn or Rustung, after the archbishop's death, was taken into
the king's favour. His daughter Anna was married or betrothed to
Earl Bothwell, who met her in Copenhagen in 1560, but he deserted her
in the Netherlands. Later, in 1563, she followed him to Scotland,
remaining at the Court until 1565, when she went to Norway. On
Bothwell's flight from Scotland he was driven by storm to Norway,
and taken a prisoner to Bergen. Here Anna called him to account
for his conduct towards her, and he had to give her a ship, and undertook to pay her a sum of money. Bothwell was then taken to
Denmark, where he died in prison. Anna lived for a long time afterwards at Seim, in Kvindherred, where she was known as *Skottefruen*, from
her connection with Earl Bothwell.

help from that quarter. The position of the primate was indeed a difficult one. There was only one of his suffragans who could be said to be on his side. The bishop of Oslo had agreed to recognize Kristian, so had the bishop of Stavanger. The see of Bergen was vacant, but the man who had been chosen by the chapter, was an open ally of the Danish monarch. Only the bishop of Hamar was ready to aid the archbishop, but he possessed little influence outside his own immediate district. Had Archbishop Olaf been a man of greater power and force of character, and one who had made himself loved and respected, he might still have rallied the bulk of the clergy and people to his side; but he was not the man to head a great national movement, even had one been possible at this time. His vacillation in moments when he should have stood firm, his alternate oaths of allegiance to different kings, and his inability to rule in the high office which he held both in Church and State, left Norway defenceless and without a champion of her rights.

Now that Copenhagen had fallen, and the attention of the emperor had been diverted by the war with France, Kristian felt himself secure. He knew but too well that Norway was at his mercy; all the strongholds of the country—Baahus, Akershus, and Bergenhus—were in his power; all the chief men were on his side, and he could afford to delay crushing the only antagonist he had left— Archbishop Olaf.

How far Kristian III. was sincere in his zeal for Lutheranism it is hard to determine. He had been, for some years before his father's death, a supporter of the Lutheran preachers in the country, and possibly may have had a genuine belief in their tenets; and at any rate it cannot be said of him that he had ever given a solemn assurance, as his father had done, to suppress the teaching of the German reformer; but his action now left him open to the charge of professing such opinions, in order to enrich himself and his followers.

He now determined on a bold stroke, which would destroy for ever the power of the Church in Denmark, and overturn the ancient ecclesiastical order of that kingdom.

When Copenhagen fell into his hands, he found that his troops were clamouring for their pay, and that his treasury was an empty one. Money must be found to satisfy these demands, and the nobility were not likely to be able to afford him the necessary assistance. In this emergency he decided to seize the episcopal revenues—for the bishops also declined to help—and to transfer them to the royal coffers. On August 11th he called together a meeting of his principal officers, and there unfolded to them his plans, which at any rate had the merit of simplicity. It was simply this—to arrest all the bishops he could lay his hands on, and to annex the property of their sees. The officers readily fell in with this suggestion, and by breakfast time the next morning the bishops of Skaane, Sjælland, and Ribe, were taken prisoners and placed in the castle. Kristian then called together the lay members of the council, and they were forced to agree to the king's plans.* They signed a declaration in which it was announced that for the future the government of the kingdom of Denmark should not depend upon " either archbishop or other bishops, but the government of the kingdom of Denmark shall be and remain, with his royal Majesty and his successors, kings in Denmark, and with the temporal council of the kingdom, and with their successors." The council further pledged themselves, that no bishop hereafter should have any part

* An interesting account of these proceedings has survived in a letter written by Johan Pein, a Prussian admiral in the service of Kristian, to Duke Albert of Prussia.—See C. Paludan-Müller's *De første Konger af den Oldenborgske Slægt*, p. 620.

in the government of the country, unless it was with the consent of the general council of the Church in Germany and elsewhere.

In order to give the appearance of a religious movement to this scandalous military *coup d'état*, it was further added that they would not oppose "the right preaching of the Holy Gospel and the pure Word of God."

The desire of the king for the furtherance of the Gospel was seen, by his at once arresting the archbishop of Lund, Torben Bilde, and the Bishop of Roskilde, and in a month's time every bishop in Denmark had been cast into prison.

Having thus accomplished a revolution, the king proceeded to make the *Rigsdag*, or diet of the country, assent to his action. It met in Copenhagen on the 15th of October, 1536, and lasted for fifteen days. The result was the issue of two documents of the very first importance— the Royal Manifesto and the "General Recess," or statute— and they set forth plainly what was to be the new policy both with respect to the State and the Church.

The manifesto was shorter than those usually issued by the Danish kings, but the omissions were very significant. All the usual promises to defend the rights of the Church and the privileges of the bishops and clergy were left out, and in place of them we find these words: "We will and shall, above all things, love and worship Almighty God and His holy Word and doctrine, strengthen, increase, advance, maintain, protect and defend it, to the honour of God and to the increase of the holy Christian faith." It was clear from this that Kristian intended to proceed in the ecclesiastical revolution which he had initiated in the month of August, and that the measure which was meted to the bishops in Denmark would very soon be extended to Norway.

But what followed in the manifesto showed also that the king intended not merely to overturn the Church in

Norway, but that he made up his mind to crush out all
semblance of national independence as well. The third
article of the manifesto states, that " because the kingdom
of Norway is now so bereft of power and wealth, and
the people of the kingdom of Norway are not able alone to
support a lord and king for themselves, and this same
kingdom is yet bound to remain for ever with the crown of
Denmark, and most of the council of the kingdom of Norway,
especially Archbishop Olaf, who is now the greatest man in
the kingdom, within a short time has twice, with the most
part of the council of Norway, fallen from the kingdom of
Denmark, contrary to their plighted faith. We have
therefore promised and vowed to the council and nobles of
the kingdom of Denmark that, if God Almighty so ordain
it, that this same kingdom of Norway, or any of its
dependencies, castles, or districts, should fall under our
authority, or be conquered by us, so shall they hereafter be
and remain under the crown of Denmark, as are one of
these other countries, Jylland, Fyen, Sjælland, or Skaane,
and not hereafter be or be called a separate kingdom, but a
dependency of the kingdom of Denmark, and under its
crown always. But if any strife should arise from this, the
council and people of the kingdom of Denmark shall be
bound faithfully to help to support us in it."*

Thus by one stroke was the ancient independence of
Norway swept away, and its liberties ruthlessly disregarded.

The other document, the " General Recess," is, from an
ecclesiastical point of view, of course, the most important,
for it meant the utter subversion of the ancient Church in
Denmark and the substitution of the king's "evangelical
superintendents" in the place of the bishops.

This document begins by stating that the late dissensions
were caused by the bishops not agreeing with the nobles,

* C. Paludan-Müller, as before, p. 628.

and because they had refused to join with them in the election of Kristian III.

The bishops were to be replaced by evangelical superintendents, who were to teach the Gospel to the people. Any person opposing this order was to be punished by loss of life and property. The revenue of the various sees was to be confiscated to the crown, and all rights of patronage (except that possessed by the nobles) were to pass to the king. The cloisters were to remain untouched for the present, until the king and the nobles decided their fate, and the occupants to be unmolested, but free to leave.

Tithes were still to exist, and were to be thus allocated— one-third for the parish priest, one-third for the Church, and one-third for the king, (who out of them was to pay the new evangelical superintendents), and for the keeping up of the schools.

Such was the import of this document, which was a wholesale measure of confiscation of the Church's property, and which necessarily involved the complete separation of the Church in Denmark from the rest of the Catholic Church. It will be noted that it was the king who was the principal gainer by this act, and also that it seems to have been aimed mostly at the bishops, whose existence as an order in the Church was terminated, and whose incomes were swept into the royal treasury, for doubtless the new superintendents were provided with very different incomes from that of the bishops in the olden days.

In this "Recess" no mention was made of Norway, but as soon as its terms were known, it was plain to the Norwegian prelates, the treatment which was in store for them; and it was clear that unless help came from the Count Palatine and the emperor, the days of the Church of St. Olaf were numbered. In October Kristofer Throndssøn came back from his errand to Holland, and with him four ships; but these were filled with neither men nor money, and were only sent in order to provide the archbishop with a means of escape when all hope was lost.   When he learned that Frederick's expedition was not ready to start, the archbishop made one last appeal for aid, but in this case, his trusting for the help of the count or the emperor, was like trusting "upon the staff of a bruised reed," for the help never came.

Kristian III. contented himself with directing Eske Bilde to seize the revenues of the vacant see of Bergen and use them in the same way as in Denmark.   Thus matters remained for the winter of 1536—7; the Church lay powerless before the king and his nobles, who only waited for the advent of spring to come and spoil their prey.   During the winter months Eske Bilde's men had driven the archbishop's adherents out of Søndmøre and Romsdal, but want of both men and money prevented their following them up to Trondhjem.

Kristian, to make all secure, before sending his forces north, managed to arrange a truce with the emperor for three years, from May, 1537, and in this agreement a special clause was inserted, to provide for the safety of the Norwegian primate; but this was not needed.

The last archbishop of Nidaros now saw that nothing could save the situation.   There was no help to be had from any quarter.   His two expeditions had been failures, and all the strongholds of Norway were in the enemy's hands.   It would be perhaps unfair to judge Archbishop Olaf harshly at this moment, but he was not the man, unfortunately, for the time in which he was called to rule.   He had no one to support him, and there seemed no alternative but flight. The ships which had been sent from the Netherlands were lying at Trondhjem; into these the archbishop collected all the treasures he could find of the cathedral and other churches, as well as the archives of the kingdom, and, going on board, set sail on April 1st, 1537.

He was not the only archbishop who had fled from Trondhjem, or Nidaros of the olden days, but Olaf Engelbrektssøn was a very different type of man from Archbishop Eystein, or even Erik or Jon Raude. The faith and order of the Church was not in question in their days, as it was in 1537, and from the point of view of either Catholic or Lutheran, it would have been a nobler thing if the head of the Norwegian Church had stood bravely at his post, and awaited in his cathedral city, the day when he would have been called upon to endure imprisonment, and the loss of all his earthly possessions, in obedience to the mandate of the Danish king. It was not until May 1st that, after a long and weary voyage, Archbishop Olaf arrived safely in the Netherlands. He had left a garrison in his castle at Stenviksholm; but within a few weeks of the archbishop's flight Thord Roed from Bergen reached Trondhjem, and the castle soon after surrendered, and with it the last shadow of opposition to the Danish king vanished from Norway.

Kristian III. had a force ready to leave Denmark for Norway as soon as the winter was over, and it started from Copenhagen in April, and reached Bergen on May 1st, the very day the archbishop arrived in the Netherlands. Here it was joined by Eske Bilde, who then with it proceeded to Trondhjem, and received over the archbishop's castle at Stenviksholm.

No time was now lost in coercing any who remained faithful to the old state of things. Trondhjem having been subdued, and the archbishop having fled, the next attack was on the bishop of Hamar. He had been, as we have seen, one of the most zealous supporters of Kristian II. in his unlucky campaign, and had been heavily fined in consequence; he was also a supporter of the Count Frederick. After Stenviksholm had surrendered, Truid Ulfstand, who commanded the force sent from Denmark,

left Trondhjem and went at once to Hamar. The bishop
had determined to make a strong resistance, and had
prepared his palace for a siege; but at the last his courage
failed him, when he saw the force which Ulfstand had
brought with him, and after an interview with the Danish
commander he agreed to surrender. On June 23rd he
was led away a prisoner. We have a truly pathetic account
of the departure of the last bishop of Hamar from his home
by one who witnessed it :—

"As Herr Truid and the bishop went together to
Strandbakken, he fell on his knees and thanked God in
heaven for every day he had lived. Then he bid good-
night to the canons and the priests, then to his cathedral
and cloister, then to his chief men, to the common people,
both townsmen and bønder, entreating them all to pray
heartily for him, and said he hoped he would soon come
to them again. But added, 'O God our Heavenly Father,
if not before, grant that we may meet one another in
heaven.' This prayer he uttered with many tears and
added, 'Vale! Vale! Vale!'" *

The old bishop never saw Hamar again. He was taken
to Denmark and kept as a semi-prisoner at Antvorskov
cloister, where he died in 1543.

There were two more bishops still left. Bishop
Hoskoldssøn of Stavanger had the year before, along with
Eske Bilde and others, approved of the election of Kristian
III. He was a timid man, and hoped by this to avert the
hostility of the king against all members of the episcopate.
Through Eske Bilde he sent Kristian a present of a silver
bowl, and as long as he (Bilde) remained in power the
bishop was left alone. But the year after he seems to have
been imprisoned by Thord Roed in Bergen, where he soon
afterwards died.

* From a description of Hamar in "Thaarup's Magazin," quoted by
Bang, p. 359.

The remaining bishop was Hans Reff of Oslo. We have seen what sort of a man he was, time-serving and crafty, and always ready to make the best terms he could with the winning side. He had already accepted Kristian, but in spite of this he was carried to Denmark by Ulfstand, after he had seized the bishop of Hamar. When in Denmark Hans Reff used his time well. Being not overburdened by any special religious convictions, he was able to assure King Kristian, of his zeal for Lutheran doctrines, and, what was even of more importance to the king, he was ready to make a complete surrender of all the temporalities of his see into the king's hands, and then offered to Kristian and his heirs, "as he valued 'his soul's salvation,' true and faithful allegiance for all time to come."

Under these circumstances the king saw fit to reinstate him as bishop or evangelical superintendent, of the diocese of Oslo, and further, to show his zeal for "God's pure Word," the king added to Oslo (already a full burden for one man) the diocese of Hamar, which had been left without a chief pastor. Hans Reff did not remain long in his new capacity as Lutheran superintendent; he died in the summer of 1545, and next year we find a new man, Anders Matson, in his office.

There is only one more diocese of which we must speak, namely, Bergen. We have seen that after Olaf Thorkildssøn's death in 1535 the archdeacon Geble Pederssøn was chosen as his successor. This man was of a good family in Norway, and had studied in Alkmar and Louvain, where he met Vincent Lunge. In 1523 he was in Rome, where he remained for some time, and was very indignant at the abuses which he saw everywhere in that city. He seems to have always been favourable to the principles of the Reformation, and when the king decided to have his own kind of bishops he was quite willing to accept the nominee of the Bergen chapter to act as bishop of that

From a Photograph by]   *[K. Knudsen, Bergen.*

RUINS OF THE CATHEDRAL OF HAMAR.

Commenced in 1152 and finished about a century later.

[To face p. 348

important diocese. In 1537 Pederssøn went to Denmark, where Bugenhagen had come in order to "consecrate" the new Danish superintendents who were to take the place of the imprisoned bishops. By him Geble Pederssøn was set apart for the management of the Bergen diocese, and, for a time, for that of Stavanger as well. We are told he was the only one of those thus set apart by Bugenhagen, who made him a gift afterwards. Pederssøn's offering was a substantial present of wine, and the famous Lutheran on accepting it, exclaimed, "Nonne decem mundati sunt, et nemo reversus est, nisi hic alienigena."[*] Geble Pederssøn lived until 1557, when he died in Bergen.

Thus the ancient Church of Norway lay helpless and wounded at the feet of her conqueror, who for the sake "of the Holy Gospel and the pure Word of God" (as he expressed it at the time of the *coup d'état*) had imprisoned or driven away her bishops and seized on her revenues. Her natural leaders failed her in the hour of her trial, and among the general body of the clergy and laity, there was no one ready or able to strike a blow on behalf of the Church of St. Olaf and Eystein.

Archbishop Olaf did not long survive his exile. In May, 1537, he came to Brussels. By the truce concluded between the emperor and Kristian III. the personal safety of the archbishop was secured, and he retired to Lierre, in Brabant. Kristian made claims upon him for the treasures both of the State and the Church, which he had carried away with him in his flight from Trondhjem, and the family of Nils Lykke demanded an account of certain valuables of which they alleged the archbishop had charge. The latter he admitted, but before restitution was made, Olaf Engelbrektssøn, the twenty-seventh and last archbishop of Nidaros, had passed away. On March 7th, 1538, he died at Lierre.

[*] "Norske Samlinger," Vol. I., quoted by Nissen, p. 222, and L. Daae's *Geistliges Kaldelse*.

We have seen the fate which befell the other members of the episcopate in the Norwegian Church; exile, or imprisonment and death, had been their portion, with the one ignoble exception of the time-serving Hans Reff. The historic episcopate which had come to Norway, first from England, was lost for ever, and a Lutheran establishment took the place of the ancient Catholic Church of Norway.

Having gained their purpose and seized on the property of the Church, the Danish kings showed little anxiety to promote the spread of the doctrines of Luther, and for a generation or more, so far as they were concerned, Norway might have relapsed into heathenism. The new evangelical superintendents were named to carry on the oversight of the ancient bishoprics, but even with the best intentions on their part, they were practically helpless. The old priests of the Catholic Church were left, as a rule, undisturbed in their parishes during their lifetime, and when they passed away, untrained and untaught Lutheran pastors, often men of very indifferent character, were placed in charge of their parishes. The new superintendents in many instances did their best to remedy this state of things by establishing Latin schools, where the future clergy might be trained, and gradually they succeeded in sending faithful men among the people. But in the evil days which followed upon the events of 1537, many of those who were sent to minister to the people were unworthy of their calling, and the records of the times tell of frequent conflicts between them and the bønder, which in more than one instance ended in bloodshed.

It was not until the beginning of the seventeenth century, in the days of Kristian IV., who seems to have had a genuine regard for the welfare of his Norwegian subjects, that something of the old religious instincts revived among the people of Norway, and efforts were made to again beautify the churches, and to supply them with suitable ornaments and plate, in the place of what had been either devoted to the cost of Kristian II.'s expedition, or pillaged by the orders of Kristian III.

We have now traced the history of the Holy Catholic Church in Norway, its foundation, vigorous growth, decline, and fall. To English people its history cannot fail to be of interest, as from England mainly came its first teachers and bishops, and its two great kingly "nursing fathers" were so intimately associated with the Christianity of the British Isles. Had that connection with England, which was so close in the end of the tenth and the whole of the eleventh centuries, been maintained, and Oxford or Cambridge, instead of Rostock and Copenhagen, been later on, the universities of the Norwegian bishops and priests, then it might have been that the Reformation would have followed on the lines of the English Church, and not that of Northern Germany. But events determined otherwise, and the loss of the historic episcopate snapped asunder the link which bound Norway to the Church in which Olaf Trygvessøn had been baptized and confirmed, and from which the great missionary bishops of his day, and of St. Olaf's, derived their orders. From henceforth they drifted asunder, after centuries of close intercourse and communion.

As it was with the Church, so was it with the State. Its consolidation coincided very closely with the introduction of Christianity, and at first both grew together, in the closest and most intimate union. It is true that later on, as we have seen, the same fierce battle between them, which was fought out in other nations, was also waged in Norway. The days of Haakon Haakonssøn, in which Norway reached the zenith of its power as a sovereign State, was also the commencement of the Church's greatest prosperity, and in the disastrous year of 1537, both Church and State were involved in a common ruin.

In Norway, Church and State were perhaps more closely associated than in any country in Europe. In the period before the hereditary succession to the crown was finally established, the bishops had the preponderating voice in the choice of the king; and the primate not merely ranked next to the king as in other lands, but when the throne was vacant, the archbishop was *ex-officio* ruler of the country until a new monarch was chosen.

From 1537 onwards a dull lethargy crept over the land, and lasted for well-nigh three hundred years, until the old spirit of freedom was breathed once more upon the dry bones of Norway's nationality, and it again stood upon its feet, and claimed its place as a sovereign and independent State, among the nations of Europe.

We cannot better close our history than by quoting the words of one who was an eye-witness of the almost irreparable injury inflicted on his native land, by the revolutionary changes brought about by Kristian III. and his followers.

Absalon Pederssøn* wrote (some thirty years after the events we have last narrated) in his "Norges Beskrivelse" these sad but true words:—

"The churches and cloisters which our forefathers built we have pulled down and destroyed; there where our forefathers led out to battle twenty thousand men we can only bring two thousand. Our forefathers continually made warlike or mercantile expeditions to other lands, whilst to-day no one will venture from the town or district in which he was born. From the day when Norway fell under Denmark, it lost the strength and power of its manhood, and became old and grey-headed and a burden to itself. Yet a day may come when Norway may once more awake from sleep, if a ruler is vouchsafed to it, for in the

* He was a native of Sogn, and chaplain of the Castle in Bergen, and a lecturer in Theology.

nation there is still surviving some of the old manhood and strength."

The patriotic Norwegian did not live to see the awakening he longed for.   It was not for two hundred and sixty-seven years after he wrote these words, that the long, long sleep was ended and the new life began.

APPENDIX I.

"SIGEFRIDUS NORWEGENSIS EPISCOPUS."

THE identity of this man has been the subject of considerable dispute among historians. William of Malmesbury, in his work " De Antiquitate Glastoniensis Ecclesiæ," has a list of bishops who had been monks of that famous foundation in the time of Edgar—" Qui sequuntur fuerunt episcopi tempore Edgari regis in diversis locis." The fourth name, in William's list, is Sigefridus— "Nonas Aprilis obiit Sigefridus Norwegensis Episcopus monachus Glastoniæ"—and he mentions a bequest left by him of four copes.

If we are to take William literally, we must conclude that this bishop lived somewhere between 959 and 975; but, on the other hand, William only gives the day of his death (April 5th), and not the year, and some of those whom he names outlived the period during which Edgar reigned.

It may be well to examine briefly the theories which have been put forth as to who this Sigefridus was.

Absolon Taranger, in his most interesting and valuable work, *Den Angelsaksiske Kirkes Inflydelse paa den Norske*, believes that he must be the bishop that Haakon the Good invited from England, to help him in his attempt to introduce Christianity. But it must be remembered, that it is not quite certain that any *bishop* came at that time, for although Snorre in the " Heimskringla " undoubtedly mentions a bishop, the older records in the *Agrip* and *Fagrskinna* only speak of priests. Again, Haakon's attempt was made in the year 950, which is nine years *before* the time of King Edgar.

Dr. Konrad Maurer, in *Die Bekehrung des Norwegischen Stammes zum Christenthume*, believes (and his opinion is shared by Munch and Keyser) that William's Sigefridus is the same as Sigurd Monachus, who lived in the second half of the eleventh century.

A A 2

Lappenberg identifies him with Sigefrid, the apostle of Sweden.
This Sigefrid is believed by some to be identical with Olaf
Trygvessøn's court bishop of the same name, who, after the battle
of Svolder, is said to have gone to Sweden, where he worked with
much success.

A. D. Jørgensen, in *Den Nordiske Kirkes Grundlæggelse og
første udvikling*, a work of much learning and research, has another
person still, whom he thinks to be identical with William's
Sigefridus—namely, Sigurd, Knut the Great's court bishop at
Nidaros. This man, it will be remembered, was the one who incited
the people to oppose St. Olaf on his return to Norway, before
Stiklestad; and after the saintship of Olaf had been established,
he left the country.

With such a conflict of opinion it is very difficult, if not indeed
impossible, to come to any conclusion. The objection which has
been raised against Taranger's view, that he is too early, as
Haakon's attempt was made in 950, seems not altogether con-
clusive, as it is at any rate within ten years of Edgar's time;
while Sigurd the monk is considered by his supporters to have
worked in the second half of the eleventh century, which would be
at least seventy-five years *after* Edgar's reign. Taranger's bishop
(if, however, any " bishop " went from England to Haakon, which
is not clear) is at any rate the nearest in point of time to the reign
of Edgar.

Next to him would come Olaf Trygvessøn's Bishop Sigurd, who
is most probably the same as Siegfrid the apostle of Sweden,
whom Lappenberg claims as William's " Sigefridus." Olaf's
bishop doubtless came from England, and quite possibly from
Glastonbury, though we are not told so. Jørgensen is very con-
fident in claiming Knut's court bishop as the Glastonbury monk,
and if we do not take William's chronology strictly, it is quite
possible that Knut's bishop was the one mentioned by him.
We know that Knut was frequently at Glastonbury, and also
that Bishop Sigurd, according to all accounts, was the founder
of the Benedictine monastery on Nidarholm, afterwards called
Munkholm.

If the chronology can be still further stretched, we have the
claims of Sigurd Monachus to be the Glastonbury monk, and,
when supported by the authority of such great names as that of
Keyser, Munch, and Maurer, they must not be lightly disregarded,

but the period in which he lived is at least twenty years after the latest name in William's list.*

We have thus three Sigurds or Sigefrids working in Norway with the early Christian kings: all appear without doubt to have come from England. If Haakon's bishop was the Glastonbury monk it would add another to the list. If Jørgensen's theory that Sigurd the monk and Knut's Bishop Sigurd are the same man, we reduce the number a little, and make it, at any rate, possible, if not probable, that he was William's "Norwegensis Episcopus." The different date of the death of the apostle of Sweden (February 15th) appears fatal to his claim. Taranger's weakest point seems the doubt that clearly exists whether Haakon ever asked for a bishop as well as priests.

Though the question is an interesting one, we fear it must be left undecided one way or another, and it seems impossible to say with certainty that we can identify exactly, any of the Sigefrids with the monk of Glastonbury, who died on April 5th, and gave a benefaction of vestments to the great foundation of the West.

* Dr. Konrad Maurer's views will be found in his *Die Bekehrung des Norwegischen Stammes*, Vol. II., 565.

APPENDIX II.

THE NORWEGIAN *STAVKIRKER* (MEDIÆVAL WOODEN CHURCHES) AND THEIR ORIGIN.

OF the old wooden churches of Norway those which were built in what is known as the " *stav* " style at once attract the attention of foreigners on account of their curious and often very beautiful construction. There are no churches exactly like them in other parts of Europe, and there has been a good deal of controversy as to their origin, in which every possible detail of construction and ornamentation has been considered. It would be impossible here, to give more than a brief summary of the various points of importance without entering too far into detail. As there does not appear to be any work on the subject in English, it may be well to give a short note mainly on Professor L. Dietrichson's most valuable and interesting work, *De Norske Stavkirker.**

It has been roughly estimated that Norway in the Middle Ages possessed about 1,200 churches, and of these some 600 can either be seen or traced. Of these about 300 were wooden churches, and Dietrichson considers that nearly *all* of them were " *stav* " churches, and points out that in most mediæval documents where wooden churches are mentioned the wording makes this clear. These *stavkirker* were spread all over Norway, and are especially found in the Oplands and on the fjords, while stone churches are more frequent on the weather-beaten coast and islands. Of the form of these remarkable buildings much has been written, and it will be sufficient for the present purpose to indicate quite generally their main features.

The church generally consisted of a nave, a chancel, and a semi-circular apse, and was surrounded by a sort of cloister (*svalgang,* or

* Kristiania, 1892.

omgang), which was generally open except at the east end, though occasionally, as at Hedal, it was completely closed in.

The entrances to this cloister were opposite the doors of the church itself, and were often in the west end or under one of the many gables of the roof. From the cloister roof there sprang the wall of the side aisle, then came another roof, and then the nave wall supporting the largest roof, which was crowned by a pointed tower often placed on a sort of cross-roof. The chancel was similarly constructed, though the dimensions were smaller, and there was often no tower, while the apse did not generally exceed two stories, and was semi-circular in shape, often finished off in a small round tower.

The churches varied very much in size and in construction, a few of them having one transept, but the majority were oblong in shape. Out of a list of seventy-nine churches given by Dietrichson only four had a transept, and the areas covered ranged from 3,696 to about 400 square feet. The ornamentation externally consisted chiefly in the "dragon heads" on the gable extremities and the carving on the door pillars, which was often of wonderful intricacy and richness. The origin of the dragon head ornamentation has been much disputed; some writers (*e.g.*, Dahl) trace them to the dragon heads common in the Viking ships, while Nicolaysen and others are inclined to believe that both the ships' beaks and the dragon heads are the representation of the fabulous creatures of northern mythology. It seems, however, to be very likely that the ships' beaks were the actual source of the ornamentation, as dragon heads were used on them long before any *stavkirker* were built; also, in a country where the best woodworkers were shipbuilders, these would be in request for the erection of wooden churches. Professor Dietrichson, with a view to collecting materials for his book, in 1884 made a careful personal survey of the wooden churches which then existed in the North European countries between the Volga and the Thames, in the course of which he collected much valuable information.

Before giving his conclusions as to the origin of the *stavkirke*, it may be well to enumerate the main distinguishing features of the buildings in question. The curious roof and gable system is perhaps the most noticeable externally, while closer examination of the walls will show them to be curiously constructed of upright planks set into a sort of framework of beams. In buildings made of horizontal logs, the walls support as well as close in the sides of the building, while in the *stavkirker* the walls only serve the latter purpose, most of the weight being borne by the pillars at the corners. The construction of these walls is simple and effective, the corner posts are fixed to the bottom beam, and the planks, which are tongued and grooved, fit into each other and into the corner posts. These planks are put in at the two ends first, and when there is only room for two more (in the middle) a change is made in their treatment, the last but one being slightly wider at the bottom than the top, and the last plank having a tongue on both sides to fit the two grooves and being wider at the top than the bottom so as to form a wedge. This last plank is then driven in and tightens the whole frame, so that when the top beam is fitted into its place the wall is very strong and compact, and needs no nails or pegs to hold the planks in their places, though cross beams are sometimes added on the inside to give it additional rigidity.

This system gives the churches the name of *stavkirker*, *stav* meaning a rounded post or pillar. Amongst other peculiarities may be mentioned the *svalgang*, or *omgang*, as the cloister was called, and the use of " L " pieces of solid wood (*knær*) to join pillars or beams inside the church. These pieces of wood were sometimes placed one inside the other and cut so as to form arches, and are often found between the pillars of the nave and the wall of the aisle, placed so as to make a sort of "unfloored triforium." Several writers are of opinion that the *stavkirker* are of Slavonic origin, as there was a considerable connection with Norway and Gardarike and Vendland about the date when many of these churches were built. J. C. C. Dahl considers that the shape of these churches is Byzantine in its origin, and has permeated through Russia and the Slav lands to the North ; he does not consider that the English churches had any influence on the North, and entirely omits the Irish group of wooden churches.

Nicolaysen is opposed to this view, and holds that the *stavkirker* of Norway are, and have always been, unique, and have no connection with others except perhaps in Great Britain and Ireland.

Professor Dietrichson, after examining the various wooden churches of Northern Europe, divides them roughly into three groups :

1. *The Western Group :* Originating in the Roman Churches

and spreading over Western Europe, receiving additions and modifications in various countries. All these churches were frame buildings.

2. *The Eastern Group :* Originating at Byzantium and spreading over Eastern Europe. All these churches were built of logs laid horizontally.

3. *The Central Group,* combining the two former groups. Found in Bohemia, &c. These churches are partly built of horizontal and partly of vertical timbers, the latter (*reisværk*) being used for higher parts of the building, in the towers, &c.

An examination of the existing Russian wooden churches shows that they are all built in the blockhouse or horizontal style, which was used in domestic architecture of both Norway and Russia. In addition to this there are the following differences :

a. The Norwegian churches are *langkirker, i.e.,* long and rectangular, while the Russian are many sided and sometimes nearly round.

b. The windows in the Russian are square or rectangular, while in the *stavkirker* the windows, if any, are generally round ; and the Russian churches had no side aisles.

Both Norwegian and Russian had the cloister or *svalgang,* but those of the latter were seldom open or arcaded.

The conclusion arrived at is that the Russian as well as the Hungarian and West Slavonic churches had no influence on the Norwegian, though there are several points in which there is a seeming similarity. The *reisværk* German churches are the nearest of the eastern group to the *stavkirker,* but they differ in the fact that their sides are made of planks *nailed* to the crossbeams, and not mortised into them. No old wooden churches now exist in Denmark, and as that country was Christianized from Germany, it is probable that the churches were of the German pattern. Dietrichson treats of the wooden churches of Western Europe at considerable length, and lays great stress on the influence of the Irish missionaries on the style of the churches in England and the West of Europe.

The Irish method of building (which was called *Opus Scoticum* or *Mos Scotorum*) seems to have been as follows : A framework was made of beams, supported at the ends by posts, and in it were set split trunks of oak with the flat side in and the round out, the interstices being filled with clay or mortar.

No old wooden churches still survive in Ireland, but from various documents some information can be obtained. Dietrichson (p. 88) quotes Concubran's Vita St. Monenæ, whose church was built "*juxta morem Scotticarum gentium*" of flat hewn planks. Also St. Bernardi Vita St. Malachiæ, where Bangor Cloister Church (built 1149) is said to have been "of beautiful Irish work of smoothened planks firmly joined." Bede, in Eccles. Hist. III. 25, describes the church built by Finan in Lindesfarne as being made "after the manner of the Scots . . . not of stone but of hewn oak and covered with reeds." Maclear ("The Celts") says that the monastic churches in early times were often made of wood and called *duirthech*, or house of oak, and it is probable that the original buildings at Iona were of this kind.

On the Continent there were many examples of similar buildings, such as St. Martin's at Rouen ("Gregory of Tours," Op. Vol. IV. 41, V. 2), St. Boniface's Chapel at Geismar, and the old wood minster at Strassburg, which (see Kreuser, *Der Christliche Kirchenbau*, I. 332) "was built of half tree trunks, the rough sides of which were turned outwards and the spaces between them filled with earth, chalk, or other filling."

Dietrichson identifies this "Opus Scoticum" with the primitive *stav* construction, of which the only extant example is to be found at Greensted, near Ongar, in Essex. In this church, which is most interesting as being the only survival of Anglo-Saxon wooden churches, only the side walls and parts of the west end are left of the original building, and these are constructed "*more Scotorum*" of half trees let into beams at the top and bottom, and joined to each other with strips of wood, while the interstices are filled with a sort of cement.

There are several points of difference between this church and the earliest Norsk *stavkirke*, but the method of constructing the walls is the same; the frame system seems to have existed though the top and bottom beams were renewed when the church was restored, but it is impossible to see how they were joined to the corner posts, of whose *present* existence Dietrichson did not seem to be aware, though he was convinced that they *did* once exist. Dietrichson considers that Greensted is a specimen of that style of church building from which the Norsk *stavkirker* take their origin. As Greensted Church probably dates from 1012, it is therefore a good deal older than the oldest Norsk *stavkirke*

(Urnes, c. 1100), and there is a considerable difference between the two. Urnes is more elaborate, and has side aisles, while Greensted has a plain nave, and the roof of Urnes shows the curious Norsk construction, which was probably not found in the original roof at Greensted. It is true that *stav* work was known in Norway before Christianity, but " the impulse came from the place whence in the Viking times the North took the important elements of its ornamentation, namely, from Ireland and the Anglo-Saxon countries." *
So much for the wall construction. The roof and gable system seems to have been the outcome of the climatic conditions of Norway, where the old Anglo-Saxon thatch roof would be of little use on account of the heavy snowfall and frequent storms. Hence the Norwegians developed a system of steep roofs and short walls, which give the *stavkirke* its peculiar interest and beauty. The steep roof would prevent snow from lying on it, and the short perpendicular walls would minimise the resistance to the wind, while the frequent gables would serve the same purpose by offering a triangular instead of a rectangular surface. There are several points of resemblance between the construction of these roofs and that of the ships of the period, many of which are mentioned by Bruun† in his *Norges Stavkyrkor*. The method of joining cross-beams with "L" pieces of solid wood, sometimes rounded to form part of an arch, is peculiar to Norway, and is found in boats and *stavkirker;* this is corroborated by Viollet le Duc, who says ‡ that the use *"de bois courbes"* belongs to Northern people and their shipbuilding.

The *svalgang,* or cloister, is not peculiarly Norwegian, being found under various forms in Hungary, Silesia, Russia, and Bohemia, and being in use in domestic architecture before it was transferred to the *stavkirker.*

The *stavkirker* would thus seem to be a product of a rather composite nature, the original method of building the walls coming apparently from the " Opus Scoticum " of Great Britain

---

* Dietrichson, *De Norske Stavkirker*, p. 165.

† He also compares the peculiar floor work of the *stavkirker* to the deck of a ship.

‡ *Dictionnaire raisonné de l'architecture française du XI.ᵉ au XVI.ᵉ siècle*, Vol. VII., p. 38. The similarity between boat and roof construction is also noticed by Gottfried Semper in *Der Stil*, and Valtyr Gudmundssøn considers that this roof construction is of Norwegian origin.

and Ireland, the later form taken by the *stavkirker* being the
result of modifications introduced to suit the climate of Norway,
the tools, the methods, and the experience of the builders.   These
modifications have made the *stavkirke* almost unique, and Norway
may claim to have reached in them " the crowning point of the
mediæval art of wooden church building."

There are many interesting points which are beyond the scope
of this note, such as the origin of the ornamentation of door pillars
and the capitals, which has been much disputed, while the connection, if any, between the *stavkirke* and the old *hov*, or heathen
temple, has also given rise to some controversy.

Unfortunately for Norway, reckless destruction, or often want
of care, has left her only about twenty-four fairly well-preserved
specimens of these curious churches, whose peculiar beauty seems
in a remarkable degree to suit their natural surroundings.

The following list of authorities taken from Professor Dietrichson's
book may be of interest to those who wish to pursue the subject
further :—

Nicolaysen, N. — *Norske Bygninger fra Fortiden*, Kristiania,
1860—1880 ; *Mindesmærker af Middelalderens Kunst i Norge*,
and his articles on " *Hov and Stavkirker* " in the *Hist.
Tidsskrift.*, II., Vol. VI.

Bruun, Johan.—*Norges Stafkyrkor*, Stockholm, 1891.

Dietrichson, L.—*Eiendommelighederne ved Stavkirkernes Construction*, in the *Nordisk Tidskrift för Vetenskap Konst og
Industri*, Stockholm, 1887 ; also *Constructions en bois de
l'architecture Norvégienne au moyen âge*, in Vol. XXXIX. of
" L'Art," Paris, 1885.

I have to thank Professor Dietrichson for his kindness in reading
these notes, and making some valuable corrections.—O. W.

Since writing the above, I have received some particulars of
the old wooden belfry at Brookland (Kent), which in many points
resembles a *stavkirke*.   Its roof is in three parts, one above the
other ; its framework has the long corner posts, and rests on
sviller (cross beams), while its perpendicular walls are of *reisværk*,
which is nailed to the beams as in the German churches.

APPENDIX III.

THE BISHOPS AND ARCHBISHOPS OF NIDAROS FROM THE EARLIEST TIMES TO THE REFORMATION.

BISHOPS.

SIGURD (OR SIGEFRID) . .	Olaf Trygvessøn's Missionary Bishop—left Norway for Sweden, 1002.
GRIMKELL	St. Olaf's companion—last mentioned in 1046.
SIGEFRID II.	Knut the Great's Bishop —left in 1031.
RAGNAR	
KETEL	
ADALBERT	1066 (?)—apparently the first Diocesan Bishop.
THOLF	1067—1072.
SIMON	Died probably 1139.
IVAR	

ARCHBISHOPS.

REIDAR	Died 1151—on his way from Rome.
JON BYRGESSØN . . .	(Translated from Bergen) 1152—1157.

ARCHBISHOPS—*continued.*

EYSTEIN ERLENDSSØN	1157 (consecrated 1161)—1188.
ERIK IVARSSØN	1189—resigned 1205.
THORE GUDMUNDSSØN	1207—1214.
GUTTORM	1215—1224.
PETER	1224—1226.
THORE (DEN TRØNDSKE)	1227—1230.
SIGURD EINDRIDESSØN	1231—1252.
SØRLE	1253—1254.
EINAR GUNNARSSØN	1255—1263.
HAAKON	1265—1267.
JON RAUDE	1268—1282.
JØRUND	1288—1309.
EILIV ARNESSØN	1311—1332.
PAUL BAARDSSØN	1333—1346.
ARNE EINARSSØN	1346—1349.
OLAF	1349—1371.
THROND	1371—1381.
NICHOLAS RUSER (OR RUSARE)	1382—1386.
VINALDE HENRIKSSØN	1386—1402.
ASKELL	1402—1428.
ASLAK BOLT	1428—1450.
OLAF THRONDSSØN	1450 (elected), confirmed 1459—1474.
GAUTE IVARSSØN	1474—1510.
ERIK VALKENDORF	1510—1522.
OLAF ENGELBREKTSSØN	1523—1537 (died 1538).

The bishops up to Adalbert (1066) cannot, of course, strictly speaking, be said to be *bishops of Nidaros*, as there was no diocesan episcopacy in the early times; but as their work was mainly carried on in that part of the country, their names are usually included in the Nidaros list. The exact order, and the names as well, are not certain. The list given above follows Jørgenssøn in *Den Nordiske Kirkes Grundlæggelse og første udvikling.*

GENEALOGICAL TABLES.

I. THE MALE LINE OF HARALD HAARFAGRE (OVERLORD OF NORWAY, 872).

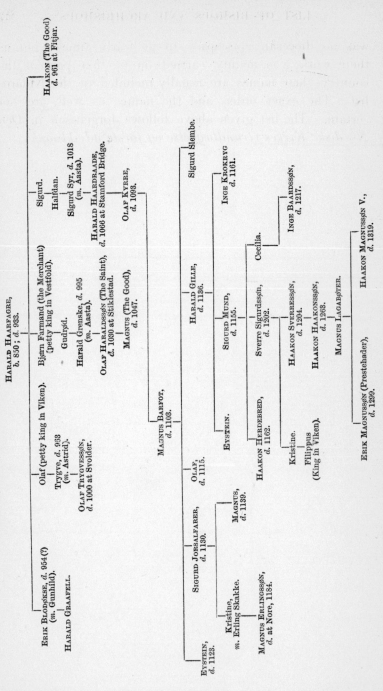

II. THE KINGS FROM HAAKON MAGNUSSØN TO THE DANISH KINGS.

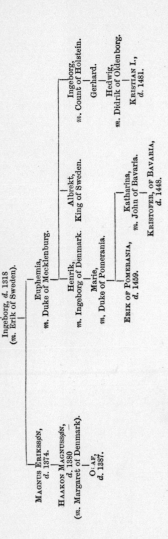

HAAKON MAGNUSSØN V.,
d. 1319 (m. Euphemia of Rügen).

Ingeborg, d. 1318
(m. Erik of Sweden).

Magnus Eriksson,
d. 1374.

Haakon Magnussøn,
d. 1380
(m. Margaret of Denmark).

Olaf,
d. 1387.

Euphemia,
m. Duke of Mecklenburg.

Henrik,
m. Ingeborg of Denmark.

Albrekt,
King of Sweden.

Marie,
m. Duke of Pomerania.

Erik of Pomerania,
d. 1459.

Katharina,
m. John of Bavaria.

Kristofer, of Bavaria,
d. 1448.

Ingeborg,
m. Count of Holstein.

Gerhard.

Hedwig,
m. Didrik of Oldenborg.

Kristian I.,
d. 1481.

III. THE OLDENBORGER KINGS OF DENMARK AND NORWAY (TO 1537).

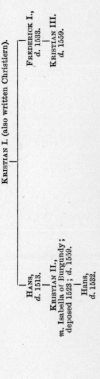

Kristian I. (also written Christiern).

Hans,
d. 1513.

Kristian II.,
m. Isabella of Burgundy;
deposed 1523; d. 1559.

Hans,
d. 1532.

Frederick I.,
d. 1533.

Kristian III.,
d. 1559.

INDEX.

NOTE.—*aa*, as in Haakon, etc., is pronounced like a long ō; the final *e* is always sounded, but as a short ĕ; *sk*, before *i* or *j*, is pronounced as *sh*; ø is like the French *eu* or German *ö*.

THE END.

BRADBURY, AGNEW, & CO. LD., PRINTERS, LONDON AND TONBRIDGE.